THE
FORAGER'S HARVEST

Samuel Thayer

A Guide to Identifying,
Harvesting, and Preparing
EDIBLE WILD PLANTS

Forager's Harvest

FORAGER'S HARVEST PRESS • BRUCE, WI

Publisher's Cataloging-in-Publication Data
Thayer, Samuel.
The forager's harvest : a guide to identifying, harvesting, and preparing edible wild plants / Samuel Thayer
p. cm.
Includes bibliographical references and index.
LCCN 205911400
ISBN-13: 978-0-9766266-0-2
ISBN-10: 0-9766266-0-8

1. Wild plants, Edible—Handbooks, manuals, etc. I. Title. II. Title: Guide to identifying, harvesting, and preparing edible wild plants.

QK98.5.A1T43 2006   581.6'32   QBI06-600299

Book Design by Fiona Raven
Photographs and artwork by Samuel Thayer, except as otherwise credited.

First Printing March 2006, 5,000 copies
Second Printing September 2006, 15,000 copies
Third Printing January 2009, 16,800 copies
Fourth Printing January 2011, 18,200 copies
Fifth Printing March 2012, 24,100 copies
Sixth Printing April 2013, 18,200 copies
Seventh Printing January 2015, 14,500 copies
Eighth Printing December 2016, 14,000 copies
Ninth printing May 2019, 12,000 copies
Tenth Printing June 2020, 17,000 copies

Printed in China

Published by
Forager's Harvest
709 West Arthur Avenue
Bruce, WI 54819
www.foragersharvest.com

Forager's Harvest

To Josh,

Not only the best friend that I have,
but the best friend anybody has.

Acknowledgements

I used to read the acknowledgements in my favorite books and wonder how a single author could become so indebted to so many people in the production of one little volume. Now I understand. Without the encouragement, ideas, and occasional pestering of my friends over the last decade, I might have never finished this book. I would like to thank all of those who patiently believed in me.

With fond memories I extend my gratitude to the many foraging companions who got wet, muddy, cold, sweaty, and bug-bitten along with me over the years, all for the thrill of eating the best food on Earth. Of these, I am particularly indebted to Mike Krause, Mark Pollock, Joe Eucolono, Jon Wheeler, and Laurie Miskimins.

I owe a huge thanks to Tammy Springer, who gave me the camera that took most of the photos decorating these pages, and Jamie Springer, who repeatedly endured sunburn, spiders, and rice worms so that I could "get my hundred pounds." Were it not for Edelene Wood, who convinced me to try teaching about wild foods, I may have never taken this path. Clayton Oslund and Bill Blackmon gladly provided advice and photographs, without which the book would be poorer. Sjana Schanning let me type early drafts on her computer, and I have not forgotten the favor. And some years ago, Tom Elpel generously extended an unsolicited yet valuable boost to my efforts.

During the extended process of writing this book, a few people have given many hours of support and help on all fronts: Glenn Schmukler, Abe Lloyd, Cindy Sakry, and Josh Morey. I can't thank you enough. For technical advice and editing, much credit is due to Mike Krebill. And even though I paid her, my book designer Fiona Raven deserves mention for holding the hand of a cautious, first-time publisher.

I would also like to thank the authors who came before me, sharing their passion and knowledge. And of course, I appreciate the plants that have sustained my life. For them I am endlessly grateful; by them I am endlessly awed. Last and first, I would like to thank God, who made all of this possible.

If I have failed to mention anybody, it is only because I'm afraid you'll want a free copy. God, you can have two free copies, but I need your address.

Contents

Introduction

One summer day when I was four years old I spotted my older brother and sister crouched under the front porch of our house. I ducked under the two-by-eights to join them, eager to share in whatever excitement had brought them there. When I got closer I found the two of them staring in admiration at a clump of small and delicate clover-like plants thriving there by grace of the sunlight that shone through the gaps in the wooden stairway. My sister plucked an entire plant and held it out briefly for me to see, whispering the word "juicies" almost as if the term were forbidden. She proceeded to eat it, stem and all, and my brother did the same with one of the plants in front of him. I followed their example and was much impressed with the lemon-like flavor.

My older siblings do not recall how they learned to eat "juicies," but they were regular fare for the rest of our childhood. It wasn't until six years later that I discovered the plant's real name. Even though my mother had sternly warned me that weeds were poisonous, I was eating a dozen different kinds by that time. I did so in secret, survived, and liked it.

When I was ten years old I discovered that there were books about wild edible plants. This opened up a whole new world to me. I started bringing home nettles and other common weeds to cook. At first this threw my parents into a panic, but by the time I was fourteen they had learned to accept my identifications without worry. I collected and ate wild foods every chance I got. My bedroom became cluttered with buckets of hickory nuts and acorns. Drying herbs adorned my dresser. The refrigerator contained things that nobody else would dare to touch, and unfamiliar smells wafted from the kitchen.

Silly dreams, of living off the land somewhere far from the city, began to form in my adolescent mind. My best friend and I went on camping trips where we would bring little or no food, forcing ourselves to forage. We'd return very hungry, but alive, and always with some new knowledge. The more I learned, the less silly my dream felt. My parents, teachers, and school counselors would have none of it – but I was determined. I kept reading, cooking, experimenting, and planning.

Today hunting and gathering is a way of life for me. Wild grains, teas, nuts, fruit juices, berries, flours, and vegetables are stored away for the seasons. And every day, at almost every meal, I eat something that was a gift of unbroken land. In a simple cabin at the edge of the woods along a dead-end country road, I am exactly where I always wanted to be.

The Meaning of Wild Food

Something about finding a wild plant and eating it appeals to everybody. Even those people who seem totally disinterested in Nature will have half a dozen questions for anybody they see pulling up a rank weed and sticking it in his mouth. This interest is more than just curious disapproval; it is a manifestation of a deeper inkling within us. Foraging is the oldest occupation of humankind. For most of our history we knew no other way of living. We are built, both mentally and physically, to be hunters and gatherers. Somewhere inside of us we are all foragers, no matter how much we have lost touch with that aspect of our nature.

Today, if cut off from purchased supplies, most of us would starve in the midst of plenty. Many people are shocked when I assert that one could subsist on nothing but food obtained from the wild. I find this amusing, since for most of human history there was no other food. Of course, I do not expect the readers of this book to go out and become full-time foragers, but anybody can conveniently and beneficially add wild foods to his or her diet as components of delicious, nourishing, and varied meals. This book can be your doorway.

One of the greatest benefits of eating wild food is that it reminds us that we are fed not by the supermarket, but by the sunshine, rain, and soil. As a society we are coming to believe the fallacy that *people* make food. Drawing even a small part of our sustenance directly from the Earth helps keep us in touch with the sobering reality that, despite our advanced technology, we cannot manufacture our most basic needs.

For many years we have been hearing of the need for greater environmental awareness. Nothing else can build such awareness as surely and powerfully as practicing the ancient ecological art of humankind – foraging. It is not observation of, but rather *participation in* the phenomena of Nature that brings us to our greatest understanding of our place in the mosaic of life.

Some people contend that hunting and gathering have no place in this modern technological age. If we seek most of all to lead healthy, peaceful, and fulfilling lives, and to leave those same opportunities for those who come after us, then foraging is as appropriate today as ever. Gathering and eating from God's garden is our direct connection to the world that he made. Like love and beauty, no progress of science can make it obsolete.

The Purpose and Organization of this Book

The *Forager's Harvest* covers edible wild plants with a thoroughness, accuracy, and detail that other references simply do not match. The information that I share about harvest and preparation is not simply taken from other literary sources; it is based on or verified by my own experiences. At the same time, I have given great attention to botanical accuracy. The result is a wild food book like no other. Follow me through these pages and into the woods for an adventure that will change your life.

The text begins with a discussion of the history and philosophy of foraging. After visiting the basic concepts of gathering wild food, there is a discussion of safe and responsible foraging practices, including a step-by-step tutorial to plant identification. After this I cover many of the skills involved in harvest, preparation, and storage of different types of wild produce. I have designed a calendar to help the forager keep track of harvest times for the many wild foods discussed in the text. The bulk of the book is composed of 32 chapters, each covering the identification, range, habitat, season of availability, edible parts, harvest methods, conservation, and preparation of a specific plant or a group of similar plants. A glossary, index, and list of references are also included.

Some wild food books are arranged with the plants in alphabetical order by their common names, others by season. Realizing that most readers are not botanists, I am still partial to the standard taxonomic order that botanists use. Common names are inconsistent, and each plant usually goes by several of them, making the alphabetical organization problematic. Many plants have multiple edible parts available at different times of year, making it difficult to organize them by season of availability. Following taxonomic order so that related plants are found next to each other has important benefits for the reader; it presents similar plants side-by-side, aiding identification, and it reinforces an understanding of the relationships between the plants. Once the standard order is learned, it becomes easy to locate the plant in any book so organized.

The first time that a plant is mentioned in the account, the Latin or scientific name is given; it is used occasionally thereafter, particularly where it seems appropriate to avoid ambiguity. Some people are turned off by scientific names, but they are absolutely necessary. In fact, few plants have a widely accepted or standardized common name the way that birds or mammals do. Using scientific names is the *only* way to communicate about plants with certainty; it pays to get used to them.

The scientific name consists of two parts. The first name is generic (indicating the genus, a closely related group of plants); it is *always* capitalized. The second name is specific (indicating the species within the genus); it is *never* capitalized. The scientific name is written in italics. The genus name is often abbreviated when the context makes it clear which genus we are discussing. The abbreviation "spp." means "species, plural" and indicates the discussion of multiple species within one genus.

Plants with similar common names are not necessarily related; mountain ash, white ash, and prickly ash are all in different families. I generally use the most familiar common name for a plant, but I think that good foods deserve good names, so occasionally, when the more familiar name is awkward, confusing, or derogatory, I use a less common name that seems more appropriate. I sometimes use multiple common names in order to familiarize the reader with those most likely to be encountered in the wild food literature.

Perhaps there is a plant that you were disappointed to see left out of this book. It is simply impossible to cover every edible wild plant in sufficient detail and fit them all into one book. I had to either omit detail or omit plants; I chose to omit plants. Not to worry, however – this book is the first in a series. Subsequent volumes will cover many more species.

This book is not intended to be a regional guide. As with all other guides, a regional bias is built into it simply because I live in a particular place and my experiences are concentrated there. I have not tried to cover my favorite plants, the best plants, or the most common ones. The species in this book were chosen to represent a variety of food types, seasons, and habitats. They were selected from among those plants for which I felt that I had sufficient information, experience, and photographs to produce a satisfactory account. The selection of plants will prove most applicable to the Great Lakes, Midwest, Northeast, and the southern part of eastern Canada. It will prove only slightly less useful to readers in the Rocky Mountains, the Pacific Northwest, the Northern Plains, the more northerly parts of Canada, and Alaska. However, the information will be highly valuable to wild food enthusiasts in any part of North America.

There is a strong tendency to assume that a book on edible wild plants will also discuss their medicinal qualities. I have generally stayed away from that in this book. While a good diet is vital to good health, the subject of remedies and medications is largely distinct from that of food and nutrition. I take medicine perhaps once every two years but I eat food several times a day, so I have a lot more experience with food. I am not an herbalist, so I do not feel qualified to write on that topic. Furthermore, there is much debate and controversy about the effectiveness of certain herbal medications, and which ailments they should be used for. There is no questionable placebo effect with food; no calories means you starve. While this guide can help with plant identification, readers primarily interested in herbal medicines should be able to find several other books written specifically on that topic.

There are four goals that I labored to accomplish with this work. These goals distinguish this book from the many other books on edible wild plants:

1. To provide a thorough account of each plant's use, based on my own experiences.

In my opinion, most wild food books cover way too many plants in far too little detail. With all the species crammed into them, there isn't room to provide enough information to guide the novice forager through finding, harvesting, and preparing the plants. Neither are such books very useful to the seasoned food gatherer, for in such limited space the author cannot fit any information besides the basics that have already been repeated in two dozen other guides. Thus they serve as little more than long lists of edible plants – perhaps exciting to the armchair forager, but not very useful to those who really want to get out and collect some food.

All too often, authors of wild food books try to cover all of the plants known to be edible in a particular region, or all of the "best" edible plants covered by other texts already in print. This inevitably forces them to include plants that they have little or no firsthand experience with. Because, as authors, they are supposed to be experts on the topic, they often feel compelled to hide their lack of experience with a particular plant by writing what they presume is true or rewording what other authors have written.

When Robert Henderson (2000) mistakenly draws four pictures of *primrose* to accompany his description of *evening primrose* – a totally unrelated and dissimilar plant that just happens to share a similar common name – it strongly suggests that his account of the flavor and use of evening primrose root is based on literary accounts rather than his own experience. Yet he neglects to explicitly reveal this in the text. Likewise, when Lee Peterson (1977) writes that hog peanuts occur in underground "pods," it is hard to believe that he has actually collected them – for surely he would have noticed that these seeds have no pods at all. Such attempts to pass off another's experience as the author's own are rampant in the wild food literature. Obvious as they are to a seasoned forager, they create serious cases of misinformation that catch the beginner off guard and often result in disappointment, frustration, and eventual disillusionment with wild foods.

All of the accounts in this book are based on my own experience; I have gathered and eaten every plant covered in the text dozens of times – most of them hundreds of times. If my firsthand knowledge of one of the particular uses of a plant is limited, I have tried to make that fact evident in the discussion. Readers deserve to know this.

I have often heard frustrated beginners seething about the vagueness of statements found in wild food books or bemoaning recipes that were absolute disasters. In so many books readers are told that a plant has an edible tuber – but not how big the tuber is, where and when to find it, how difficult it is to collect, how it should be cooked, or what its texture and flavor are like. When we pick up a wild food book, these are the things we want to know – so that is what I have set out to tell you. An author can't do this if he hasn't put in the "dirt time."

The Forager's Harvest shares the discoveries that many years of avid use of wild plants have brought me, so that other wild food enthusiasts can benefit from that experience. This information is highlighted by stories from my own life that hopefully will give the plants character and help readers remember the important facts about them.

I make no claim of covering the best, best-known, or most common edible wild plants, or all of the worthwhile plants of any particular region. Books making these claims never live up to them – but more importantly, no wild food enthusiast needs such a book. Whether highly experienced or just starting out, the only proper way that people learn to identify and use plants is one at a time, with great care, excitement, and attention to detail. I have formatted this book with that in mind. I do not include a large number of species, but each plant included is covered in great detail.

2. To discuss plants, plant parts, uses, and techniques that are largely ignored in the wild food literature.

While certain wild food plants are covered thoroughly elsewhere, there remain many excellent species for which one can find virtually no useful information. Such little-known plants are not necessarily inferior in flavor or texture to those that are well-known, nor are they less common or harder to collect. There isn't much written about them simply because most of the information available on wild foods is derived from a small number of original sources which happened not to cover them.

It does not take a wild food collector very long to notice that there is an eerie similarity between the various popular foraging books. Not only do they cover largely the same plants, but they also say mostly the very same things about them. Yet even when it comes to these widely discussed wild foods, there is a great deal more to learn about them than what commonly finds its way into print. I hope that this book will be a breath of fresh air for those who are tired of this timid repetition of worn opinions.

3. To provide the tools and images necessary for confident identification of the plants, showing them in their edible stages.

Plant field guides and identification keys are very helpful and all foragers should use several of them, but they are not designed with the wild food gatherer in mind. They generally depict plants in the flowering stage, which may be the best time to identify them but is usually not when the plants are collected for food. Field guides and floras often employ dichotomous keys, which are great tools but do not provide the level of certainty that a forager requires. Only a fool would eat a plant that he hadn't identified with great care; gatherers of wild food need a higher degree of confidence when identifying a plant for the first time than a passive naturalist does. That is the reason that foraging manuals always tell you to cross-reference your plant in several field guides.

For plant identification, most foraging books pass the responsibility on to "reliable field guides." As an identification tool, this book is superior to any field guide (for the small number of plants that it contains) because it is designed with the forager in mind. Multiple photos of each plant clearly show all parts and stages of growth that are needed for positive identification. Unlike other field guides, this book also shows the edible parts of each plant in the proper stage and condition for harvest. The text descriptions of the plants are more elaborate than readers will find in most foraging guides, emphasizing a great number of easily observed characteristics that can be compared to plants in the field. The step-by-step tutorial to positive plant identification found later in the introduction will help the reader feel comfortable when identifying a plant for the first time.

The text will occasionally mention edible plants that are not covered in detail in this book. Readers are responsible for finding adequate and reliable resources for identifying these plants, as well as information pertaining to their use and preparation, before consuming them.

4. To provide reliable information.

A large number of wild food references contain accounts of the various water lilies of the genera *Nuphar* and *Nymphaea*. Most claim that the "sweetish" tubers or rootstocks can be boiled or roasted like potatoes. Some contain recipes for using the tubers in stews. Books covering these "edibles" include Lee Peterson's *A Field Guide to Edible Wild Plants*, Bradford Angier's *Field Guide to Edible Wild Plants*, and Elias and Dykeman's *Field Guide to North American Edible Wild Plants*. These creatively titled books are probably the three best-selling wild food guides in the country. One or more of them resides in nearly every bookstore and library on the continent. They are printed by large, respected publishing houses. But the rootstocks and tubers of most, if not all, species of *Nuphar* and *Nymphaea* are poisonous. If these authors had actually eaten the plants in question, the mistake would never have been made.

Elias and Dykeman's book contains a photo on page 78 that is labeled "stinging nettle, young plants" but which actually shows wood nettle; on page 218 the photo of "common barberry" is actually of Japanese barberry. Not only can wood nettle and Japanese barberry be easily told apart from the plants they were mistaken for, but the differences between them are very important to a food gatherer. These are just a few examples of the erroneous information and sloppy scholarship that plague the wild food literature.

Many of the books in print on edible wild plants are written by inexperienced and unqualified people. There are no degrees in this field, no certifications, no regulatory body or professional association to approve texts, no widely accepted authority that can verify the accuracy of statements found in print. Since *nobody* has a degree in "edible wild plants," *anybody* with a degree in a peripherally related field can be passed off as a wild food "expert" by himself or his publisher.

No degree abbreviation follows my name, but you can rest assured that this book is free of egregious botanical errors such as those discussed above. I make claims based on my experiences, not on some unacknowledged, uncited literary source. I don't need to claim to be an expert; I'll just share what I know and hope you find it useful.

The History of Foraging and Wild Food Literature

Although collecting and hunting wild food was universal only eight thousand years ago, its practice has been declining steadily since then. As agricultural economies, with their higher densities of people, expanded across the world, they were constantly in need of new soil to till. This expansion put them at odds with foragers, who occupied the coveted lands, every step of the way. Not only because human societies tend to despise their economic competitors, but also because foragers represented an entirely different socioeconomic system that threatened the very stability of oppressive, feudal agrarian civilizations, hatred of hunter-gatherers became the universal dogma of civilized cultures. A prejudice was born that wild food was beneath the dignity of real human beings, and that those who lived upon it were subhuman. It was alright to kill or mistreat them, and conquering their land was virtuous. This attitude continued until foragers were exterminated or their way of life had been destroyed.

To accompany the more obvious campaign of violence against Native Americans, the Europeans who settled North America tried (and for the most part succeeded) to make the defeated Indians ashamed of their traditional diets. They stigmatized wild foods, pretending that they were disgusting, rough, poor fare fit only for beasts. While most Native Americans in the East and South subsisted heavily on agricultural crops, all tribes had economies that incorporated wild plant foods to a significant extent. This knowledge was almost completely lost with the European conquest.

The discipline of ethnobotany did not exist until the late Nineteenth Century, so very little was recorded about Native uses of wild plants, especially in eastern North America. People did not see any value in recording the knowledge of "backwards savages," except perhaps as a curiosity. What was recorded was filtered through biased minds, leaving us with a great deal of nonsense. By insisting on the unpleasantness and crudeness of Native fare and exaggerating the difficulty of using it, explorers justified their conquest as bringing civilization to miserable savages. These early accounts often misidentified the plants that the Natives used because proper identification was often unimportant to those who wrote them. The few who valued accuracy were bound to make mistakes because they were *observing* rather than *doing*. Errors also arose because the English names of North American plants were not standardized, creating confusion as to the interpretation of older accounts.

Just before the last of the traditional Native cultures were destroyed in the late 1800s and early 1900s, a few anthropologists made serious efforts to record their plant uses. While much of our information on edible wild plants comes from this work, it was too little too late. An enormous amount of detail was lost.

It is commonly believed that European peasants and early settlers in North America made extensive use of wild plant foods. Although they used such plants far more than people do today, it is misleading to say that they were expert foragers. For the most part, the settlers despised wild foods because of the stigma attached to them and made every effort not to eat them. Most wild plants were eaten out of necessity when crops or transportation failed, and this wasn't very often. The settlers didn't care to become proficient at the use of these foods, or to develop good recipes for them, because they were for temporary, emergency use only. In every region there were only a few wild foods that became acceptable for white folks to gather on a regular basis. These were non-staple foods or staple foods used in ways that were very different from how hunter-gatherers had employed them.

The settlers did use a number of quasi-wild, human-dependent agricultural tag-alongs that came from Europe. This had always been a part of the European peasant economy, and many rural folks from a few generations ago were fairly well versed in the use of some of these plants. This is what I call "farmer folk knowledge" of edible wild plants. It pertains only to a particular group of plants that are similar in their habitat, origin, life cycle, and in the kind of food they supply. Such human-dependent food plants include dandelion, chicory, plantain, stinging nettle, curly dock, sow thistle, common chickweed, lamb's quarters, amaranth, purslane, winter cress, sheep sorrel, black mustard, and many others.

If you've read a little on this topic you've probably noticed that these plants dominate the literature on wild foods. This is not because they are outstanding in flavor, abundance, or ease of collection – despite the fact that the authors who focus on them repeatedly make such claims. These plants are in the spotlight simply because they are the plants that European peasants used, and the dominant culture of North America is the heir to that peasant tradition.

You've probably never seen a book called "How to Drive a Car," just as nobody in eighteenth century New England was reading about horsemanship.

We don't write books about the mundane things that all people are expected to know. So by the time that popular books began to appear on edible wild plants, such as Charles Francis Saunders' *Edible and Useful Wild Plants of the United States and Canada* in 1920 and Oliver Medsger's *Edible Wild Plants* in 1939, we know that folk knowledge of wild foods was disappearing, and probably already an uncommon thing. These works helped to keep it alive, and to collect information from accounts of Native American uses of plants so that it could be easily accessed by those interested.

But as the old Indians died, the food scare of the first World War ran its course, and the Great Depression ended, North Americans found themselves less and less interested in traditional wild sources of nourishment. During the middle of the 20th Century a few books came out on this topic, such as Nelson Coon's *Using Wayside Plants*, Fernald and Kinsey's *Edible Wild Plants of Eastern North America*, and Ben Charles Harris' *Eat The Weeds*. But the knowledge and interest continued to fade.

Then came Euell Gibbons with his 1962 classic *Stalking the Wild Asparagus*, which has had more influence in the field of wild foods than any other book. He followed this with *Stalking the Blue-Eyed Scallop, Stalking the Healthful Herbs*, and some lesser-known works. Gibbons was a curious experimenter, passionate forager, and marvelous cook; his work stood out for this reason, capturing the imagination of millions. He became a celebrity and got many people interested in foraging. It became trendy, at least in some circles.

Several publishers perceived that foraging was a hot topic, and that few titles existed in that niche. Money was to be made, so books were written and published. A large number of mediocre wild food guides appeared, written by people who overstepped the bounds of their knowledge to create a finished product that they or their publisher thought would sell. Many of them were evidently unqualified to author such works. Even more importantly, the wild food literature since Euell Gibbons has been characterized by an abject stagnation of knowledge; most such books contain little or nothing that is new or original.

Most recently published books are thinly disguised regurgitations of the same information contained in the original seven books mentioned above. These originals contained some outright errors and several inadequately or poorly described plant uses; plagiarists were unable to discover and deal with these problems. Thus mistakes, opinions, and particular interpretations of experiences became "well known facts," found even in the best-selling wild food books on the market.

If a wild food book is truly based on the author's own experiences it will not closely resemble another's account. There is so much to learn about each plant, so many possible ways of doing things, so many superb recipes, and so many edible plants, that it is unthinkable that even two foragers with great experience, much less two dozen, would all emphasize the same recipes, species, and ideas. The fact that wild food books read like a bunch of fifth grade science reports all based on the same encyclopedia points to copying from common sources.

There are many knowledgeable foragers out there, but unfortunately, few have written books. The deplorable state of information on edible wild plants can be cleared up over time if those who write on the topic exhibit professionalism and follow a few simple guidelines:

1. Everything we write should be based on our own experience (unless #2).
2. We cite the source for any opinions or observations that do not come from our own experience.
3. We should make a reasonable effort to let readers know our level of experience with a plant, and not to exaggerate it.
4. We should not condemn a plant based on limited experience with it.
5. We should verify the accuracy of our plant identifications, referring to and using scientific names.
6. If we have experience with one plant, we should not assume that a related plant has identical qualities.

A revolution is coming to the wild food literature. When the works of authors who abide by these principles come to supplant those of sloppy scholarship, the study of wild food plants will be taken seriously again, and the oldest and most beautiful pastime in human history will rise from the ashes.

Getting Started
With Edible Wild Plants

Why Forage?

There are a number of practical reasons that one can cite for collecting wild food: nutrition, taste, variety, thrift, emergency preparedness, convenience while on the trail. But these are the benefits, not the reasons. People gather wild food for the same reason that people go camping, fishing, hunting, bird watching, or just walking in the woods; it puts them in touch with a natural world that dazzles, excites, and amazes them; it provides a deep and primal satisfaction; it feels beautiful and sacred. It is this satisfaction that holds a person's interest in wild foods – but the benefits are great as well.

If you are willing to put in the necessary time you can expect a great deal from wild foods: gourmet meals that no amount of money can buy, better health, a lower grocery bill, and exciting times that you will remember for the rest of your life. You can expect to experience a special camaraderie with foraging companions and a new facet of outdoor thrill. You will have a wonderful means by which to baptize acquaintances, child and adult, in the blessing of Nature. Most of all, you can expect to enjoy food in a way you never knew was possible.

For me, foraging is also a spiritual experience. The food gatherer has countless hours of quiet and reflective time in the divine gift called Nature. Small miracles are witnessed: a newborn fawn, a hidden spring, an ancient tree left standing. Through these we come closer to understanding the larger miracle that gives us life.

Do Wild Plants Taste Good?

Many people assume that wild plants just don't taste good; they are last resorts, food for survival emergencies only. If that were the case, I would have lost my interest in foraging long ago. Others say that if these plants were truly good, they would be cultivated. But luckily, the truth is that wild foods taste better than cultivated ones.

Few who have delighted in the experience of a wild strawberry or blueberry can fail to be disappointed by the bland, overgrown ones found in the produce aisle. Yet most of our wild foods have no cultivated counterpart and are thus unique and incomparable experiences. Many wild foods exhibit perfection in texture, flavor, and appearance and can stand up against the best of cultivated produce; they are gourmet by any definition and could be served to the most finicky palate without any excuses being made on their behalf. In fact, it is invariably wild, not cultivated, foods that fetch the highest prices at the classiest restaurants and markets.

The primary reason that so many people consider wild plants crude and unpalatable is the deep prejudice that our culture fosters against these foods, but other factors have conspired to promote this reputation. One is the fact that so many who teach about wild plants have chosen to emphasize ubiquitous but mediocre edibles such as dandelion and common plantain. Dandelion is a bitter green that nearly everybody dislikes on the first try, and I can find nothing positive to say about the flavor or texture of plantain greens. If somebody is introduced to wild foods via these plants I cannot blame him for thinking that we neo-primitive food gatherers are force-feeding ourselves for the sake of having a hobby.

Certain wild plants do require one to cultivate a taste for them, just as we do with coffee or beer, but there is no reason to use these potent herbs to introduce people to wild food when so many delicious and mild vegetables, which will please the newcomer on the first taste, are at hand.

One November, I was walking with an acquaintance along a boardwalk through a marsh in a local park. He asked me, "Cattails are edible, aren't they?" I told him yes. Before I could say another word he leaned over, grabbed a dry, fluffy cattail seedhead, and took a huge bite. The down puffed out in his mouth and he coughed it out, then threw the seedhead aside and commented, "Don't know why they'd eat it, though – it's not very good." Dismissing cattail as unpalatable from this experience would be like refusing to eat apples because the branches are too hard to chew.

Just as with cultivated produce, wild plants have specific edible parts; the wrong parts can be inedible or poisonous, and even the right parts will be tough and distasteful if harvested at the improper stage. Oftentimes the beginning forager is simply unaware of what the plant should look like when it is ready to harvest, or even what part should be collected. Such ignorance has led to many experiences that turned people away from wild foods.

Of course, everybody is not going to like every food. But let me assure you that if you learn to identify the plants in this book, collect them at the proper time, and prepare them in a sensible fashion, you will like most of them. Even more than that, after a while you will crave them – and you may find it hard to imagine life without them.

Eating Wild for Health

I am asked quite frequently about the nutritional composition of wild foods. Unfortunately, very few of the plants covered in this book have been subjected to nutritional analysis, so I cannot answer this question with specific figures for each plant. However, the small percentage of wild edibles that have been analyzed have produced exciting results.

Wild plants have been shown, on average, to have a far greater content of vitamins and minerals than similar domesticated crops – often boasting twice the content or more. This trend has been demonstrated across different produce types and the sample of plant species analyzed is large enough to safely assume that the trend is general. While we may not be able to provide the specific nutritional profile of every plant or plant part, we can reasonably say that each wild food is probably an excellent source of vitamins and minerals.

This should come as no surprise; wild plants are not bred for size or keeping quality, nor are they forced to grow on impoverished soil. Furthermore, wild foods are fresher than anything you can buy, decreasing the portion of complex vitamins lost through deterioration.

We should not forget another great health benefit of wild food – to both humans and the environment: the fact that they are not doused with highly toxic pesticides or herbicides like the bulk of our cultivated produce.

There can be no doubt about it; eating wild is extremely healthy.

Foraging for Thrift and Self-Reliance

Not only is foraging an inexpensive pastime, it can also significantly reduce one's grocery expenses. Wild foods are an immense and underutilized resource for those who would rather spend time than money – whether they find themselves in a wilderness homestead or an urban apartment. Many edible wild plants grow in profusion and can be harvested as easily as the vegetables in a well-tended garden. The experienced forager rarely has to wander and search; if she is in her own neck of the woods she generally knows when and where to find what she needs, and in an unfamiliar area it usually does not take her long to discover more food than she could possibly carry home.

Not only does the forager have free access to unique, delicious, and astoundingly healthful foods that are unavailable in any supermarket, she also experiences a steadily increasing feeling of independence from the market economy. Through learning to forage, she can one day have the reassurance of knowing that even in the worst of times she can feed herself and her family.

Foraging: The Ultimate Survival Skill

While I don't promote foraging primarily as a way to prepare for worst-case-scenarios that the majority of readers will never experience, that preparedness is on the minds of most people who study wild foods. Wilderness skills have become increasingly popular over the last thirty years, with numerous survival schools popping up around the country and hundreds of books being published on the topic. While food is not the first priority in a wilderness emergency such as getting lost or stranded, having even token meals gives people a feeling of security and helps them stay focused. Fear of starving to death can send people into a self-destructive panic even when starvation may be weeks away.

You can't make yourself learn about wild foods because you are afraid that someday you will be forced to eat them by dire circumstances. You have to practice foraging as you learn it, and learn it as an exciting pastime, a labor of love. Otherwise, when that "survival situation" comes up, you will be totally unprepared for it.

But the "Earth skills" movement entails much more than preparation for emergencies; most people involved are looking for a deeper connection to Creation, an understanding of the proper human place in the ecosystem. Many of these people dream of living primitively or simply one day – disconnecting themselves from a society they see as immoral and destructive. The survival schools and publications that cater to this movement focus on fire making, shelter building, hide tanning, flint knapping, and a small number of related skills that produce a visible artifact that can be shown off.

But the truth is that once shelter, clothing, and a few other basic necessities are taken care of, the primitive will spend more of his working time hunting, gathering, and preparing food than doing all other tasks combined. Fire-by-friction can be learned in a weekend and mastered in a month; it will take years to become a competent forager. In a short-term survival situation, when food is a comfort rather than a necessity, knowing about wild edibles is important. In a long-term survival situation, wild edibles are everything.

Conservation

Some people insist that there are too many of us for anyone to go "live off the land." I wonder what such people suppose that we live off of now? In fact, foraging is an ages-old, time-tested, low-impact, and sustainable use of natural resources. Responsible wild food gatherers are deeply concerned about the plants that they harvest as well as the habitats they are found in. They strive to exercise good judgment and responsible moderation in their harvest. In this respect, people who forage plants for their personal consumption should not be confused with ginseng collectors and other wildcrafting profiteers who have seriously overharvested certain species.

The responsible wild food gatherer should treat the landscape like a sacred garden that she has been privileged to harvest from; ecology should always be on her mind while collecting. The basic rules of conservation for gathering wild plants are to **never take more than the remaining population can easily replace**, and to **always harvest in the way that does the least damage to the plant and its surroundings**. Understanding the life history of each plant that you collect is the key to implementing these rules. The individual plant accounts in this book outline conservation considerations in more detail when appropriate to the species under discussion.

Another ecological concern that foragers should be aware of is harmful invasive plants. Invasives are exotic species (some introduced accidentally, but most of them intentionally) which take over natural plant communities, crowding out native plants and destroying the habitat for native wildlife. Many of these species are edible, and harvest can help to reduce their prevalence. Whether or not you are collecting invasives for food, you should consider expending some effort controlling these plants in the areas where you harvest. For example, every year I have participants in my workshops take some time to weed garlic mustard out of hardwood forests where it is invading.

All of the plants in this book are abundant in some areas but rare in others. It is important to know if the species you intend to collect is legally protected in that area. But since legislators aren't running around the woods to see what plants need protection, *take the initiative yourself of determining which plants are abundant enough to be collected*. This is your sacred responsibility as a forager.

The plants that are most susceptible to overharvest are perennial herbs from which we harvest **single underground storage organs** such as roots, corms, or bulbs. When the storage organs are harvested, the entire plant is killed. These plants generally do not produce many seeds because they are adapted to living long life spans. Although often numerous, such species can be easily overharvested because they reproduce so slowly. Gather them by thinning out a small portion of the population where they are thriving. Be conscious of any long-term change in population and adjust your harvest accordingly.

Perennials that produce multiple **tubers** are less susceptible to overharvest because they produce extras to compensate for those that are consumed by animals. A small number of them are almost always left behind to begin the next season's growth. However, even with these species, overcollection can eliminate or greatly reduce local populations – so be sure to leave a fair number of tubers behind.

In general, collecting **rhizomes** can adversely affect plant populations more easily. A single rhizome may produce several large stalks, so it is rather easy to get carried away and uproot most of a colony. Inadvertently breaking or cutting rhizomes into small pieces while collecting will result in many smaller plants where before there had been a few large ones. These smaller plants may be unable to compete with the surrounding vegetation. With rhizomes, be careful to take only a small portion of the colony from which you are harvesting.

When the edible **roots of biennials** are harvested, the entire plant is killed. Never collect all of the roots in a colony; let at least half of them go to seed the next year. Since biennials are strong producers of seed and have short life spans, their populations naturally fluctuate more than those of perennials – but they also recover faster. If you want to keep a supply of these plants available, bring seeds as you harvest and scatter them over the disturbed soil where you have dug the roots.

When gathering **leafy greens from perennials** you can generally take about a third of the volume without unduly harming the plant, but don't collect from the same plant repeatedly during the growing season. This will not only prevent the plant from producing seed, it will also exhaust its stored energy, causing it to shrink and, if continued, eventually kill it. Weedy **annual greens**, however, are so prolific that they can generally be collected without restraint.

Shoots of perennials should be collected once per season from each colony, and even then less than half of the total number of shoots should be taken. Wild perennials that have all of their shoots cropped year after year will get gradually smaller until they are crowded out by uncollected neighboring species. They also produce shoots of poorer quality when stressed by constant collection or mowing.

Fruits, berries, seeds, and **nuts** are the gift of the plant and they are meant to be harvested. Your collection of them will rarely harm the reproduction of these species because all of them produce vastly more seeds than can possibly grow into adult plants. However, keep in mind that these are important food sources for wildlife.

Where to Forage

There are edible wild plants in every landscape in North America – although some areas are certainly more productive than others. In this book I have chosen plants to represent a wide range of habitats, from wild forests to urban lots. A particular habitat tends to produce many similar foods concentrated in one or a few periods during the yearly cycle. For example, pine barrens have many fruits in mid to late summer, but few edible greens or roots; while mature hardwood forests have few fruits, many roots, and a smorgasbord of greens in spring. An avid forager will want access to a variety of habitat types in order to obtain a good supply of produce for as much of the year as possible.

Because the popular wild food literature is so focused on farmer folk knowledge it tends to emphasize disturbance-dependent plants. This has unfortunately caused some authors to ignore foods of the forest or even disparage the wilderness as a foraging site. In fact, remote areas often offer superb opportunities for collecting wild food.

You don't need a wilderness area to forage, however; a mixture of farmland and woodlots provides a very productive landscape. Urban areas harbor disturbance-loving weeds and an unpredictable allotment of food-bearing trees, shrubs, vines, and herbs in waste places, parks, empty lots, and ornamental plantings. Every person on this continent lives within walking distance of worthwhile foraging opportunities, and most of us are surrounded by more wild food than we'd ever know what to do with.

There are many places, urban and rural, open to the public, but one must determine if harvesting plants is legal before collecting on these lands (or be ready to run and hide). Most large public forests are open to harvesting fruits, nuts, berries, and mushrooms, and a chat with a ranger or forest employee will likely secure permission for a modest harvest of greens or shoots.

Rural roadsides are treated as public property in many areas. Especially if you are clearly picking berries or nuts *right beside the road*, few people will give you any grief. Many thousands of people forage on roadsides annually; in fact, it is probable that more wild food gathering takes place here than anywhere else. If you forage on the roadside, do so with some common sense: don't pick near a home where it might seem intrusive, don't pick anything that appears to have been planted or tended, and certainly don't gather where somebody is likely to suspect you of doing something illicit. Resist the temptation to go even a little distance off the shoulder of the road. This arouses suspicion, anger, and the territorial instinct – and it makes you a legitimate intruder. You may someday encounter a person who approaches you angrily, claiming to own the shoulder of the road. He is probably not worth arguing with; leave meekly.

Private lands offer great foraging opportunities but you should *always* receive permission before using them. For many people, approaching a stranger and asking permission to collect plants is intimidating – but it is worth it.

There are a few things that you can do to increase your chances of securing permission. The first time you talk to a certain landowner, ask permission to harvest a specific plant that can be seen from the road; make it something like elderberries or butternuts that the landowner is likely to have heard of before. Offer to share your harvest with him. (Don't worry, he won't want any.) If the landowner was kind and the property seemed like a promising one that you'd like to return to, bring a gift of some foraged product, such as a jar of jam or jelly, as a thank you at a later date. After feeling assured that foraging really is a hobby of yours and that you're not up to anything else, the landowner will trust you more. Contrarily, if a landowner is grumpy and begrudgingly grants access to his property, it is probably best not to take him up on the offer (unless you see a really, really good butternut tree).

Cooking With Wild Food

At first you will probably use wild plants as substitutes for familiar cultivated ones in recipes. This is fine, but you need to keep in mind that these wild foods are not the same as the cultivated plants they are intended to replace; each has a unique combination of flavor and texture.

Enjoy wild foods for what they are, not for what they almost are. A wild vegetable may be frequently likened to a particular cultivated vegetable in the literature; many of these cliché comparisons are totally inaccurate. For example, jerusalem artichoke is regularly described as a "potato substitute," even though, besides the fact that is a tuber, it has no outstanding features in common with the potato. There have been thousands of frustrating unsatisfactory attempts to prepare this wild tuber in a fashion reminiscent of mashed potatoes. Throughout this book I try to make such comparisons only when they will be meaningful and helpful to the reader.

The first time that you prepare a certain wild food, I recommend cooking it all by itself and eating a small serving. It will probably be bland and boring – but taste carefully. Experience and analyze the flavor and texture, trying to imagine what would complement them well. Envision which traditional dish your new food may fit into. Start with simple combinations and see how they strike you, then reform or elaborate on your ideas until you develop recipes that work for you.

If you substitute a single wild ingredient in a familiar recipe and the result is disappointing, you may consider the recipe a failure but don't give up on the plant – it may be perfect for another dish. Be patient – it can take a while to figure out how to cook with an unfamiliar vegetable, especially those for which we don't have culinary traditions to guide us.

As people cook less and less, cookbooks become ever more popular. They fill up shelves with thousands of recipes in many a home – but few of these recipes will ever be tried. A recipe needs a cook to bring it to fruition. If you have no inclination to cook, wild food recipes will do you no good; whereas if you enjoy cooking you will quickly devise your own ways to incorporate wild plants into your everyday cuisine. For this reason (and because few readers are likely to have all the wild ingredients that are necessary to prepare one of my recipes assembled at one time) I have chosen not to include recipes in this book.

For a variety of more conventional recipes including wild foods I recommend *Stalking the Wild Asparagus* and *Stalking the Healthful Herbs* by Euell Gibbons, and *Abundantly Wild* by Teresa Marrone.

Plant Identification and Foraging Safety

How Euell Gibbons Didn't Die

Like millions of other old people, Euell Gibbons died of a heart attack. Yet the myth that this foraging celebrity was killed by the wild foods that he extolled, either in the form of stomach cancer or simply by consuming the wrong plant, sprung up quickly after his death and is still more widely believed than the truth. Our civilization's collective conscience is somehow comforted by the thought that wild plants kill people.

Most people get sick from restaurant food several times in their life, and many die from such food poisoning every year. One never hears that "If you eat at restaurants you'll probably die," yet I hear the same said frequently about collecting wild food, despite the fact that foraging deaths are almost unheard-of.

The fear of eating the wrong plant and being poisoned runs deep for many. Some people talk as if toxic plants are lurking in the woods, waiting to jump into our mouths and slither down our throats at the slightest *faux pas*. But foragers are not a bunch of toddlers who walk about the forest sticking random plants in their mouths. The consumption of an object is a deliberate act and can therefore be done with care and scrutiny.

Anybody can avoid eating the wrong plant by following one simple rule: **never eat any part of a plant unless you are 100% positive of the plant's identification, and certain that the part you intend to eat is edible in the condition in which you have harvested and prepared it.** Plant poisonings are *always* the result of this rule being disregarded.

Another danger sometimes associated with wild food is that of pollution. Certainly, it is wise not to collect plants for food if they are beside well-traveled roads, in recently sprayed agricultural fields or lawns, or other obviously polluted sites. However, the irrational fear that typically accompanies wild food has often caused warnings about such things to be overblown. People who live in the city and eat from their own vegetable gardens tell us not to forage in the city because the plants found there may contain pollutants, and people who grew up picking berries from country roadsides find themselves warning others not to, since such plants may be contaminated by exhaust. Henderson (2000) goes so far as to state that "water pollution and biological contamination have poisoned all the wild watercress in North America . . . foragers should steer clear of the wild watercress they encounter in streams and ditches, no matter where they are."

The truth is, we live in a polluted world; we breathe dirty air, drink tainted water, and get most of our food from chemical-laden farm fields – and we survive. Wild plants are part of that world and should not be neglected because of an unexamined double standard.

In short, while foraging entails some inherent risks, as does any activity, these risks are relatively small. With the application of common sense and reasonable caution, risks associated with gathering wild plants can be reduced to a minimal level. Foraging is no more dangerous than the average hobby – and the primary danger associated with wild food, that of eating the wrong plant, can be completely eliminated.

Identifying Edible Plants: A Step-by-Step Tutorial

The process of identifying an unknown plant can be difficult for beginners – and for experienced foragers it is still an exacting and carefully administered task. If a wildflower is misidentified in a photo album or an herbarium, it's not really a big deal. But if a plant that you are going to eat is mistaken for another, the repercussions can be serious. Thus wild food harvesters need a higher degree of confidence in a plant's identity than your average wildflower enthusiast or botanist does.

Wild plants are no harder to tell apart than cultivated vegetables; they only seem confusing to the beginner because they are unfamiliar and because there are so many of them. With practice, however, you can learn to recognize a wild food plant as easily and with the same level of confidence with which you recognize apples, carrots, or strawberries. This section describes the identification process that is used to get to that confident level of recognition. This is a vital first step for each plant, but once it is achieved, that same plant will be recognized easily upon future encounters.

Sometime while walking outdoors you'll see a plant and think, "Hey, that plant is in my wild food book." Then you'll go get the book and page through it until, if you're lucky, you find the plant. This is your ***tentative identification***; it is only the beginning of the identification process.

Sit down beside your tentatively identified plant and observe it carefully. Compare every available part of the plant to the verbal descriptions as well as the photographs or drawings in the book. Your plant should closely match the description and the image. Sketching the plant and accompanying the drawing with written observations is a superb way to get yourself to look more carefully at details and to help you remember those details later on.

Do not ignore the description just because you like the picture better. No matter how good a plant photograph may be, written descriptions play a vital role in identification because they tell you which features to look at and which you should weigh most heavily. Often the more important identifying characteristics are not the first ones noticed.

As you compare the characteristics of a real plant to a book's description and image, it is vitally important that you **do not mentally force your plant to fit the description**. If the leaf is supposed to have smooth margins, do not look at a leaf with very small or blunt teeth and say, "Well, it looks smooth enough." Do not call any cluster of flowers a raceme just because a raceme is a type of flower cluster. You may be very excited and really want to have found a certain edible plant, you may want to prove your tentative identification correct, but do not be brash; observe and appreciate the subtlety of Nature. Convincing yourself that a plant fits a description when in fact it does not is a dangerous habit, and no description can safeguard against it. Your plant should fit the description easily and reasonably, without any lenient comparisons or stretched definitions.

Certain identifying characteristics are more constant than others. Plant

Note the great difference between these two common burdock leaves found near each other. The odd form (left) was caused by abnormal growing conditions. Such drastic variation is not rare and may be caused by genetics, injury, or growing conditions. Also, plants may look surprisingly different at different stages of growth.

identification manuals usually focus on *the form and arrangement of the flowering and fruiting parts* because these are the parts preserved in herbaria and they are often the most reliable features to use for plant identification. *Stem cross section, scent, leaf pattern* (whether they are compound or simple, alternate or opposite, etc.), *leaf form* (venation, dentation, thickness, texture) and *type of root or other underground storage organ* are also generally very reliable characteristics. *The least reliable characteristics are those of habitat association, phenology, absolute size of the plant or plant parts, and color.* These less reliable traits should still be considered seriously, but they should not be given as much weight as the more consistent ones listed above. With all plant parts, form is far more important than size or color.

Many newcomers expect each plant to have one or two unmistakable characteristics which positively identify it. This is unrealistic; wild plants don't come with labels. Every feature of a plant can vary from the norm in certain circumstances – even the most reliable ones. For this reason you should absolutely **never identify a plant by a single characteristic**.

During the process of identifying your plant you will encounter botanical terms such as *alternate*, *pinnately compound*, and *umbel*. If you don't know what such words mean, look them up in the glossary. (Any plant book without a glossary is probably poorly designed for identification and should not be used for this purpose.) You need to understand this basic botanical vocabulary to positively identify an edible – and you will see these terms again and again as you learn about plants.

If, after carefully, impartially, and reasonably comparing your plant to the description and image in your first book, you feel confident that you have identified it correctly, run through the same process with several more field guides to double and triple-check your identification. Read about "look-alikes" and use the descriptions of those plants to ascertain that your plant is not one of them. Then go find several more specimens of your plant, preferably in diverse growing conditions, and examine them to get an idea of your plant's range of variability.

Before you eat a plant you need to be absolutely positive that you have identified it properly; you need to be sure enough to bet your life upon it. There should be as little doubt in your mind about what kind of plant you are eating as there would be if you were eating a banana. You need to have what I call ***contradictory confidence*** in your identification of the plant. If you reach this level of certainty you will immediately contradict *anybody* who tells you otherwise, despite his rank and title. The President, the Pope, and the produce

---

The Five Steps of Identifying Edible Plants

1. **Tentative identification:** You have located what you think is a certain plant.

2. **Compare your plant to a reliable reference:** Do this carefully, thoroughly, critically, and reasonably.

3. **Double and triple check:** Compare to several more reliable references.

4. **Find more specimens:** Do this until you can effortlessly recognize the plant; it may take minutes, hours, days, or even years.

5. **Assess contradictory confidence:** Do you really have it? Are you sure? Are you willing to bet your life? Would you proclaim it in front of a group of botanists?

---

manager wouldn't be able to convince you that an apple is an orange: that's contradictory confidence at work, and that's how sure you need to be.

Here's another good rule to follow: **if you need to use a book to identify a plant, you are not ready to eat it**. You should never eat a plant until you know it well enough that you can easily and instantly recognize it without a book. You may reach this point on the first day you encounter a certain plant, or it may take many encounters over a period of months or even years. How long this will take depends on many factors: whether the plant is in an easy or difficult stage to recognize, the quality of your field guides, and most of all, your own level of experience with plant identification. Your first few plants will be the most difficult, and you should take great care not to rush the process.

Sometimes you may know a certain plant in one stage of growth but not in another. The slightest hesitation or doubt indicates a lack of contradictory confidence regarding the specimen in question. This means the field guides must come out again to verify the identification. If your guides do not adequately display the plant in a certain stage of growth, you may need to mark the plant and observe it through the seasons, waiting until next year to harvest it.

Some Advice for the Complete Novice

People who have absolutely no experience with studying or observing Nature are at a disadvantage when it comes to foraging; they tend to underestimate the subtlety and variability of plants. Some people are unaware of the most basic notions about plants in general, such as the facts that some herbs are perennial and flowers become fruits. This is alright, but people at such a level of botanical knowledge need to recognize that they need a basic education in Nature observation, which will require some time, effort, and an open mind.

First of all, I suggest that you try to identify and learn the most common plants in your area, whether or not they are edible, using reliable field guides such as *Newcomb's Wildflower Guide* or Pojar and Mackinnon's *Plants of the Pacific Northwest Coast*. It may take you hours or even days to get your first unknown plant identified, but this will be your introduction to field botany. After you have identified and sketched about a dozen plants you may be comfortable enough to consider identifying plants for consumption. Trying to jump right into foraging without this basic training is like trying to read a Tokyo newspaper with a Japanese-English pocket dictionary.

Identification, Recognition, and the Search Image

I once took a group of fifth grade boys at a summer camp on a wild food hike and showed them sheep sorrel. I pointed out how the leaves flared out at the base and grew in a rosette, then asked them to bring back some sheep sorrel to pass my inspection before they could eat it. Several kids brought me handfuls of leaves that did not have any lobes at the base – generally considered one of the plant's distinguishing features – and the naturalist at the camp, who was assisting me, admonished them for paying such poor attention. But in fact, every leaf they brought back was a sheep sorrel leaf – many just lacked the characteristic lobes. So how did those kids recognize the sheep sorrel leaves that were so utterly different in shape than those that they had been shown?

When you become familiar with a plant your mind begins to develop a file of information and characteristics associated with it. This file, or set of associations, is what I call a ***search image***. People do not recognize familiar things, whether a plant species or one of their parents, by specific distinguishing characteristics. Instead, we recognize them with their respective search images, which contain far more details about their physical aspect than we could ever consciously remember. The search image contains more nuances of texture, shape, position, color, smell, and other such things than could possibly be conveyed verbally.

A distinguishing feature of clover is that it has three leaflets, as any plant guide will tell you. But our search image of a clover not only tells us that a four-leaved clover is still a clover; it is so keen that most of us can instantly recognize a fraction of a clover leaflet stuck to a lawnmower blade. Those fifth-grade boys recognized sheep sorrel because it had sheep sorrel's color, texture, size, petioles, and growth form – leaf shape was only one of dozens of features contained in their search image of it.

Identification and recognition are two completely different things. Identification comes first; it is a careful and deliberate process that one must go through as she becomes familiar with a particular plant. Recognition occurs when a functioning search image is built through repeated positive identification. Every subsequent encounter with that plant will enrich and refine the search image until recognition is instantaneous and effortless.

The well-developed search image involves so many identification characteristics that it is essentially foolproof. It is the incredible tool that allows one to recognize an elm tree in a pasture a quarter-mile away, or to spot a familiar wildflower along the interstate in a quarter-second glance. Once you learn to recognize a plant, you will not have to go through the tedious process of identification every time you harvest it.

Look-Alikes, Look-Similars, and Poisonous Plants

There is no such thing as a look-alike; there are only look-similars. If people couldn't tell the plants apart, they wouldn't be considered separate species. Any edible plant can be consistently and reliably distinguished from similar-looking toxic plants by the trained eye – but your eye is trained only after you have carefully gone through the process of identifying the plant and developing a search image of it. Before collecting an edible plant that has a dangerous look-similar, you should memorize a few features that distinguish the edible species from the toxic one. Even if you confidently recognize the edible plant, use these features to double-check every specimen that you harvest.

Some edible plants do appear similar to harmful plants, and such similarities can fool those who practice insufficient care in plant identification. A good example is common milkweed and common dogbane. Although there are a dozen easily observed differences between these two species in the shoot stage, and a person familiar with them can differentiate them with ease, many foragers have been fooled by their similarities.

The danger involved with mistaking similar-looking plants varies according to the plants in question. The usual result of mistaken identity would be having to spit out something that tastes terrible, but a few plants are so toxic that you could be seriously harmed by a small sample. Therefore, **it is absolutely unacceptable to taste or eat any part of any unidentified plant under any circumstance**.

In the individual plant accounts I have tried to mention toxic plants that seem likely to cause confusion with the plant under discussion. However, it is impossible for me to list every potentially confusing species. I suggest familiarizing yourself with look-similars as you learn the edibles that they resemble, since this will make you feel much more comfortable with the edible plant's identification. If the similar-looking plant is extremely poisonous, you should refrain from eating the edible plant that it resembles until you can confidently identify *both* species. I also recommend that you wait to eat any plant with a truly dangerous look-similar until you feel proficient and experienced at plant identification in general. However, do not let the horror stories of ill-informed people scare you into a state of hypercaution that prevents you from using perfectly good food plants.

Learning From Others

One of the best ways to learn about edible wild plants is to accompany an experienced forager into the field (and hopefully the kitchen as well). Having somebody else identify a food plant for you is certainly far easier than going through the process on your own. However, if you do this you need to keep in mind that you are trusting your life to another person.

Poisonings have been known to occur when some careless person tells another that a certain plant is edible when it is in fact toxic. Some people say such things to show off their "knowledge," perhaps not considering that somebody might actually put their claim to the test. When a misinformed person does eat the plant, the misinformer may say nothing rather than lose face by admitting that he didn't really know what he was talking about.

However, it is not very hard to tell who the real foragers are. Ask them questions; they should know a lot about the plant that they claim is edible. They should have eaten the plant previous to making such claims, and they should be happy to eat the plant again with you in attendance. (Most people want to look smart, but few will put their lives in jeopardy to do so.) The simple moral here is to be careful whom you trust.

Food Allergies and First-Taste Procedures

So, you have gone through all the hoops; you've identified your plant with a mountain of references and they all concur; you've examined it inside out, upside down, and half-to-death, and it fits the descriptions like a glove. You've found it growing all over the field by your house and in a dozen other places. It's now the right time of year to collect it; you have a pile in the refrigerator and you want to see if it was worth all the effort.

The first time that you eat the plant, exercise some restraint. Cook it by itself and taste a small portion carefully. If it is bitter or otherwise distasteful, spit it out. This is an extremely important secondary line of defense. The tongue was designed to tell us which foods are safe and which aren't, and it does a remarkably good job of this. Most toxic plants taste terrible. (Of course, this does NOT mean that you should go around tasting plants to see if they are safe to eat, because there will be exceptions to the rule, and some plants are so toxic that only a taste could be harmful.) For example, if you mistook dogbane for milkweed, your shoots would taste incredibly bitter. That bitterness practically screams "Don't eat me!" But I know of a few people who, confident that they had milkweed, and thinking that milkweed was supposed to be bitter, forced themselves to choke down the dogbane. Not surprisingly, they got sick. One of the most important safety rules in foraging is this: **if it tastes bad, don't eat it**.

A problem arises here, much like the problem that I earlier called "making it fit." Somebody can be so excited about foraging that she convinces herself that a plant tastes good when in fact it does not. Some people even think that wild food is supposed to taste bad, so they judge it differently than they would judge cultivated food. Not only is this an insult to foraged food, but it is also dangerous because things that taste bad are almost always bad for you.

If, on the other hand, you like the taste of your new plant, go ahead and consume a small serving. Even if it's really good, resist the temptation to pig out. Wait a day and see how the plant affects you. (Refrain from eating two or more new foods on the same day, otherwise, if there is a problem, you will not be certain which food caused it.) Perhaps this particular plant, though edible, disagrees with your metabolism and gives you gas or nausea. Most likely, however, you will feel great afterward. If all goes well, treat the plant as you would any other vegetable with similar qualities, incorporating it into your diet in a sensible fashion.

There is a slight possibility that you could be allergic or intolerant to a plant that is normally edible. This phenomenon is fairly well known with such familiar foods as peanuts, almonds, mangoes, and cashews, as thousands of people are affected by them. People are usually exposed to most of the foods that they will eat for the rest of their lives during early childhood; it is a rare event thereafter to consume a totally new food product. But the forager is exposed to new foods on a regular basis, which increases the likelihood of experiencing an allergic/intolerant reaction.

Food allergies are serious and can make a person extremely ill. Symptoms of the first reactions are usually similar to food poisoning or stomach flu; the body purges itself of the unwanted substance by vomiting and diarrhea, accompanied by nausea and general physical discomfort. Certain groups of plants, such as nuts and legumes, cause allergies more frequently than others. Unfortunately, these reactions do not necessarily occur upon the first exposure to a plant; you might eat it safely several times before your body develops the allergy or intolerance. If you ever get unexpectedly ill from a plant food that you know to be edible, suspect such a reaction. If you confirm that you are allergic or intolerant, treat the plant as if it is toxic, since symptoms generally get more severe with each exposure.

Food allergies are an inescapable and unpredictable fact of life. To collect wild foods you must assume this risk. However, don't let this scare you off; such reactions are rare, and they are no more prevalent among wild foods than among cultivated ones.

Edible and Poisonous: What Do They Mean?

Most people believe that there is a clear dichotomy between edible and poisonous plants. The common notion is that you can eat an edible plant without harm, but if you ingest a poisonous plant you soon drop dead, or at least get rushed to the emergency room. This view is misleading. One's understanding of diet, nutrition, and the edible plant literature is impaired without a realistic grasp of the concepts of *edible* and *poisonous*.

Many edible plants are poisonous and many poisonous plants are edible: the two properties are not mutually exclusive. All of us eat poisonous substances on a regular basis. Before continuing, let us define an *edible* plant as *a plant that produces one or more parts which can be consumed without negative health repercussions*; and let us define a *poisonous* or *toxic* plant (the two terms are used interchangeably) as *a plant that produces one or more parts which can cause negative health repercussions if consumed.* This is how the terms are conventionally used in the discussion of wild plants.

The same plant can produce one edible part (potato tubers) and one toxic part (potato leaves), but this is not my point. Neither should I need to reiterate that certain plant parts may be toxic if harvested at the wrong time, or that certain plants are poisonous unless subjected to specific treatments that render them edible. These things are widely known and well understood. What many people don't seem to understand, however, is that *the same part of the same plant, harvested at the same time, usually fits the definitions of both terms, edible and poisonous:* It is possible to consume it without harm, and it is possible to consume it until it harms you.

Rather than a dichotomy of edible and toxic, there is a continuum between two extremes. At one pole you have potent, deadly plants such as water hemlock, while at the opposite you have rather benign foods like the apple. However, every food and drink has the potential to harm you if you consume too much of it. The kidneys and the liver are major features of human physiology because *every* food we eat contains substances that are toxic and others that produce toxins upon metabolism and breakdown. The proper question, then, is not *if* a substance can harm you but *how much* will it take to harm you.

When I was a child I loved green bell peppers. One time when I was six years old I was helping my neighbor weed his garden and he kindly rewarded me by offering "as many green peppers as you want." I grabbed one and ate it right away, and a little while later I returned for another. Not wanting to squander my special privilege, within a few hours I had eaten five whole, raw green peppers. Most people would agree that green peppers are edible, but my small body felt very ill after that.

In 1915, more than 10,000 Americans died of pellagra (Wardlaw, 1999), a niacin deficiency disease that results from eating corn (maize) as too great a proportion in the diet. Thousands still die annually of this condition in poorer parts of Africa and Asia. It might not be fair to call corn toxic if it just happened to lack niacin, but this isn't the case. Corn actually contains a fair amount of niacin; it causes pellagra, however, because it contains molecules that bind to niacin and make it unavailable to the body. A superfluous corn intake can lead to a niacin deficiency that results in pellagra, even if you are consuming sufficient niacin.

If your diet consists wholly of protein for a prolonged period (as might occur if you were incarcerated in a refrigerated semi trailer full of lean chicken breasts with a grill and a warm sleeping bag) ammonia and urea will be produced by the protein's metabolism faster than the liver and kidneys can handle their excretion. They will build up in the system and can eventually cause death.

Most of our common spices and seasonings are toxic enough that consuming a few ounces would make a person very ill; in large enough doses they could be fatal. But who eats a few ounces of rosemary, mustard, or nutmeg? Who slurps down a glass of horseradish? What person, given alternatives, would choose to eat maize gruel as the main course of every meal for months on end? And who in the world gets locked in the chicken truck?

We eat things in safe portions because our bodies tell us when to stop. Cravings and revulsions keep our diets in line. As a culture we have developed norms and habits regulating the use and consumption of familiar foods. Baked garlic served as a dinner entrée would certainly raise some eyebrows – and that's a good thing, because anybody who ate two cups of it probably wouldn't feel well afterward. However, we have not developed such norms for wild foods, increasing the likelihood that somebody will overindulge and suffer the results of poisoning.

When a wild food is consumed in an unreasonably large portion and it makes somebody sick, this will be attributed to the *plant's toxicity*, but when the same occurs with a cultivated plant the event will be attributed to the *person's stupidity*. When I got sick from green peppers, my parents chuckled and made that'll-teach-ya type comments. If a wild plant had caused identical symptoms they probably would have rushed me to the hospital in utter terror, had my stomach pumped, and warned me to forever avoid that terrible plant – or worse yet, all wild plants. The story might have made the local newspaper, striking fear into other mothers with small children.

Wild foods tend to be judged by different standards than familiar cultivated ones. If a wild plant, unfamiliar as a spice, had the same physiological effects as a small quantity of jalapeño pepper (burning sensation in the mouth and throat, irritation of the digestive tract prompting often severe diarrhea, to name the more obvious) it would be universally and unequivocally called toxic. Jalapeños *are* toxic; we just eat them anyway. Traces of solanine are said by many to make the fruit of wild *Solanum nigrum* poisonous, while the same chemical in cultivated tomatoes, potatoes, eggplants, tomatillos, and bell peppers is dismissed as insignificant. Wild food authors warn us repeatedly of the oxalic acid in vegetables such as wood sorrel, sheep sorrel, and lamb's quarters – while conventional cookbooks never warn us about the same substance in rhubarb stalks, spinach, and garden sorrel.

Hopefully the reader can begin to understand how so many wild plants are called both edible and poisonous in the literature: They can be eaten in moderation without worry, but can make one sick if consumed in abnormally large amounts. Do not let terms such as "mildly poisonous" elicit undue fear when used in reference to known edible plants that have been consumed for generations.

None of this is meant to imply that some plants aren't dangerous to consume. Certain species contain extremely potent or destructive toxins, or extremely high levels of toxins, and these should never be consumed in any amount. Such plants should be unambiguously called *poisonous, toxic,* or *deadly.*

Some books, especially those focusing on survival, assert that one plant or another is "edible but distasteful," "marginally edible," or "fit for emergencies only." This is misleading. A plant that is universally considered distasteful is toxic. It may be only mildly toxic, allowing you to eat a little without harm, but any portion large enough to contain a significant number of calories will make you sick. After consuming a certain quantity you will find it revolting. If you do force yourself to continue eating it you will either vomit or become ill, either of which is costly in a survival situation. Such plants are worthless as food sources.

I am often asked questions like, "If I eat these wapato leaves when they are mature they won't taste good, but they won't hurt me either, will they?" They will. If they aren't for you, they are against you. Your kidneys, liver, and intestines have better things to do than deal with such foolish notions. You might be amazed at how precisely your cravings, revulsions, and taste preferences regulate your diet, and how extraordinarily difficult it is to override them; you should not be surprised at how consistently your well-being will be negatively impacted when you do ignore them. This illustrates the last rule of safe foraging: **Plants are edible only insofar as they taste good and are pleasant to eat.**

Children and the Foraging Instinct

Many parents are justifiably nervous about the prospect of letting their children forage, especially alone – but often there is little they can do to stop it. Children who are allowed to spend a good deal of unsupervised time outside, especially with other children, will almost always begin eating a small number of wild plants. Usually these are the same few species: sheep sorrel, wood sorrel, and grape tendrils being the most common. Children love and seem to crave the sour flavor of the oxalic acid found in these plants, and it is mysterious and amazing how so many children, even in this modern, anti-foraging culture, learn of their edibility. I regularly discuss this with groups of adults in my workshops, and roughly half of them claim to have eaten one or more of these plants during childhood – but few can recall how they learned of it.

I have done a small number of wild food programs for children, or that included children, and I have been impressed with their aptitude. A group of fourth through sixth graders at a boys camp amazed me: I did a four-hour collection and preparation session with nine kids, showing them about twenty species of edible plants. When I returned two weeks later for a follow up, most of the same kids attended, plus several new ones. Every participant from the first session remembered several plants, and one bright boy could perfectly and confidently identify all the plants we had discussed, rattling off identifying characteristics with ease. The veterans had already taught many of the plants to the newcomers.

At another weekend camp for parents and children, I taught the group, ranging in age from five to fifty, nine of the most common trees, shrubs, and herbs around camp. On the last day, the only person who could identify all nine was the precocious five-year-old.

I have been repeatedly amazed at the ability of children to observe plants and to recognize those previously shown to them upon spotting them again. When shown a properly identified plant, the search image seems to form easily in their minds. In fact, the worst mistakes of identity that I have witnessed were all committed by adults. Perhaps there is more of a foraging instinct than we like to admit. I suspect that civilized people actually lose their foraging aptitude as they age; like a limb, it is either used and developed or it atrophies.

This is a difficult situation for parents, however, because **the majority of serious plant poisonings occur when children under five years old put unknown vegetation in their mouths** (Turner and Szczawinski, 1991). At some point, however, children become fully cognizant of the potential danger of poisonous plants, and from then on are no more likely to poison themselves than adults. It is up to each parent to decide when a child has developed to this degree and is ready to participate in foraging.

Harvest and Preparation Methods for Wild Plant Foods

The harvest and preparation guidelines outlined in this chapter are useful generalizations – even for plants not specifically covered in this volume – but before eating any plant, find detailed information specific to that species, as exceptions to these generalizations may be significant.

Some Thoughts on Using Wild Plants

For most foragers, gathering a plant is an exciting, awe-inspiring, even sacred moment, and the process of turning raw produce taken from the outdoors into fine sustenance is almost magical. In practice these two steps are inseparable: preparation begins with the selection of the plants to be harvested, and the gatherer is never finished until the food is consumed.

All wild plants, like cultivated ones, need to be harvested at the proper stage if they are to be edible or palatable. In many cases this prime condition lasts for a very brief period and collecting just a little too early or too late will yield a poor product. In a few cases, plants in the wrong stage can be toxic. After identification, then, the next step in harvesting is to find plants in the proper stage for collection. This is addressed on a plant-by-plant basis later in the book.

Plants should be harvested conscientiously with a final product in mind. That means you only pick what you will use; wild plants are too precious to waste with lustful overharvest. They should be gathered carefully: cut or pinch succulent shoots, shear or cleanly break fruit clusters, pluck only tender greens, dig roots and tubers without cutting them to pieces, and don't smash fruit. After collection, place the plants in a clean container, keep them cool and out of the sunlight, and don't let them dry out. Finally, prepare them for consumption or storage as soon as possible.

Be patient as you learn to harvest and prepare each plant; there are many special techniques and subtle skills involved in these seemingly simple tasks. There is a saying that *anything worth doing is worth doing poorly at first*. This wisdom is eminently appropriate to foraging. Your first attempts at some of the things described in this book will prove awkward and perhaps frustrating.

Do not be discouraged – efficiency will come with time, experience, and persistence.

Sand is Not a Wild Food

Dirt and teeth are enemies. For much of human history, old people commonly starved to death because their teeth were worn down to nothing, thus we have an instinctive disdain for grit in our food. It's really a bummer to expend all the effort to gather and prepare a wild dish only to suffer through its consumption or, worse yet, dump it out the kitchen window. Even if you are excited or hungry enough to tolerate a sandbox salad, anybody else to whom you feed it will be decidedly unimpressed.

I dwell on this point because, through the course of teaching many foraging workshops in which the plants collected by many different hands go into a communal pot, I have come to realize that careless contamination with dirt is an enormous problem. Some people will pull up a whole plant, root and all, and literally throw it into our salad bowl with gobs of dirt or mud attached. But unwanted grit also has more subtle ways of invading the dinner plate.

Keep on the dirt alert at all times when foraging. Low, spreading or trailing plants are highly susceptible; try to get them where they rest on leaf litter instead of bare ground, or rinse them thoroughly. Bare soil underneath any plant lower than 12–18 inches can mean serious trouble, as rain splashes the dirt up onto the lower leaves. Plants on beaches and in or beside bare crop fields, where gusts of wind pick up loose particles, are something to watch for. In spring, rivers often flood and deposit alluvial dirt on acres of otherwise perfect vegetables. Roadside dust, though not as bad as sand, has also ruined many a perfect patch of fruit or greens.

Hairy or rough plants are always more problematic in this respect than the smooth-surfaced ones. Since the dirt can cling tenaciously, it is highly preferable to find plants growing where they have stayed clean rather than attempting to wash gritty ones.

There Is no Hamburger Tree

"Nature is like a banquet," many of us have heard. "One has only to learn how to eat it."

I beg to differ. Nature is NOT like a banquet. It's not like a supermarket, either; it's not even like a well-spaced produce stand with most of the stalls hidden in the bushes.

At a banquet, the prepared meal is laid out before you; If you find that in the woods, you're raiding someone's picnic. At a supermarket you find food that's already been processed – the grain is threshed, milled, and baked, the fruit is juiced, and the vegetables are canned. At a produce stand you don't have to dig potatoes, twist off ears of corn, or pick raspberries.

I'm all for extolling the bounty of the Earth, but let's be realistic. If you really need an analogy, let's say that Nature is like a garden where you don't have to plant, cultivate, or weed. You still have to dig, pick, wash, peel, and everything else.

Many people seem to lose interest in any wild food that requires work beyond gathering and perhaps washing and cooking. This includes most wild food authors. That limitation basically leaves us with salad greens, potherbs, shoots, small-seeded berries, and mushrooms. You will find that the wild food literature focuses heavily on such plants.

I often say in my workshops that the more useful a plant is for subsistence, the less information you can find about it. I wish I were kidding. The wild food literature normally pays only lip service to staple foods because they don't fall into any of the easy-to-use categories listed above. Authors commonly try to make staple plants sound more appealing to the armchair forager by understating the time and effort required to harvest and prepare them and oversimplifying the instructions for doing so. Such naïve, sugar-coated accounts may make pleasant reading but they have little practical value.

I eat salads, berries, potherbs, and mushrooms too – but what about the roots, tubers, nuts, legumes, starchy vegetables, fruits, and grains that have always comprised the vast majority of the human diet? Well, here's a fact that you may have heard from your mama: *if you want to eat, you're going to have to work*. I can't figure out why so many people suppose that this rule shouldn't apply to foraging. Again and again I'm amazed to hear frustrated foraging "enthusiasts" complaining that wild foods take "so much work." What did they expect? Ready-to-eat, delicious, abundant, and nutritionally complete high-calorie food that grows on trees? You already know what I am going to say: *There is no hamburger tree.*

How many fishermen do you know who complain about the hours they spend on the water? How many miles does a deer hunter walk or drive for each animal he shoots? How many hours does a gardener spend tilling, weeding, and tending each pound of vegetables? Yet none of them complain; they know that effort is part of the deal. Effort is what makes these activities satisfying; without the effort, they would just be shopping. I hate shopping.

I certainly hope that armchair foragers enjoy this book, but I wrote it for people who actually plan on going afield and coming home with food to prepare. Thus I have included many plants even though they require effort, skill, and equipment to harvest and prepare.

Many wild food authors ignore or dismiss any plant that requires significant processing before consumption. Perhaps they are unaware of the large number of domesticated foods which require extended processing, and of the even greater number whose wild ancestors did. Olives are poisonous as they come off the tree; they are subject to at least a week of leaching before being consumed. Wild almonds are toxic, yet they were gathered and prepared for millennia before domestic, nontoxic forms developed. Manioc, a staple for millions in the tropics, can be deadly in the raw state. In fact, to dismiss a wild food because it requires processing – whether leaching, winnowing, parching, shelling, or some other method – would be to dismiss the ancestor of nearly every major crop plant on Earth.

In this book I will not send you looking for the holy grail of wild foods; I will not hand you the icing without the cake. Foraging is something to *do*, not just dream about. I will give you the tools to do it – but *you* must provide the work.

Greens

The term "greens" refers to the edible leafy portion of a plant. Familiar cultivated greens include lettuce, spinach, and collards. Despite the incredible array of wild greens available, they comprise a minor part of the average person's diet. Greens tend to be low in calories, high in fiber, and very high in vitamins and minerals; many are surprisingly rich in protein. Most people would be better nourished if they chose to include more greens in their diet, and wild greens are a fun way to increase one's consumption.

When gathering greens, look for the newest, youngest growth. This will taste better and have less fiber, plus it will be more digestible and contain proportionately more calories and protein. The new growth can be identified by smaller size, lighter green color, the ease with which it breaks off, and by its location at the terminal end of a branch or shoot. Some young leaves are shiny and have a rubbery feel to them; they may also droop because their stems have not yet had the time to produce tough fibers. Another test that works to see if certain greens are still tender is to pull on them gently – if they can stretch notably without tearing they are not yet fibrous.

Greens are most abundant in spring and early summer. With most perennial greens, the leaves are tender enough to eat for only a brief period during the spring. The greens of annuals are generally best when young but remain tender much longer than those of perennials or biennials; some are good through the entire growing season. On biennial plants with edible leaves, the greens to seek are usually the young, upright leaves of the second-year plant, especially the first few leaves on the newly emerging stalk. Ground-hugging basal rosette leaves tend to be unpalatable. Through late summer and fall only a few species of wild green are available, which become highly appreciated.

Collect greens into a clean bowl or bag, or directly into your hand. Pinch, bend, or cut off the greens that you pick – do not yank off whole branches or tear out whole plants. Some people use a knife or shears for collecting greens, but no tool is more effective or convenient than a thumbnail of the right size pinched against the first finger.

Greens are at their best the moment you pick them. As they age they lose flavor and nutrients, and as they dry they toughen – often dramatically. If it is impossible to use the greens immediately, placing them in an airtight container in a cool place will keep them reasonably fresh for a few hours to a few days, depending on the type.

Some greens are excellent to eat raw; these are what I call "salad greens" in the text, despite the fact that I only occasionally make a salad from them. More often, I just grab a handful and enjoy them on the spot. Besides nibbling them alone or adding them to salads, raw greens can be used as garnish or placed on sandwiches.

Cooked greens (potherbs) are usually either boiled or steamed, although they can also be wilted in oil, added to stir-fry, or used in dishes like lasagna. Almost any salad green is acceptable as a cooked green, too. Steaming retains more of the nutrients and flavor than boiling, but either method is acceptable. Most greens shrink dramatically when cooked, so keep this in mind as you collect. Some are very tender and need only brief cooking, while others are tougher and warrant longer cooking. There are a small number of greens that carry an unpleasant flavor which can be removed by boiling and then draining and discarding the water.

Different greens have different purposes. Some are bitter, spicy, or aromatic and should be used sparingly, while others are mild and hearty and may be served in larger portions. Many wild food authors comment on the North American palate's abhorrence of the bitter flavor, particularly in greens. While this is partly true, more often it is used to counter the prevalent dislike of certain common wild foods such as dandelion and chicory. There seems to be some confusion about *the purpose of bitterness*. People can tolerate, and often learn to appreciate, a small serving of bitter greens, but most would be disgusted if you tried to serve them these same greens in a larger quantity. It is probably true that Americans do not eat enough bitters, but bitter greens are never a primary source of calories in any culture.

I like a small serving of potherbs with almost any meal, unadulterated or perhaps with a touch of salt. Others like to add pepper, butter, cream, melted cheese, croutons, or similar embellishments. I also enjoy greens in many of the soups, casseroles, and hot-dishes that I eat on a regular basis.

Shoots and Stalks

Shoots are the young, tender stems of various plants. They are produced when biennials or perennials grow rapidly using previously stored energy, and they are tender because the plants have not yet had the time to produce cellulose in their stems. With the exception of fern fiddleheads, most shoots appear spear-like. They usually have a few small, immature leaves on them but differ from greens in that the stem comprises the majority of their bulk. People tend to eat shoots as a larger part of the diet than greens, but they are still a minor source of calories. The only well known cultivated shoot vegetable is asparagus, but there are dozens of wild ones.

Other plants have stalks that are edible or have an edible portion in the center. Two well known cultivated stalk vegetables are celery and rhubarb; wild plants provide a wide selection of these, too.

Edible shoots and stalks are available primarily from the middle of spring into the early part of summer. Generally, the same species of shoot will come up one to three weeks later in a field than in a forest. This habit is a response to the greater likelihood of frost in the open; it greatly extends the season for many shoot vegetables.

Although the wild food literature is replete with injunctions to collect various shoot vegetables only when under a certain height, you should ignore such instructions. Height is the wrong indicator of prime condition. Look for robust shoots with a high thickness-to-height ratio, tiny or unopened leaves, and stems that are tender and flexible.

It is common for the bottom section of a shoot to be tough and woody while the upper portion remains tender. When harvesting shoot vegetables, feel along the stem to determine the extent of the *bend-easy zone:* this will tell you how much of the shoot will be tender enough to enjoy. You will have to learn through experimentation how easily each species should bend to indicate tenderness.

When gathering shoots or stalks, do not tug straight up on them; bend, pinch, or cut them off at the proper point. Yanking them out pulls up unwanted plant material that will just need to be trimmed later, may get the food dirty, and often damages the root system.

As with greens, use the shoots as soon as possible. If you can't get to them right away, they last a little longer than greens in the refrigerator – just make sure to keep them from drying out. Most shoots will toughen dramatically when stored for a few days, however, so it may be necessary to cut off the tougher bottom ends before consumption.

I like shoots steamed or boiled and served with a little salt or butter. They are also delicious in soup and a great many other dishes. In general, just boil shoots long enough to make them as tender as you like; the cooking time will vary according to your texture preference and the particular kind of shoot being prepared. Most shoots and stalks are edible raw but people tend to prefer them cooked.

Since shoots are often found in great abundance they are good vegetables to store in bulk for use later. Most are too succulent to dry well, but they can be frozen after a quick blanching or pressure-canned.

Underground Vegetables

Greens and shoots are good, nutritious food, but underground plant organs are much better sources of calories. Usually less fibrous and milder in flavor, they are more digestible and better suited to serve as the bulk of a meal. Most of the calories in underground storage organs are in the form of carbohydrates.

Some foragers are turned off by the prospect of having to dig for food, but these people are missing out on some of the best vegetables that Nature has to offer. Furthermore, knowledge of subterranean vegetables could be invaluable in a survival situation, since for much of the year there is no other readily available source of concentrated calories.

Most underground vegetables are at their best from late fall through early spring – corresponding to the time when the above-ground portion of the plant is dormant. They can also be collected for a few weeks on either side of the dormant period, but at these extremes they will not be of the highest quality. Rather than describe this period of availability for every underground vegetable in the book, I refer to it simply as the *root season*. Spring ephemerals are the primary exception to this pattern; their roots can also be gathered during the summer, since the plants are dormant at that time.

Confusing Terminology of Underground Plant Parts

Most people call any plant part that is underground a root, but botanists don't. If you're going to learn about edible plants it would be wise to learn the difference between the various types of underground storage organs that plants produce. Understanding plant parts and what they do helps one understand the life cycle of the plant and can aid in identification.

Root	The underground part of the plant designed to anchor it as well as absorb nutrients and water.
Stem	The structures of the plant designed to transport water and nutrients between the roots and the leaves, flowers, etc. Stems can be under, on, or above the ground.
Taproot	A thick, tapering root, usually fleshy and growing downward. Examples include carrot, parsnip, and evening primrose. Most plants with edible taproots have a biennial life cycle. During their first year, biennials exist as a basal rosette without any stalk. The sole purpose of this rosette is to photosynthesize and store energy in its root. The root is then used to fuel extremely fast growth of a flowering stalk in the second year. After flowering and producing seed, the plant usually dies. Collect biennial roots only from plants in the rosette stage, which lack a stalk.
Tuber	An enlarged portion of a stem (usually underground), used to store nutrients. Examples include potato, wapato, and jerusalem artichoke. Normally, a single plant produces many tubers each year, and these serve as its primary form of reproduction. Tubers usually have significantly less fiber than roots.
Rhizome	A horizontal underground stem, sometimes enlarged to store food. Examples include cattail and ginger. Rhizomes have two purposes: they store energy and provide a means by which the plant can move a short distance every year. Many are too fibrous to chew, so an edible starch is extracted from them, while others are much less fibrous and can be eaten whole.
Bulb	A subterranean bud having thick, fleshy, modified leaves for storing nutrients. Examples include onions and garlic. Bulbs are mostly confined to plants of the lily family. They store energy from one year to the next but only have a limited role in spreading or reproduction.
Corm	An enlarged section at the base of an upright stem, usually found at or just below the surface. There are no well known cultivated examples, but jack-in-the-pulpit has a corm. Corms generally serve for energy storage only and not for reproduction.

Many edible underground parts contain appreciable amounts of a non-digestible complex carbohydrate called *inulin* (not insulin). Inulin is held responsible for the excessive flatulence produced by some root vegetables, especially when they are eaten raw or undercooked. This substance passes into the lower digestive system unabsorbed, where it is broken down by bacteria, producing gas. Roots contain the greatest quantity of inulin in early fall, but this gets gradually converted into simple sugar in preparation for growth the following spring, making them taste sweeter while increasing their usable calories and decreasing their propensity to cause gas.

Inulin can be broken down into digestible sugars by prolonged cooking. Most root vegetables, especially when collected early in the season, should be cooked thoroughly before consumption to break down some of the inulin and render them more digestible.

Try not to damage subterranean vegetables during harvest; any damaged ones should be used up first. After collection keep them moist, cool, and out of the light. Underground vegetables can be stored dirty but should be cleaned well before cooking or eating. Pay special attention to knobs, eyes, or places where roots fork or branch, as a pocket of dirt is often hidden in such places.

Taproot vegetables are a traditional standby in soups and casseroles, and many are good eaten alone. Wild roots can be used in any of the ways that you would use cultivated roots, but the flavors and textures will vary. A few wild roots are even excellent munched raw like carrots. Tubers lend themselves to most of the same culinary uses, but they are also popularly baked, boiled and mashed, or sliced thin and fried. Even more so than roots, tubers are suitable to serve as the main source of calories in a meal. Rhizomes, bulbs and corms are a varied lot and it is hard to generalize about their culinary use.

About Shovels, Trowels, and Digging Sticks

For digging wild roots and such you can use any kind of shovel, but I prefer one with a short handle – mostly because they are easier to carry and fit more readily into the trunk of my car. Don't buy a shovel with a handle made of plastic, PVC, or fiberglass. The manufacturer might guarantee the handle to never break, but they neglect to mention that it will come loose from the blade. Wooden-handled shovels are both cheaper and better, and their breakage is usually the result of misuse.

The shovel is useful for digging many underground vegetables, but it is most often used for excavating taproots, which normally run straight down into the soil. After watching hundreds of students attempt to dig out roots I have realized that the ability to properly use a shovel for this task is a rare skill these days, so I'll take a minute to explain it.

Place the tip of the shovel blade on the ground two to four inches from

the root you intend to dig out (the higher figure for larger roots). Ideally the root will be in the middle of the scoop of dirt you upturn. Now here's the important part: *The blade should be oriented* **vertically***, so that it goes into the soil* *parallel to* *the root rather than at an intersecting angle which will sever the root partway down. This means that* *the shovel handle should not be vertical; it should be angled away from you.* Holding the shovel in this position, jump up and

This small digging stick, held in one hand, is used to unearth ground beans, toothwort tubers, and other small, shallow underground vegetables.

This digging stick, perfect for many roots, bulbs, and tubers, is held with two hands.

land with both feet on the top of the blade, thrusting down with the feet if necessary to drive the blade into the soil. (Note: jumping is optional for the accident prone.) If the targeted root is very small, don't drive the shovel deeper than necessary to unearth it. Once the shovel blade is driven properly into the soil, pry slowly back toward you until your scoop of dirt comes loose. (Shovel handles often break when yanked or pulled mercilessly at this juncture; if necessary, rock back and forth, alternately applying pressure on the handle and then relieving it. You may need to insert the shovel on the opposite side of the root as well to loosen the entire scoop of dirt. If the dirt is very firm do not drive the shovel blade all the way in before prying on the handle.) Break the scoop in half if necessary, then pull the root free. The entire process described above takes five to thirty seconds to execute.

A trowel is a small shovel held in one hand, often used by gardeners. It does not work nearly as well in the rocky, hard, root-filled soil of the wilds as it does in the loose, friable loam of a well-tended garden. Nevertheless, a trowel is a nice tool to have for digging out many underground vegetables. A dandelion digger is similar to a trowel, but the blade is narrower and longer. With either tool, get the sturdiest, highest-quality one you can find.

Some people chuckle at me when I mention the use of a digging stick, as if I would only use such an inferior, outmoded tool on account of some quaint desire to feel more like my Paleolithic ancestors while foraging. I laugh back. My digging stick and I can outdo any shovel-wielding competitor collecting ground beans or spring-beauty roots.

In fact, I use two distinct kinds of digging sticks. The first has a long, narrow blade, about 12 × 2.5 inches (30 × 6.5 cm) long, and a handle about 8 inches (20 cm) long, widening at the top to provide a larger handhold. It allows more precise and efficient digging than a trowel, plus it is far more sturdy, allowing one to pry forcefully with it. This two-handed digging stick is used to unearth individual bulbs, tubers, or corms without having to turn over a big scoop of dirt, and it is used to work around rocks or roots where a shovel would be useless. My second kind of digging stick is much smaller, slightly curved, and is held in one hand when in use. It is designed specifically for gathering ground beans but is occasionally used for other plants.

When I am on a long hike it is simple to carry a digging stick, while a shovel is a cumbersome annoyance (unless I am confronted by a belligerent bear, in which case a shovel is much more comforting). Thus, when only a tiny portion of my time is spent digging, I might take a stick instead of a shovel even where the shovel would work better.

Fruits and Berries

Wild fruits come in a dazzling array of colors, flavors, shapes, and sizes. An important part of a healthy diet, they provide many important nutrients, including calories in the form of simple carbohydrates and vitamin C. Wild fruits were collected and eaten in great quantity by every Native culture in North America outside of the Arctic.

Harvest Methods and Tools

To reduce crushing, pick berries into a wide, shallow container rather than a tall, deep one (especially very soft berries like raspberries or strawberries). This will extend their shelf life by several hours. Plus, shallow containers will be less prone to disastrous spills. I pick fruit directly into a one-gallon container that I tie around my waist. I empty this into a squat 3.5-gallon tub with a cover that serves as my bulk container.

I learned recently that in some areas a strap-on berry picking container such as the one I use has been dubbed a *blickey.* I immediately adopted the term because I am sick and tired of saying "strap-on berry picking container." The blickey is a godsend to a serious berry picker. With it, you'll never have to keep track of where you put your pail, you'll never have to bend over in awkward positions to drop fruit into a bowl or waste time picking the container up and moving it around, you'll never spill your berries, you'll always have both hands free for picking, and you can even climb trees with a container! The only time the blickey doesn't help is when you are picking berries that grow low to

A blickey being used to pick thimbleberries.

the ground and require you to squat. For such berries, I just set a bowl on the ground and scoot it around as I pick.

To make a blickey, select a box-like plastic tub that is as deep or deeper than it is wide. (The deep, flat edge against your belly stabilizes the container, which is very important.) Drill a hole in each of the two top corners of the side that will rest against your body, run a small rope through them, tie the ends behind your back, and *voila*, you have the greatest berry-picking invention since the container itself. (Because the blickey is deep, you may want to empty it before it is full when collecting soft berries to keep from crushing them.)

Berry hook with a foot loop being used to hold down a chokecherry limb.

The next best tool for the wild fruit picker is the *berry hook*. This is a rod 4–6 feet (1.25–2 meters) long with a hook on one end and a loop of rope tied to the other. This implement is used like an extension of the arm to grab high branches or the upper trunks of flexible shrubs and pull them down within reach of eager hands. After pulling down the limb, put your foot through the loop to hold it there, leaving both hands free to gather fruit. Hook branches as far out or as high up as you can reach to reduce the strain placed on them when they are bent down. If necessary, grab the branch with your hand once it is within reach and readjust the position of the hook to reduce tension. If a stem is very hard to pull down you should probably leave it alone or it is likely to break.

Preparation

Small, soft berries should be dealt with as soon as possible after collection. During hot weather they will often mold or spoil within a few hours, especially if smashed during collection. Refrigeration will only extend the shelf life of such fruit to about a day, and careful initial handling can perhaps double that. To avoid waste, you should eat, cook, or freeze these soft berries immediately. Fruit with thicker skins, such as blueberries, chokecherries, and plums, will last a little longer but should still be used promptly. Some fruits, such as apples and cranberries, naturally have a much longer shelf life.

Many wild fruits and berries are delicious to eat right from the plant without any preparation, and these tend to be the most popular species. Other wild fruits are too sour or tart by themselves for most palates to enjoy. However, these potent fruits often make unsurpassed jams, jellies, juices, syrups, sauces, fruit leathers, pies, baked goods, wines, and other products.

Juice: Juicing can be an end in itself, but it is also a necessary first step in making jelly, wine, or fruit syrup. For juice you generally want totally ripe fruit because it is softer and juicier, but some kinds taste better when a portion of the fruit is under-ripe. There are two basic methods for making juice: crushing and pressing raw fruit, and straining cooked fruit.

Wild fruits that I prefer to juice raw include grapes, autumn olives, apples, and highbush cranberries. I usually crush the fruit with a wooden pestle (which I call my "stomper") in a clean, sturdy pail or tub. Then I place some of the mashed fruit in a jelly bag and squeeze it as hard as I can to wring out the liquid. (Adding a little water to the fruit as you mash it will dilute the flavor but will also allow you to extract significantly more juice. I do this with some fruits that have extremely strong flavors.) Raw fruits can also be pressed in a cider or grape press, if you have access to one. Fresh-pressed juice will usually have a lot of particulate matter in it. In apple cider this stuff is good, but in many other wild fruit juices the crud that settles to the bottom is distasteful and should be left there. In this case the brighter, cleaner-tasting juice at the top should be poured into a different container.

I like fresh-pressed juice the best, but this process doesn't work well for most fruits. Any fruit that can't be juiced effectively raw will have to be boiled or simmered to break down its tissues and release their liquid. Very tart, seedy fruits are often good candidates for juicing because in this form they are easy to combine with other ingredients. I use this method to juice blackberries, chokecherries, currants, and many others. Cooking alters the flavor; boiled juice will rarely match the taste of the fresh fruit.

Add one to two quarts of water to each gallon of fruit (depending on how juicy and how potent they are) and let it simmer on low heat until the fruit begins to break down and liquefy. Then you can turn the heat up if you wish – but not too high, because if you scorch it the flavor will be ruined. When the fruit has boiled gently for a while and seems to be well softened, mash it up a final time to release all of the juice.

Pour the hot, mashed fruit into a jelly bag or cloth suspended over a container. If you want really nice-looking juice or jelly, let it strain by gravity alone for several hours. If you're not so picky about the look of the finished product, you can squeeze out the juice by hand, which is much faster and yields a little more volume – just be sure to let the mash cool down enough to be handled safely.

Juices should be refrigerated for short-term storage. For long-term storage, fresh-pressed juices should be frozen, as canning alters their flavor. Cooked juices can be stored by water-bath canning.

Straining Fruit: Straining separates the seeds and skins from the pulp of the fruit. Most wild fruits need to be strained or juiced for easy and pleasant consumption. Anyone who ignores this majority in favor of the few exceptions is missing out on much of what Nature has to offer. Plus, fruits that require straining are usually far easier to collect than those that don't, which more than makes up for the extra step in processing. Wild fruits that I strain include cranberries, plums, various species of cherry, nannyberries, pawpaws, gooseberries, autumn olives, apples, and many others. The fruit pulp produced by straining is called *puree*; it can be used for jam, pie, sauce, spread, fruit leather, or for baking and other types of cookery.

Villaware fruit strainer, assembled, that has just been used to strain chokecherries.

The simplest tool used for straining is the colander. A colander is basically a bowl or pot with holes in it. Mashed fruit is placed in the colander then stirred and pressed; the pulp is supposed to exit through the holes while the seeds and skins remain inside. This only works for fruit with seeds larger than the holes in the colander, but if you get a colander with very small holes it is nearly impossible to get any pulp to go through. Thus, there is only a narrow range of seed size for which the colander is an effective strainer.

A step up from the colander is the simple rotary strainer or Foley mill. This is basically a flat-bottomed colander with a blade and a handle attached to a shaft. You crank the handle, which turns the blade, which moves material in a circular fashion and presses pulp through the holes in the bottom.

The best tool for straining fruit is a more complex mechanical strainer that mounts to a table or shelf. These have a hopper that empties into a cavity where a corkscrew pushes material against a funnel-like screen. The seeds and skins exit at the narrow end of the screen, where they fall into an awaiting container, while the puree drips (or squirts) through the holes along the length of the screen into another container. Manufactured primarily for making apple and tomato sauce, these strainers can be made to work effectively with almost any small-seeded fruit. Options include different sized corkscrews and screens with different hole diameters. Some fruits strain better than others and it may take some trial and error to get the apparatus to work with a particular fruit. For example, mine clogs with chokecherry pits unless I leave the tension spring out, and I can't run nannyberries through it unless they are steaming hot. However, these strainers are so effective that I recommend them to any forager serious about wild fruit. Common brands include Villaware and Squeezo.

Seeds and Grains

Grains have a fascinating story as a human food source. Today they are by far the world's most important source of nourishment, yet just a few thousand years ago, when the world was populated by hunter-gatherers, grains were a minor component of most people's diets. While there are hundreds of species of plants which produce edible seeds, the preponderance of them are simply too small and labor-intensive to be worth utilizing as food. However, North America is home to several species of wild grain that are worthwhile to harvest.

Depending on the species, grains are harvested by knocking or beating them into a basket or other container, or by stripping the seedheads off by hand. One can also harvest the entire plants and let them dry – which will often cause more seeds to ripen – then beat (thresh) the plants so that the seeds fall off onto a tarp or cloth.

Harvested grains always come with varying amounts of unwanted, coarse, inedible material such as pods and husks, collectively called *chaff*. The edible seed will often be fully enclosed in the chaff, as is the case with most grass seeds. Breaking up and removing this chaff from the desirable seeds is the most time-consuming task involved with the harvest and processing of grains, and billions of people have spent much of their lives performing this task.

Grains should be dried after collection to avoid molding or other spoilage. Placing the material on a tarp in the sun for a day or two is usually sufficient, depending on the type of grain. A cookie sheet or other such tray can be used indoors for smaller amounts. The material doesn't have to desiccate very quickly, so you can let it dry at room temperature for a few days if you want. Once the grain is dried it can be stored for a long period, if desired, before being processed further.

Parching: Parching is the process of heating up seed material (grain and chaff) in order to make the chaff more brittle. (This step is unnecessary for some grains.) Parching can be done in a metal container over virtually any heat source (but not a volcano; that's dangerous). I use a washtub, modified barrel, or large pot over an open flame. Smaller batches are done on a stove or in the oven. Stir the seed material constantly while parching to avoid scorching it; you want to get it hot, dry, and brittle, but you don't want it burnt.

Rubbing: Whether or not you parch your grain, it needs to be rubbed to cause the chaff to separate from the seeds. Rubbing is most effective when done promptly after parching, because this is when the chaff is the most brittle. Let the grain sit and the chaff will absorb moisture from the air, becoming more supple and harder to break. If you are going to rub a grain that has not been parched, make sure that it is thoroughly dry before proceeding. It is also a good idea to sift your seed material through a colander before rubbing in order to remove any unwanted pieces of leaf, stem, or other large debris.

Most likely, your first experiments with rubbing grain will involve simply rubbing between the hands. In this case, take a small handful of seed material and hold it tightly between your palms pressed together flat. Maintaining a good deal of pressure, rub the material vigorously while holding your hands over a container to catch the seeds that work their way out. Rub until all of the seed material has worked its way out of your hands, then pick up another handful and repeat the process. Do this until the majority of the hulls have been loosened from the seeds.

A slightly more effective method, and one that is easier on the palms, is to place a small amount of the seed material on a rubbing surface (such as a thick piece of rubber or leather) and apply pressure with a small rubber or leather pad held in the hand. Rub the material around vigorously until you can see many kernels loosened from their chaff.

Winnowing: This is the final step in finishing grains. Winnowing is the process of separating the desirable seeds from the loosened chaff (called *trash*) by using the different rates at which they travel through the air. Winnowing is one of the most important innovations in human history – making it possible to utilize small seeds, which would otherwise be prohibitively difficult to separate by hand, as a food source. Large species of grain are easier to winnow than smaller ones because the seeds are heavier.

The simplest kind of winnowing is done by slowly pouring the grain-chaff mixture from one container into another in a breeze. Theoretically, the chaff, being lighter than the grain, will be blown aside by the wind, while the seeds will fall into the container. The winnower needs to adjust where she pours the grain so that all of the kernels fall into the bottom container but as much of the chaff as possible is blown aside. Higher winds mean you need a shorter drop to accomplish this, while gentler winds necessitate a higher drop. You will never remove all of the chaff in a single pouring, so repeat the process many times until only an insignificant amount of trash remains. Results are best with steady rather than gusty winds. It is possible to create your own wind on a calm day, or even to winnow indoors, by using a fan.

With many small grains such as amaranth and lamb's quarters, winnowing will remove a large number of "empty" seeds, which are lighter in weight and color than normal, viable seeds. If you see seeds blowing aside, stop and examine them. If they are good seeds, adjust your pouring height and position so as not to lose any more. On the other hand, if they are empties, be glad that you are getting rid of them.

After the first winnowing you are almost certain to find that a substantial portion of the chaff has not separated from the grain. In this case, rub the seeds again to loosen the remaining chaff, then proceed with a second winnowing. Repeat this process as many times as is necessary to achieve the clean final product that you desire.

In old photographs you may see Native American women, or women from subsistence cultures elsewhere in the world, winnowing seeds with a winnowing tray. Unlike the pour-in-the-wind process described above, tray winnowing is difficult to explain and even harder to do. However, it has the advantages of requiring only one container and not being dependent upon the cooperation of the wind. Once you become proficient, it may also be faster. For a more thorough explanation of tray winnowing, see the chapter on wild rice.

Milling: Once the grain has been winnowed, it is ready for milling into flour – if that's what you want. Flour is required if you intend to make baked goods, flatbread, tortillas, pancakes, gravy, or pasta from your grain. However, keep in mind that flours from wild grains will not behave like wheat flour when used for these products, since they lack wheat's quantity and kind of gluten. To get a finished product resembling the wheat-based goods that you are familiar with you will need to mix your wild flour with wheat flour.

You can make flour by pounding seeds between two properly shaped stones, a *mano* and *metate*, but these are harder to come by than flour mills, which can be purchased through Lehman's catalog and in some hardware or specialty stores. Flour mills come in various sizes, but most commonly they are about the size of a small meat grinder. They generally clamp to a tabletop or counter and are cranked by hand, although some electric models are available.

The two pieces of the mill that do the actual grinding are called *burrs*,

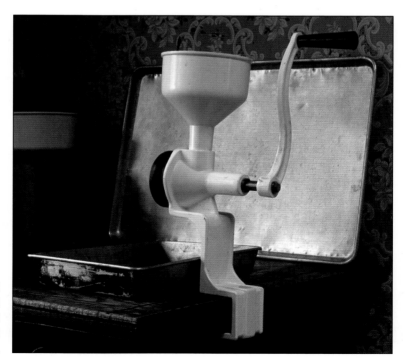

Hand-turned flour mill assembled and mounted for use.

and these are usually made of either iron or stone. Most stone burrs, whether natural or synthetic, only work well for soft, low-oil grains such as wheat, rye, and barley. For anything else (i.e. wild food) you want to use iron burrs.

Using a flour mill is simple: put the grain in the hopper, turn the crank, and flour comes out. Tightening or loosening the burrs adjusts the flour's consistency. Read the manual for your particular mill, if it comes with one, and follow any instructions it may contain. A flour mill can be used to grind many foods besides grain, including nutmeats, dry beans, and diced and dried tubers. If you try such projects, just make sure that the pieces you are attempting to grind are small enough to feed into the mill properly. If the crank becomes very difficult to turn as you use the mill, try to get past the tough spot by alternately cranking forward and backward. *Do not put extremely hard pressure on the handle if it feels stuck* – I have seen parts of flour mills break under this kind of misuse. If you can't manage to get past the jam, take the mill apart and clean it rather than try to muscle the material through. Find out what caused the jam and don't put it in there again.

If you choose not to make flour, wild grains still have excellent culinary uses in their whole form. They can be boiled into hot cereal or gruel, added to soup, or used in hot-dishes as one would use rice or barley.

Seed Terminology

The term *grain* is held by some to refer specifically to edible grass seeds, but in this book I use the term in its wider sense to also refer to other small seeds of herbaceous plants. *Seed* is used to denote legumes and other edible seeds larger than the typical grain, although this designation can correctly include all grains and nuts as well. A *nut* is a seed, usually large, enclosed in a hard shell. "True" nuts have no fleshy fruit around them, but this is a useless technicality that almost everybody ignores. A *stone* is a hard-shelled seed of a fleshy fruit. Hard seeds of fruits are also called *pits* and sometimes *pips*. A *kernel* is the edible portion of any type of seed, especially one that is hard, and a *meat* (as in *nutmeat*) refers to the edible portion of a nut or seed, especially those that are soft or oily.

Nuts

Nuts often served as dietary staples for hunting and gathering peoples and are among the most abundant and practical food sources found in nature. A few of them, such as acorns and chestnuts, are comprised primarily of starch along

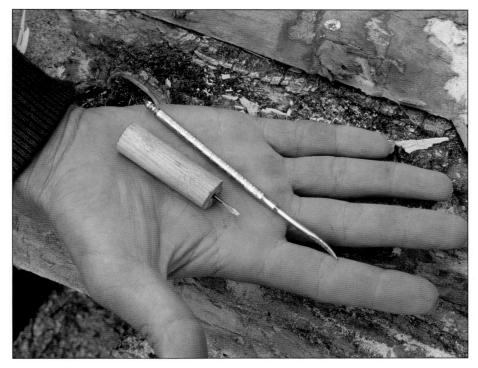

Store-bought and home-made nut picks.

with a little oil and protein, while most others consist primarily of oil along with a substantial amount of protein and some carbohydrate. This nutritional profile makes nuts among the most concentrated sources of nutrients and calories found in the wild.

Some nuts are picked directly from the bush or tree upon which they grow, but the more common practice is to pick them up off the ground after they have fallen. Sometimes, when the tree is laden with nuts, shaking the branches or hitting them sharply with a heavy stick will cause hundreds to fall. If nuts are out of reach, a three-foot long stick about an inch and a half thick can be thrown end-over-end like a boomerang to dislodge them – it works surprisingly well.

At harvest time one needs to discern which nuts contain good kernels and which are empty or wormy. This can be a tricky task. One relies on different visual cues for each species; I cover these in the specific accounts.

Nuts are among the most easily stored wild foods. Most of them keep well in their shells for a year or more if they are stored in conditions that are not extremely hot, wet, or dry. A shallow pail or tub in the basement will work fine. Most nuts have some inedible flesh or husk which encloses their hard shell (such as the green stuff on walnuts or the sheath on hazel nuts). This should generally be removed before the nuts are stored for the long-term. If you store nuts in a place where squirrels have access to them they will soon disappear, and mice, especially deer mice, can pilfer away a pile surprisingly fast.

Different nuts are cracked in different ways. Nutcrackers work for some, but most often a hammer is the better tool. Set the nut on a block of metal, stone, or wood. While holding it there with one hand, use the other to strike it with a hammer. Wear a thin glove on the hand holding the nut to avoid "shell shock." Many people are intimidated by the thought of using a hammer this way, but it pays to get comfortable enough with one to use it. You can also buy heavy duty nutcrackers made especially for black walnuts and other large, hard species.

After cracking, the nutmeats can often be picked from the shells with the fingers alone, but a nutpick is extremely useful for those species with convoluted chambers inside the shell. Store-bought nutpicks are designed for large, cultivated nuts and are too large to work well on some of the smaller wild nuts. It is easy to make a better nut pick on your own by pounding a nail part of the way into the end of a short wooden handle, cutting off the nail's head with a hack saw, then pounding the protruding end of the nail on an anvil to make it flattened and slightly curved. Some people like to use wire cutters to help them snip open sections of nutshell that haven't cracked right, but I feel that this is too much work and usually just throw the difficult pieces outside for the chickadees and mice.

Nutmeats can do wonders to liven up baked goods, desserts, or a bowl of hot cereal. Raw or roasted nuts are popular as snacks, but nuts also lend themselves to a great variety of lesser-known culinary uses. Some are great in salads, while in soup both the texture and flavor of many species is reminiscent of beans; their oils add heartiness to the broth. Ground up nuts can be a main ingredient in hot dishes or casseroles, and when combined with flour, egg, and seasonings, they can be made into burgers or patties.

Nuts also have some specialized uses. Those that consist mostly of starch are often ground into flour. Oily nutmeats can be ground into nut butters. It is also possible to extract pure oil from many kinds of nuts; the leftover meal can be used as a high-protein flour additive.

For those interested in survival or foraging for subsistence, no group of wild foods is more important than the nuts.

Storing Wild Foods

Food preservation is vital to a self-sufficient food economy and it is the hallmark of a thrifty kitchen. Perhaps more importantly, it allows one to indulge in the summer or fall's adventures even while winter's cold winds batter against the window panes. The hunter-gatherers who once populated North America assured themselves of a year-round food supply through ingenious and effective methods of storing seasonally harvested food products. The modern casual forager has even more methods of food preservation at her disposal.

There are four principal methods of long-term food storage: canning, freezing, drying, and cold storage or root cellaring. Less important methods include fermentation and chemical treatment (such as salting). All of these storage methods work because, in one way or another, they prevent bacteria and other microorganisms from spoiling the food.

Each of these techniques is suitable for some, but not all, food products. Many items can be stored using all four of these primary methods – although which one you choose will greatly affect the finished product (compare canned tomatoes to sun-dried tomatoes). Your choice will depend on your taste preferences, your level of experience with the various methods, the equipment and time available to you, and the amount of surplus food that you have harvested and wish to store.

Freezing

Freezing is perhaps the easiest of the four principal food storage techniques. While it does require a very complex and expensive piece of equipment – the freezer – this happens to be something that most of us already own. Other than a freezer, the only equipment that you will need is some containers that seal well.

There are two major advantages to freezing food products: it requires less preparation time than other food storage methods, and it preserves food closer to its fresh state than canning or drying.

The greatest drawback of freezing is that it is energy-intensive to keep the food frozen. If you plan on storing a significant portion of your food supply you will very quickly run out of freezer space unless you own several such appliances. And unfortunately, much food never gets eaten until it is three years freezer-burnt simply because it is so inconvenient to dig through a full chest freezer to get at a bag of strawberries that you think might be at the bottom somewhere.

Living most of my adult life without a freezer has taught me that this appliance is completely unnecessary for a self-sufficient food economy, but also that one can be incredibly convenient. The freezer is a very useful appliance, but don't plan on using it to preserve everything. It is best suited to store meat, fresh-pressed fruit juices, and small, uncooked fruits and berries.

It is highly preferable to freeze fresh-pressed juices, as canning greatly alters their flavor. When you thaw some juice six months after freezing, it will be almost as good as if it was pressed an hour ago. When you freeze juice, be sure to leave about ten percent of the container empty to allow for expansion as the liquid solidifies.

Before freezing vegetables, boil them for about five minutes (one minute for greens) – this is called *blanching*. Normally, a living plant that is frozen undergoes physiological and chemical processes detrimental to its culinary quality. Blanching kills the plant's cells and denatures certain enzymes, preventing this from happening.

Canning

Canning is the storage of sterile food in sterile containers that are impervious to organisms that cause spoilage. The food and the containers are sterilized simultaneously by heat. There are three basic types of canning: pressure, water-bath, and sterile-product. Each is appropriate for certain types of food and not others.

This section only gives a brief overview of canning; my intent is to make you aware of and excited about its possibilities. Before canning you should obtain and read a canning reference manual such as the *Ball Blue Book* or the USDA Extension Service's *Complete Guide to Home Canning* (Agriculture Information Bulletin No. 539).

Almost any food can be canned, but the flavor of some foods is affected more than others. Wild produce items that I like to can include bracken and ostrich fern fiddleheads, asparagus, milkweed shoots and pods, fruit spreads, juices, and wild leek bulbs. Soup is an excellent candidate for canning because it is cooked for a long time anyway, and it is very convenient to be able to open up a single jar of soup rather than having to make a whole pot from scratch. The beauty of canning is that once the food is processed, it requires no energy to keep it preserved.

There is a persistent myth that home canning is dangerous. Certainly there are some risks involved, as there are in any activity – but these risks are minimal. Unless you are ignorant of canning safety procedures, or you disregard them, you are safe. It's that simple. Don't let anyone scare you away from canning because it's "dangerous." In fact, due to better technology and better understanding of food safety, canning is safer today than ever before.

The common danger associated with home canning is that of food poisoning. This danger is exaggerated to an absurd degree; you are, in fact, many times more likely to experience food poisoning from eating at a restaurant. The more realistic fear is that of being scalded by the contents of the canner due to a spill or explosion. Such accidents do occur, but simple precautions can prevent them.

The real reason that canning is perceived so negatively is that in the middle of the 20th Century, when freezers were becoming a commonplace household appliance and commercially canned goods were becoming more regular grocery items, canning was seen as the old-fashioned, outmoded way of doing things. It was associated with poverty, the past, the Great Depression, and everything backwards and rural. As is always the case when people disdain or desire something for social reasons, they must contrive economic ones to justify their position. Although we have forgotten that context, the scorn of canning and home-canned food persists.

Equipment

For canning you will need a canner, canning jars, two-piece lids, tongs for handling hot jars, and a clean cloth for wiping the jar rims.

Pressure canning should be done only in a canner manufactured specifically for that purpose (Presto and Mirro are the main brands). Water-bath canning can be done in any deep pot with a lid, as long as something is placed inside to keep the jars from resting directly on the bottom. Sterile-product canning does not require a canner.

The standard sizes for canning jars are half-pint, pint, and quart. Half-pints are good for anything you won't normally eat much of at once, especially products that don't store well after being opened. Quarts are used for things that get consumed quickly. In large families, quarts will prove to be the most convenient size, while a single person is likely to store everything but juice in pints or half-pints. Old canning jars can often be obtained very cheaply at garage sales or auctions, but the older jars break more easily during canning than new ones.

A few commercial products are sold in jars that can be re-used for home canning. The best are those that have the emblem of the Arkansas Glass Company (a picture of Arkansas containing the diagonal abbreviation AGC) on the bottom; these are used by many small food-processing companies. You will know they are the right size because standard jar lids will fit them.

Jar openings and lids come in two sizes: standard and wide-mouth. Which you choose is a matter of personal preference. Wide-mouth jars take up more space and the lids are more expensive, but they are easier to clean and get the food out of. Don't use the old-fashioned French lids that clamp onto the jar. There is no need to use paraffin on jelly jars, either. Only use two-piece closures that are composed of a lid and a screw band to hold it on. Re-use the screw bands but not the lids.

Pressure canning

Pressure canning is the only safe way to can low-acid foods such as asparagus, beans, corn, meat, fish, greens, soup, dairy products, and all non-acidic fruits and vegetables. The purpose of pressure canning is to kill the spores of the bacteria that cause botulism, which can survive normal boiling temperatures. The high pressure inside the canner causes water to boil at a higher temperature, killing these spores.

Botulism bacteria live in dark, moist, oxygen-poor environments; they are commonly found in soil. A byproduct of their metabolism is an extremely potent toxin called botulin. The majority of botulism cases occur at foodservice establishments, but those that are caused by home-prepared foods are most commonly associated with low-acid fruits and vegetables, because some people mistakenly presume that they are not as dangerous as meat and dairy products and therefore don't pressure can them (Ray, 1996).

The safest way to pressure can is to *buy a new canner, carefully read the instruction book that comes with it, follow the instructions, and keep the booklet for future reference.* Canner companies print accurate, safe, up-to-date, and easy-to-understand instructions for pressure canning. The directions found in your canner's instruction booklet should override those you read here wherever the two differ.

Pack the food to be pressure canned into clean jars. (Although many people do so religiously, there is no need to sterilize jars by boiling before any type of canning.) The food can be pre-cooked (called hot-pack) or it can be packed in the jar raw (called cold-pack or raw-pack). Cold-packed foods will require more processing time in the canner. Certain foods, especially those that are likely to have many air pockets when raw (leafy greens, for example), should not be cold-packed. (The canner booklet will tell you which ones.)

Never put hot product into cold jars, or it may crack them. Keeping newer jars at room temperature is usually enough to alleviate this problem, but older jars should be soaked in hot water for a few minutes before filling them.

With hot-pack, pour some of the cooking water into the jars along with the food. When raw-packing, pour boiling water into the jar after the food is packed in, then press along the sides and agitate the contents with a wooden spoon or soft spatula to release the trapped air bubbles. Add boiling water to make up for the volume of air released. In either case, the liquid should completely cover the food and should come no closer to the jar lid than one inch.

Make sure there are no bits of food or nicks on the jar rims, for these can cause them not to seal, or cause the seal to break during storage. Place new lids on the jars and apply the screw bands to hold them firmly. Then they are ready to go into the canner.

You should have water in the canner heating up while you are doing all this. Ideally it's just beginning to boil right now. The amount of water you need in the canner depends on its size (check the manual for your model) but it will not be enough to cover the jars. The canner should come with a raised and perforated metal shelf that sits in the bottom to hold the jars. Place your jars of food onto this shelf, otherwise the bottoms can get too hot, causing the jars to crack.

Properly screw on the lid of the canner. Let it boil until steam starts to shoot steadily out of the valve, then let it steam like this for another 7–10 minutes. Put the pressure-cap on. When the pressure in the canner reaches the desired level (usually 10 or 11 pounds, depending on your canner and the altitude) turn the heat lower and begin counting down your "processing time" as listed in your canning book's time chart. Adjust the heat to keep the pressure at or just above the desired poundage. Do not let pressure build up to dangerous levels, and never leave the canner unattended.

If you are pressure canning wild plants, it is unlikely that you will find recommended processing times listed for most of the foods you are dealing with. Use the recommended time and method for a domestic vegetable that is physically similar. When in doubt, play it safe and process for longer.

When your food has undergone the recommended processing time, turn the heat off and let the canner release pressure by itself. Do not take the pressure cap off, or the sudden change in pressure can cause the jars to eject contents and wreck their seals.

Do not remove the canner's lid until there is absolutely no pressure in the canner – which means that when you take the pressure cap off, no steam or hot air will shoot out. If you fail to heed this last warning you could get seriously scalded. When the pressure is totally released, open your canner and remove the jars, using tongs if necessary.

After the jars have been out of the canner awhile, their lids should "pop" as they get sucked down by decreasing pressure in the jars. If you press on the center of these lids they should not move. If the lids have failed to seal they will move and pop each time they are pressed in the center. If any failed to seal, refrigerate them and use the contents soon. Try to figure out what you did wrong to cause the seal to fail.

After the jars have sealed, take the screw bands off. There is no reason to leave them on; the suction pressure is what holds the lid on after sealing. Then you can use the screw bands on your next batch, or you can clean them right away so they won't rust.

Store your jars in a cool, dark place, as sunlight can adversely affect the food. You don't want your jars to freeze, but if they do it does not always cause them to crack or break their seals. Label your lids with the contents and date canned, and try to use the oldest stuff first.

Now it is time for the last line of defense against food poisoning. Botulism usually does not create bad odors, but if you have any reason to suspect the food, throw it out. Boiling food for five minutes destroys botulin, so it is recommended that you do so before consumption.

Water-bath canning

Water-bath canning is much simpler than pressure canning. It is used for high-acid foods such as fruit, fruit spreads, juice, and a few acidic vegetables such as rhubarb. Since botulism bacteria cannot survive in acidic environments, pressure canning is unnecessary for these foods. Water-bath canning is inappropriate for fruits that are not acidic, such as figs, dates, olives, and some varieties of peaches and tomatoes. Do not pressure can anything that can be canned in a water bath, for pressure canning will be detrimental to the flavor.

In water-bath canning, the jars of hot product are placed in a canning kettle with boiling water that covers the lids by at least an inch. (Never cold-pack for water-bath canning.) The water is boiled for a period of time so that the jar and its contents are sterilized. The boiling time depends on the size of the jar and the texture of the product you are canning. Juices circulate in the jar to facilitate heat exchange, so they heat up evenly and rather quickly, while thicker products do not circulate and therefore heat up slowly, from the outside in.

Sterile-product canning

Sterile-product canning involves heating food to boiling temperature and then, immediately after removing it from the heat, pouring it into clean jars. Immediately screw clean, two-piece lids onto the jars and turn them upside-down for a few minutes. The heat of the product sterilizes the inside of the jars and the lids.

An assortment of canned goods from my cupboard. Top row: apple butter, milkweed white, huckleberry, ostrich fern. Middle row: thimbleberry jam, pin cherry jam, milkweed shoots, venison. Bottom row: plum sauce, tomatoes, bracken shoots, venison stroganoff mix. Figure out which method was used for each one.

Sterile-product canning is used primarily for jam, jelly, and concentrated sugary syrups. These foods are not susceptible to botulism because the bacteria cannot survive in such high-sugar environments. They don't need to be canned in a water-bath because the increased density caused by the large proportion of dissolved sugar substantially raises the boiling temperature. Even after cooling a little as it is transferred to the jar, the jam or syrup will still be safely above the sterilization temperature. However, half-pint jars used for sterile-product canning should be soaked in hot or boiling water beforehand because their higher glass-to-product ratio may cool the food down too much to fully sterilize it otherwise. Jars smaller than half-pints should not be used at all for this process.

Don't be scared away from canning by unrealistic worries. After a few batches, all of the safety precautions will start to feel like instinct. You'll wish you had learned earlier. And you'll be able to use this ditty: "I can can, can you can? If you can't can I can teach you to can."

Drying

Dehydration has always been the most important method of long-term food storage. We are so accustomed to dry goods – flour, sugar, grains, breakfast cereal, chips, and even oil – that we tend to forget that these items keep at room temperature because they contain little or no moisture.

Drying, like canning, is advantageous in that once the food is prepared properly for storage it can keep for years in that state with no further investment of labor or fuel in its maintenance. It also has the additional advantage that dehydrated food takes up less space than other means of storage. The wild foods that I dry include greens, berries, seeds, grains, nuts, and flours from various starchy vegetables.

Foods can be dried either in the sun, out of the sunlight in a warm place, in a food dehydrator, in an oven on low heat, or above a woodstove. Each of these methods has its advantages and disadvantages.

You can place the food to be dried on cloths, screens, or even boards. Some years ago I purchased several large baking trays and these have proven to be incredibly convenient drying surfaces, making me the envy of my foraging friends. I built myself a rack to hold fifteen of these trays so that I can dry many gallons of nuts, grains, or roots indoors at one time without taking up a lot of space.

Drying seeds, **nuts**, and **grains** is fairly easy because these items are not particularly high in moisture to begin with. They can be dried at room temperature in an open, shallow container or on a tarp laid in the sun.

Thin, leafy **greens** should be dehydrated out of the sunlight, as sun-bleaching damages both their flavor and nutritional qualities. (Because greens have so much surface area in proportion to their volume they desiccate quickly and do not need the sunlight to hurry them along anyways.) Leaves can be spread on trays, cloths, screens, or another clean surface, or the leafy tops can be tied in loose bundles and hung in an out-of-the-way place. Once the greens have dried you can place them into an airtight container. Thick, succulent greens are poor candidates for drying because they tend to toughen in the process.

Dehydrated greens can be used in most dishes that call for cooked greens. They can also be crumbled into a fine powder by rubbing between the hands. This leaf meal can be used to thicken soups or casseroles and it can be mixed with flour to enhance pasta, tortillas, or bread.

Shoot vegetables dry poorly, in my experience, because they are so thick and juicy. The only shoot vegetable that I regularly dry is bracken fern fiddleheads. I do this by blanching the shoots for about a minute and then laying them on a tray placed out in the sun. On a hot day they are hard like uncooked spaghetti after only about six hours.

Roots and **tubers** can be dried as well; for best results they should be diced or sliced thin first. I dry both wapato and hopniss tubers after they have been peeled, boiled, and mashed, sometimes grinding them into flour or meal after they are dry. Dried starchy tubers get very hard but can be used in cooking after being rehydrated. I also dry the cores of cattail rhizomes after they have been cut into short sections. After this they are ready to be ground into flour at my convenience and will store in perfect condition for years. I have never tried drying the less starchy taproots such as evening primrose and parsnip, but if I did I would grate them or cut them very fine or try blanching them first to keep them from getting tough.

Drying **fruit** is trickier than drying grains, nuts, or greens, but the final product is so delightful that it is worth the effort.

Small fruits and berries can be dried whole, but I have only found this to be practical with an electric food dehydrator. Otherwise they simply do not dry fast enough and either spoil or loose much of the freshness of their flavor. Electric food dehydrators work great, but they suck up a lot of energy and they are small; for the quantity of fruit that I dry they are not a practical option.

Once berries are crushed they will dry much faster, making it possible to dehydrate them quickly in the sun without spoilage while retaining much of their fresh flavor. I dry many gallons of berries every year and have come to the conclusion that sun-drying is the most practical way to do it.

My favorite fruits to dry are serviceberries, chokecherries, blueberries, huckleberries, autumn olives, apples, and nannyberries, but at one time or another I have dried almost every wild fruit that I could get my hands on. Fruits with stones or troublesome seeds should be strained before drying; the dehydrated puree is called *fruit leather* and is a wonderful snack food. Some fruits must be cooked before straining, otherwise it is preferable to make leather from raw fruit. Larger, firm fruits can be sliced thin before drying in a dehydrator or in the sun.

I dry crushed fruit and fruit leather on large baking trays placed outside on a hot, sunny day. (If it is not sunny, I switch to freezing or canning the berries.) Sometimes, if I am picking all day, I bring the trays with me; as soon as I get a half-gallon of berries I crush them, spread them on a tray, place it in a sunny spot nearby, and continue picking. When I start the drying process right away like this the final product tastes noticeably better. Good places to put the drying trays are on the roof of your car or on the roof of a house or shed; try to get them off the ground in any case so they can warm up a little more. Angle the trays toward the sun if you can. Be careful where you put them; I have had

Crushed serviceberries, tapped-out and ready to dry.

children and dogs step on my drying fruit, and once a tray was even run over by a truck.

I crush berries right on the drying tray, using my hands or a heavy, flat-bottomed glass. Then I spread them out as evenly as possible, no more than a quarter-inch thick.

For fruit leather it is very important to spread the fruit puree evenly and not leave any empty spots on the tray. Uniform thickness is important because any thin spots will dry first, sticking to the tray when you try to flip the leather over. Spreading crushed fruit is more of an art than it sounds. First, plop about a half-gallon of puree on the tray and spread it around. There will be thick spots and bare spots. After the initial spreading, let the puree sit on the tray for a minute or two to "bond" with it. Then push down the high spots and fill in the empty ones by quickly and repeatedly tapping the mashed fruit with your fingers, coaxing it in the right direction. (If your fingers touch the fruit for more than a fraction of a second, the pulp will stick to your fingertips and mess everything up.) I call this "tapping out" the fruit, and it takes a while to get the knack of it.

After five to eight hours in the sun, depending on weather conditions and how thickly you have laid them upon the tray, crushed berries are ready to be

Chokecherry fruit leather, one tray cut and flipped.

flipped over. Flipping is indispensable because it keeps the fruit from sticking to the tray; it also facilitates faster drying. You want to flip the fruit when the top is dry but the bottom is still moist; it should come off easily with a straight-edged wooden or plastic spatula. After flipping, the fruit will require another three to six hours in the sun to be adequately dry.

If you are making fruit leather, use the edge of the spatula to cut it into strips two to four inches wide, and loosen around the edges of the tray before trying to peel the strips so that they come off without ripping. At the right time for flipping, you should be able to gently pick up the fruit leather in long strips; if it falls apart it is probably not quite dry enough to flip yet. Fruit leather dries a little more quickly than crushed berries because it does not contain skins to impede the flow of moisture; it may dry in three to six hours on the first side and two to five hours on the second side.

Sun-drying fruit requires sunny weather and a temperature of at least 65° F (18° C) for one to two days. The hotter and sunnier the weather, the better. Never crush berries and spread them on the tray and then wait to put them out to dry. They will mold or spoil very quickly once crushed – even faster than the fresh fruit. Try not to start berries drying in the late afternoon, either; make sure they have several hours of good drying time on the first day. Most drying occurs between the hours of 10:00 AM and 5:00 PM, so try to have your fruit out during this entire period if the weather is cooperative. Bring the trays in before the dew starts to settle.

If flies become a nuisance you can cover the trays with a screen or light cheesecloth, but this will slow down the drying process since it does cast some shade.

You know your berries are done when they are hard and not sticky. If you can get some pulp to rub onto your finger, or if you can easily pinch through a piece of the fruit, it is not yet dry enough. It does not need to be crispy; dried fruit remains somewhat supple. A little trial and error is required to properly judge when the fruit is sufficiently dehydrated, but always dry it for longer if you are not sure. Insufficiently dried fruit may mold weeks or months later in storage, while fully dried fruit will keep for years in perfect condition.

Cold storage

A parsnip is a living organism. Like a person, if it becomes too dehydrated, it will die. It can survive a light freeze, but bringing its temperature too low will kill it, too. Once you let a plant die you must freeze, can, or dry it in order to prevent it from spoiling – but as long as you can keep it alive, it will prevent itself from spoiling. If the parsnip gets too warm, however, it will try to grow, drawing sustenance from the enlarged taproot and causing it to shrink and lose quality. The aim of cold storage, then, is to keep the plant alive but dormant. Cold storage can be done in a refrigerator, but the space and energy costs are limiting. For larger amounts of food, a root cellar is the most practical means of cold storage.

A root cellar is an underground chamber that utilizes the Earth's relatively constant temperature to maintain a cool, moist environment in which to store certain vegetables and fruits. Some people have a small, enclosed room in the basement that they use for this purpose, but the classic root cellar is a structure separate from the home, built into the ground, especially where there is a hillside or mound of dirt.

If you don't have a root cellar or even a basement, you can still apply the same principles to storing vegetables. For example, you can keep a bucket of wild roots outside covered with a pile of leaves until the weather gets really cold and then bring it in to the coolest part of the house. This will not be as effective as a root cellar or refrigerator, but you should still be able to keep certain vegetables for many months this way.

Cold storage has some distinct advantages over other storage methods. First, it preserves food in its natural, unaltered state, providing fresh fruits and vegetables long after their harvest. (No dried or canned goods compare to fresh produce in the middle of winter.) Secondly, it requires little effort to prepare foods for such storage and little energy to keep them preserved.

The number of foods that can be stored for the long-term with this method is limited, however. Only *entire organisms*, those produce items fully capable of growing or reproducing, are candidates. This excludes leaves and stalks (unless stored as a whole plant) and most fruit. Furthermore, these items can generally only be kept alive for the duration of their normal dormancy period in Nature or perhaps slightly longer. In temperate regions this means that suitable foods can be stored in a cellar from fall through spring – and if you're lucky, into the early summer. Although its application is limited, cold storage is a superb way to keep those food products that are well suited to it.

Only a very small number of wild fruits can be stored in this fashion. Cranberries and apples are common examples, and Turner (1978) reports that natives in British Columbia had a special cold storage technique for blue elderberries. Only attempt to store fruits that are undamaged. Place them gently in a box or crate and cover with wood shavings, newspapers, leaves, or something else to impede the flow of air so that moisture loss is minimized.

Cold storage is employed primarily for underground vegetables that can be readily collected in volume. Examples include wild carrot, evening primrose, parsnip, burdock and thistle roots, hopniss, jerusalem artichoke, and wapato. You can take any of these roots or tubers and pack them loosely in bins or buckets, then cover with moist sand, sawdust, leaves, newspapers, or sphagnum moss, cover the container, and the vegetables should keep for at least a few months in a cool place. Since the top few inches of the ground typically freeze during some part of the winter in temperate North America, these wild root vegetables are adapted to withstand being lightly frozen. In this respect they are far more hardy than most cultivated vegetables, but they should still be protected from a hard freeze.

It is easy to store most roots for a month or two, but if you plan to keep them all winter you need to treat them gingerly. Dig them carefully and try not to nick, cut, or bruise them. Any that you inadvertently damage should be the first ones used up. Pack the roots so that they touch minimally and check every few weeks to make sure the packing material has not dried out. If possible, keep the roots right around the freezing point without much temperature fluctuation.

If the whole point of cold storage is to mimic natural dormancy conditions, why not just leave the roots growing wild?

This is a very good question. In fact, I recommend leaving the roots where they grow as long as they are accessible (i.e. the ground is not frozen), and not trying to store more than you will use before they become accessible again. Use the Earth as your cold storage facility as much as possible.

For more information on cold storage and root cellars, I recommend the book *Root Cellaring: Natural Cold Storage of Fruits & Vegetables* by Mike and Nancy Bubel, Stackpole Books, 1991.

Timing the Wild Harvest

The wild foods available change constantly, and many are in season for only a few weeks each year. It can be frustrating and surprising how quickly the season for a particular edible plant passes, and it is difficult to keep track of such a great number of wild foods. Over the years I have kept note of the phenology of the wild foods that I collect. (*Phenology* refers to the timing and sequence of seasonal biological events.) I have used this information to prepare a phenology chart or biological calendar that foragers can use to plan their harvest of wild plants.

The chart shows the seasonal availability of all the major food products covered in this book. The numerical dates are estimated averages of the dates that I have observed in central and northern Wisconsin over the last 15 years, at approximately 45° N latitude and 1000 feet (300 m) elevation. The dates provided will be most applicable where the climate is comparable, but they can also be adjusted to correspond to different regions.

In spring, add roughly a week to these dates for each 100 miles (160 km) north and subtract a week for each 100 miles south. (One degree of latitude is equal to 69 miles or 111 km.) Also add a week for each 1000-foot increase in elevation and subtract a week for a 1000-foot decrease.

A plant that is available for three weeks according to this chart may be in season for five weeks in the Southeast but less than two weeks in northern Ontario. This is because, as the growing season becomes shorter, the period of time allotted for each phenological event also becomes shorter. In other words, as you go north, biological events of spring happen later, but more quickly, and fall events happen sooner and more quickly.

As summer progresses, the calendar adjustment criteria that apply in spring fail to hold true. Many northern plants catch up to their southern counterparts over the course of the summer due to longer day length and their biological programming for shorter growing seasons. For example, butternuts in Virginia flower in late April and ripen in September, while those in my area flower in early June but still ripen in September. By autumn, those phenological events stimulated by shorter day length and colder temperatures, such as leaf fall and the ripening of many fruits and nuts, occur earlier in the north than in the south.

Plants tend to ripen in the same sequence regardless of the specific dates.

The phenology chart is set up so that the reader can use one event to indicate the concurrence of others. If you see black locust flowering, the chart tells you that it is also time to harvest sumac shoots, burdock stalks, evening primrose stalks, wapato greens, and goosefoot greens. This is really the most accurate way to use the chart, since even in the same locality phenological events can occur several weeks later during an abnormally cold year than during an extremely hot one.

Unfortunately, there can be cases where the sequence of phenological events is not the same as that shown on the chart. This is because different plants respond to different stimuli. The Pacific Northwest Coast has long, cool springs, and certain plants can grow steadily in this mild weather. Other plants grow poorly at moderate temperatures and don't really take off until the weather is truly hot. It is thus possible for a cool-weather plant to ripen before a hot-weather plant in a mild climate, but for the sequence of the same two plants to be reversed in a hot climate. It is even possible for such a flip-flop to occur in the same locality between a hot spring and a cool one.

Another important consideration, as you look for plants in the proper stage for harvest, is *microclimate*. Raspberries usually ripen a few days earlier on the north side of an east-west road due to the south exposure. The difference between phenology on the north and south slopes of the same hill can be as much as two weeks. In the spring, plants growing at the base of a cliff or building wall, especially the south side, may ripen precociously by as much as a month.

Those who live in mountains have the advantage of being able to change their climate drastically by traveling relatively short distances; I know a couple in West Virginia who, using elevation to their advantage, harvest blueberries from July to early October. The Great Lakes produce similar effects, delaying phenology on their shores by a week or two. Where I live, deep waterless depressions on sandy soil, called frost pockets, experience a nearly arctic climate due to cold air drainage at night; in these I can collect fiddleheads as late as July. Many plants, particularly shoot vegetables, come into season much later in fields than they do in woodlands. A savvy forager is always thinking of microclimate and how it can be used to her advantage.

Plants put their energy into different parts at different times of the year. Edible calories tend to be concentrated wherever the plants are putting the most energy at any one time. Below I list some major divisions of the growing season and the food types that are most abundant during those times, in order of relative importance. While a few wild foods of each type are available at any time during the growing season, you will find that your foraging efforts tend to be concentrated as follows at different times of the year:

Early Spring: Underground storage organs, perennial greens
Mid Spring: Underground storage organs, perennial greens
Late Spring/Early Summer: Shoots and stalks, greens
Mid Summer: Small fruits, annual greens
Late Summer: Fruits, seeds, nuts
Early Fall: Nuts, fruits, seeds, underground storage organs
Late Fall: Underground storage organs, nuts, seeds
Winter: Underground storage organs, nuts, seeds

Key: P = Peak of Season; I = Coming into/out of Season

Dates correspond to an average growing season at 45°N latitude and 1000 ft (300 m) elevation.

Dates correspond to an average growing season at 45°N latitude and 1000 ft (300 m) elevation	Early Spring (Mar 25–Apr 25)	Mid Spring (Apr 25–May 10)	Late Spring (May 10–June 5)	Early Summer (June 5–July 1)	Mid Summer (July 1–Aug 10)	Late Summer (Aug 10–Sep 10)	Early Fall (Sep 10–Oct 10)	Late Fall (Oct 10–Nov 15)
Ostrich fern fiddleheads		I	P	I				
Cattail leaf bases		I	P	I				
Immature cattail spike				P	I			
Cattail pollen				P	I			
Cattail lateral				P	P	P	I	
Cattail rhizome	P	P	P	P	P	P	P	P
Wapato tuber	P	I				I	P	I
Wapato green		I	P	P	P	P	I	
Wapato flower shoot stalk				I	P	P		
Wild Rice						I	P	I
Wild leek greens	I	P	I					
Wild leek bulbs		I	P	P	P	P	I	
Smilax shoots			P	I				
Smilax greens			I	P				
Butternut						I	P	I
Siberian elm samaras (green)			I					
Siberian elm samaras (ripe)			P	I				
Stinging nettle greens		P	P	P	P	P	I	
Wood nettle shoots		I	P	I				
Wood nettle greens			I	P	P	I		
Sheep sorrel greens		I	P	P	P	P	I	
Goosefoot greens			I	P	P	P	I	
Goosefoot seeds						I	P	P
Spring beauty root	P	I						
Spring beauty greens	I	P	I					
Marsh marigold greens		P	I					
Swamp saxifrage stalk			P	I				
Serviceberry				I	P			
Chokecherry						I	P	I

■ = Peak of Season   ▨ = Coming into/out of Season

Dates correspond to an average growing season at 45°N latitude and 1000 ft (300 m) elevation	Early Spring (Mar 25 – Apr 25)	Mid Spring (Apr 25 – May 10)	Late Spring (May 10 – June 5)	Early Summer (June 5 – July 1)	Mid Summer (July 1 – Aug 10)	Late Summer (Aug 10 – Sep 10)	Early Fall (Sep 10 – Oct 10)	Late Fall (Oct 10 – Nov 15)
Pin cherry					■	■		
Ground bean – aerial						■	■	■
Ground bean – subterranean	■	■	■					
Hopniss tuber	■	■	■	■	■	■	■	■
Black locust flower			■	■				
Black locust beans					■	■	■	
Sumac fruit					■	■	■	
Sumac shoot			■					
Riverside grape							■	■
Basswood greens			■	■				
Basswood flower/bud				■				
Evening primrose root	■	■					■	■
Evening primrose greens			■					
Evening primrose shoot			■					
Evening primrose flower/bud					■	■	■	
Parsnip	■	■	■	■	■	■	■	■
Common milkweed shoot			■	■				
Common milkweed flower/bud				■	■			
Common milkweed pods					■	■		
Virginia waterleaf greens	■	■						
Virginia waterleaf stalks/buds			■					
Nannyberry							■	■
Highbush cranberry							■	■
Burdock root	■	■					■	■
Burdock petiole			■	■				
Burdock stalk			■	■				
Thistle root	■	■	■				■	■
Thistle petiole	■	■	■				■	■
Thistle stalk			■					

This calendar may be photocopied and altered for private use.

Ostrich Fern

Matteucia struthiopteris

The glossy form of ostrich fern fiddlehead, growing in a river floodplain forest, at the ideal stage for collection.

In May I walk down to the stream near my house with a fishing pole, some bags, and a trowel. I dig up a few wild leeks, placing any earthworms that I encounter into a small jar. When satisfied with my take of either bait or vegetables, I drop my line into the clay-tinted rushing waters to entice a hungry brook trout from his undercut bank. Before I depart with a couple of fish, I stop to add a handful of ostrich fern fiddleheads to my bag. The warblers are singing, flitting among the treetops that are just beginning to don the fresh green of spring, and the spring peepers chirp from every pond or puddle. On the way home I encounter a black bear, feeding as I am on the bounty of the spring woods.

How much easier and how much more fun it is to harvest from God's garden than to toil in your own!

Description

The ostrich fern is among our largest ferns; its deciduous leafy fronds frequently grow to 6 feet (2 m) long. Like many ferns, it has two kinds of fronds: large, green, infertile, leafy ones that photosynthesize, and much smaller, brown, fertile ones that serve only to produce the spores. The infertile fronds are arranged in a rosette of 5–7, forming a large funnel shape. The fertile fronds are found in the center of this rosette, standing upright rather than spreading. All of the fronds grow from a raised rootstock that looks like a scaly mound. The leafy fronds are much wider above the middle and they end rather abruptly at the top. Going down from the middle towards the base, the feathery side-branches (called pinnae) get gradually smaller and smaller – the lower ones being miniscule. This shape reminds some people of ostrich plumes, hence the name. The tips of ostrich fern pinnae are limp and often droop, overlapping the next pinna below them, creating a cascade-like pattern.

Brown, fertile fronds of ostrich fern.

The stalk of the frond has

79

a deep, U-shaped groove running its entire length on the top (the side facing the center of the rosette), similar to the groove in a celery stalk. The presence of this groove distinguishes ostrich fern from interrupted or cinnamon fern, two other large, rosette-forming species which are often confused with the ostrich fern. When the frond first emerges in spring it has a coiled top. The shoot at this stage is called a *fiddlehead*. The curled top of the ostrich fern fiddlehead has some thin, papery, brown scales very loosely attached to it, but the straight part of the stalk does not have any scales or wool adhering to it. This also distinguishes it from interrupted and cinnamon ferns, both of which have very woolly fiddleheads. However, ostrich fern shoots are found with two distinct surface textures: some are smooth and bright glossy green, while others are covered with a thin whitish layer of very fine fuzz or powder.

The fertile fronds are typically only about 2 feet (.5 m) tall. They are stiff and straight, becoming dark brown when mature, with side branches only 1–2 inches (3–5 cm) long. These fronds often persist upright through the winter and are commonly collected for dried flower arrangements.

Look-Similars and Health Concerns

There is probably more confusion and misinformation surrounding fern fiddle-heads than there is with any other wild food. While it is true that the ostrich fern is among the best-known wild vegetables in North America, it is usually called by the ambiguous name of "fiddlehead fern." This name prompts many people to erroneously assume that all ferns with fiddleheads are ostrich fern – or at least are edible.

In the literature, one occasionally runs across reports of people getting sick from fern fiddleheads, and in some cases ostrich fern is specifically implicated as the culprit. Two well-known cases of fiddlehead poisoning occurred in 1994: one in New York State, and the other in a chain of restaurants across British Columbia, Alberta, and Saskatchewan. In the reports detailing the in-vestigation of these incidents (MMWR, 1994; Morgan P. et al, 1994) I find no evidence that the investigators confirmed that the fiddleheads involved were actually *Matteucia struthiopteris*. It seems doubtful that the investigating agencies had a person capable of confidently making the distinction. In fact, they seem to regard specific identification of the ferns as an incidental and insignificant detail in their reports.

Canadian health officials presume that ostrich fern occasionally contains a "mystery toxin" which is destroyed by thorough cooking, but both the logic and the evidence supporting this conclusion appear flimsy. The disturbing prevalence of fiddlehead misidentification makes it seem far more probable that the ferns in question actually belonged to a species other than ostrich fern. In the 1994 Canadian case, a single commercial collector was responsible for supplying all of the fiddleheads causing sickness; this also points to misidentification as the most likely explanation.

Like any other edible plant, ostrich fern has the potential to cause allergic reactions and may be otherwise disagreeable to a few people. However, I believe that it is responsible for few, if any, of the cases of illness that are commonly attributed to it.

It is not surprising that the general public is confused about fern identification and edibility. I have seen photographs of interrupted fern *Osmunda claytonia* and cinnamon fern *Osmunda cinnamomea* labeled as ostrich or "fiddlehead" fern in local newspapers, on websites, in national magazines,

Fiddleheads of cinnamon fern *Osmunda cinnamomea* (left) and interrupted fern *O. claytonia* (right). Note the woolly covering. Do not eat either of these species.

and even in edible wild plant guides – the resources that we are supposed to be able to turn to for clearing up this kind of confusion. For example, the Basic Essentials series field guide *Edible Wild Plants and Useful Herbs* by Jim Meuninck shows a photograph of cinnamon fern fiddleheads on page 44, in the section on ostrich and bracken ferns. Several other books have drawings, labeled as ostrich fern, that resemble the *Osmunda* ferns, accompanied by verbal descriptions which obviously pertain to the wrong species, suggesting that the author has not correctly identified the fern that he is collecting, using, and writing about.

There has long been debate about the edibility of cinnamon and interrupted fern fiddleheads. Many books claim the cinnamon fern to be edible, but other sources call them inedible. I have never heard the interrupted fern specifically called edible, but it seems to be collected at least as often as the cinnamon fern. Every spring, thousands of people across the continent gather these species for food. I don't know *why*, since both cinnamon and interrupted ferns taste terrible; most people can stomach no more than a few of these fiddleheads. However, if you chop them up small and dilute them with other vegetables in a stew, their bitter flavor is drowned and the whole stew might taste passably good. Many people have eaten these fiddleheads for so long (perhaps believing that the bitter is good for them, or that wild greens are supposed to be bitter) that they insist that cinnamon or interrupted fern is the right species to collect.

I had gathered samples of both cinnamon and interrupted fern fiddleheads occasionally over the years, trying some raw and some cooked. I never found them palatable and therefore never considered them edible. I suspected that the distasteful qualities indicated harmful constituents. I also suspected that the cases of sickness attributed to ostrich fern probably resulted from consumption of these species. Faced with so many people who claimed that these ferns were perfectly fine to eat, I decided to test my hypothesis. A friend and I consumed 10–12 raw interrupted fern fiddleheads one day in May. Not surprisingly, we got sick. Our symptoms were identical: severe headache, nausea, dizziness, lethargy, and general malaise. Later, I forced myself to eat a serving of cinnamon fern fiddleheads boiled. The symptoms were similar but milder, and the fiddleheads were so repulsive that I had to force myself to swallow them.

Many wild food authors state that all fern fiddleheads are safe to eat, varying only in their palatability. Do not believe this claim – collect fiddleheads only from species that you have identified and that you know are safe. Cinnamon and interrupted ferns are apparently unsafe to eat raw, and, although their toxic qualities might be reduced by boiling or steaming, I also strongly advise against eating them cooked.

With all of the confusion about fiddleheads, you might think that these two species were hard to tell from ostrich fern, but this couldn't be further from the truth. They are remarkably easy to distinguish, and there is no excuse for misidentification. A six-year-old, once shown the difference, could get it right a million times out of a million. Cinnamon and interrupted fern fiddleheads are thickly covered with wool and lack the deep groove running the length of the stem.

The literature contains many warnings about the ostrich fern's content of thiaminase, an enzyme that breaks down thiamine. Such warnings are typically accompanied by an admonishment to eat the fiddleheads only after thorough cooking. However, the thiaminase in fern fiddleheads becomes a significant health concern only if you eat large servings of raw fiddleheads on a regular basis for a prolonged period; livestock have been known to suffer from thiamine deficiency when pastured where they were forced to eat large quantities of ferns for extended periods. I know of no cases of this occurring in human beings. I consider it safe to occasionally consume a few ostrich fern fiddleheads raw.

Mature ostrich fern rosette, with fronds about 5 ft. tall.

Range and Habitat

In the United States, ostrich fern is found in the Midwest as far south as Illinois, Iowa, and southern Ohio, the Northeast (south to Virginia in the mountains), and the southern half of Alaska. In Canada this species occurs from east coast to west, and north almost as far as there are forests.

The primary habitat of the ostrich fern is river bottom forests, where it normally forms huge, dense colonies. There are many river valleys across the continent where the luxuriant rosettes of this fern are thick for mile after mile, covering thousands of acres. Due to this localized superabundance, ostrich fern is among the few wild greens harvested on a commercial scale, and the fiddleheads are available in season in many restaurants and produce markets. Smaller colonies of ostrich fern can also be found in rich woods, especially near ponds, ravines, dirt roads, and steep slopes. In these places the plants are usually smaller than those found in river bottoms. This fern needs bare soil for its spores to germinate, which accounts for its occurrence being largely limited to places prone to erosion by floods or human disturbance.

Harvest and Preparation

The time to collect ostrich fern fiddleheads is in the middle to late part of spring. The first shoots appear at about the time that the trees begin to leaf out, and the last fronds are unfurled just before the tree leaves are fully formed. As with most shoots, those growing in the open come up a week or two later than those found in the shade. Where I live, the collecting season is roughly three weeks, from about May 10 to June 1.

You can pick the fiddleheads as young as you want, but I generally choose to let them get at least eight inches tall before collecting them, otherwise it seems like a lot of potential is wasted. You will often read that the fiddleheads should not be picked when over eight inches tall, but nowhere have I found any reasoning expounded for this contention. I pick mine as long as the stems are tender and the tops are still tightly curled; the average size being about 12 inches (30 cm) and the maximum about 28 inches (70 cm). I harvest them by simply cutting or breaking them near the base. The bottom inch or two is generally tough, and on larger fiddleheads the tough portion can be as much as a foot in length.

Most of the edible volume of the fiddlehead is contained in the straight part of the stalk rather than the coiled top. Some people, however, collect only the

The powdery form of ostrich fern. Note the deep groove in the stalk and the way that some of the fiddleheads lean backward just below the curled top. Compare this to the woolly, straight, ungrooved fiddleheads of the *Osmunda* ferns.

coiled disc at the top of the fiddlehead – which I consider an egregious waste. This still kills the frond, but it only utilizes a third or a fourth of its volume. Furthermore, in my opinion the flavor and texture of the straight section of the stalk is superior to that of the coiled top.

When you gather fiddleheads, don't pick all of the fronds from a single rosette; take two out of five, or three out of six. Don't pluck fiddleheads from the same rosette more than once per season, either. Use discretion and conscientiously avoid overharvesting. Although ostrich fern may be abundant and vigorous, asking too much of a plant will cause it to shrink as it expends its energy reserves, and eventually it will die altogether. Sustained heavy harvest has eliminated some ostrich fern colonies near human population centers.

Ostrich fern fiddleheads are crisp and sweet, making a pleasant nibble or addition to salads when raw. Most often they are boiled or steamed until tender and served like asparagus. Their mild flavor and pleasant texture go well in just about any soup, stir-fry, or other vegetable dish.

Before eating the fiddleheads, be sure to wash off any sand or mud that might be clinging to them; this problem is especially prevalent when river bottoms are flooded after heavy spring rains. You may also want to rub off the rusty-colored papery scales nestled in the coiled part of the fiddlehead.

When ostrich fern is in season, I eat it almost daily – but I eat it on a regular basis during the rest of the year, too. Since these fiddleheads grow in such abundance and can be so efficiently collected, they are excellent candidates for bulk storing by canning or freezing. Every spring I can several dozen jars of these, so that I can open them and add them to a meal at my convenience all year long.

Collected as a spring rite by traditional Earth-cultures across the northern hemisphere, the ostrich fern has been a friend to humans for untold generations. Long before agriculture began, vast plantations of this delicious vegetable stretched luxuriantly for acre upon acre in the clean springtime sunshine, offered for free to the bears, deer, and people who would partake of them. In all those years, some good things, fortunately, have not changed.

Cattail

Typha angustifolia, T. latifolia

Marsh of common cattail in early summer. This is an ideal gathering site, since the plants are robust and spread out in soft mud.

I spent part of my childhood living beside a cattail marsh that covered a few hundred acres at the edge of a large lake in southeastern Wisconsin. The red-winged blackbirds nested there by the thousands, and every dawn in autumn they formed a raucous crowd atop the weeping willows in our yard. There was a pool of open water amidst the marsh plants where painted turtles basked on floating pond lily roots, snapping turtles lurked in muddy shallows, teals and mallards raised their broods, and great blue herons stalked anything small enough to swallow. Muskrats lived in carefully assembled heaps of gnawed-down vegetation that dotted the marsh. Every April, garter snakes and mink hunted the golden-eyed leopard frogs who groaned and grunted from the sparse cattails that had been beaten down by the winter's wind and snow and then flooded by the spring melt.

I played for hours on the floating cattail mats, which sank under my weight until my calves were soaked. Occasionally I would find a raft of cattails that had broken loose during a violent storm and float around the lake on it for a while. I used to pull up armfuls of the young cattail stalks and throw them into my neighbor's poultry pen, watching with great satisfaction as the geese gobbled down the long leaves like giant green noodles. But it never occurred to me that cattails might be edible for humans. In fact, ever since the time that my sister fed some to her gerbils and one of them died, we considered them poisonous. When I first read of cattails being used as food, I was skeptical. But I was wrong.

Euell Gibbons (1962) called cattails the "supermarket of the swamps." While this may be a slight exaggeration, the cattail is a remarkably versatile food source. This amazing plant produces four delicious vegetables, plus a rhizome that is packed with nutritious, edible starch; finally, its beautiful pollen provides an interesting, protein-rich flour. This great variety of edible parts, combined with year-round availability in superabundant quantity, makes the cattail among the most useful wild edibles to learn.

Description

The cattail is one of North America's best known plants. It grows from 5–9 feet (1.5–3 m) tall, usually in dense pure or nearly pure stands. All of the leaves are basal and stand very erect; they are packed into a tight cluster until two or three feet above the ground. Cattail leaves are long, sword-like, and thick with air-filled cavities. They lack a distinct midvein, hairs, and teeth. The stalk is round, very straight, and solid all the way through. It bears inconspicuous flowers and, later, the familiar hot-dog like seedheads that persist through the winter.

There are only a few other marsh plants with similar form that might be confused with cattails. One of them is the sweet flag *Acorus calamus*. This plant usually occurs in small pure stands in hard-bottomed marshes, but it does not grow as tall as the cattail. The flower spike of sweet flag hangs off to the side partway up one of the leaves. The cattail flower head is always at the top of the stalk and points vertically. Sweet flag can easily be distinguished by its strong, pleasant odor. Another group of plants that can cause confusion is the irises. Irises are not nearly as tall as cattails and their leaves usually grow at an angle, unlike cattail leaves which are nearly vertical. Most significantly, iris leaves grow in clumps that are flattened in cross section at the base, while cattail leaves form a round clump. This distinction is easy to observe and is unmistakable.

Two species of cattail range widely in North America: the common cattail *Typha latifolia* and the narrow-leaf cattail *T. angustifolia*. The two plants are similar and can be used for food in the same ways, except that rhizomes of the narrow-leaf cattail are smaller and harder to collect and utilize. Narrow-leaf cattail inhabits slightly drier situations than the common cattail, and thus it is often difficult to dig for the underground parts because the roots are entangled with the sod of wetland grasses. Common cattail often grows in water a foot or more in depth; it is more commonly found where the mud is soft and the rhizomes are easy to gather. The main difference between the two is the thinner leaves, stalks, and seedheads of the narrow-leaf cattail. Another distinguishing feature is that the male (top) and female (bottom) parts of the narrow-leaved cattail's flower spike have a noticeable gap separating them, while those of the common cattail do not. The two species often hybridize.

Range and Habitat

One or both species of cattail are found in nearly every part of North America. They thrive on wet ground at or near the water table. Common cattail usually grows slightly shallower than wapato or bur reed and much shallower than wild rice and pickerelweed. Cattails need sand, gravel, or muck where there is a good deal of sunlight. While cattails require exposed mud to germinate, they often grow out from the shore into deeper water, either as a floating mat (where there is loose mud) or on the stream or lake bed (if the bottom is harder).

Harvest and Preparation

Spikes: In the early part of summer, flower spikes first appear on the cattail plants. These are located atop the stalk and, while they are still immature, will be wrapped in a leafy sheath. The spike is divided into two sections; the top is male and produces pollen while the bottom is female and produces seed. Thousands of tiny flowers are packed tightly along the stalk to form this spike. The individual flowers are so small as to be virtually indistinguishable to the naked eye, making the whole spike appear as a solid green mass.

While the spike remains immature, the top (male) section makes a decent vegetable. The whole spikes are difficult to break off by hand, but there is no need to do this. All you want is the top section; this breaks away from the lower section very easily when bent quickly at a right angle. Thus you need no shears or knife to harvest them.

You can boil the spikes briefly and then nibble the flower buds off the stalk (many have likened this to eating miniature corn-on-the-cob) – or you can scrape them off with a knife and use the resulting yellowish-green material in many cooked dishes. You can also eat them raw. The flavor has a hint of sweet corn and a hint of mushroom, but is entirely cattail. There is some question as to the food value of these spikes, since they seem to pass through the system hardly digested.

Pollen: If you don't cut the immature spikes, the male part will begin to release pollen in a few days. In a small region, cattail pollen ripens over a surprisingly long period due to variations in water temperature and microclimate, but in one particular marsh the season is brief and easy to miss. At the right time, the pollen head will be yellow and a tap on the stalk will release a cloud of yellow pollen.

Cattail pollen can be collected by leaning the heads over and shaking them over or into a container. (Be careful, however, because it is very easy to lean them over too far and cause the stalks to snap.) Another good collecting method is to cut a small hole in the side of a clean, dry, one-gallon milk or

Immature cattail spike with sheath peeled off; the top section is "cattail on the cob."

Flower spike loaded with pollen.

water jug about 3.5 inches (9 cm) up from the base. Insert the pollen-bearing head of a standing cattail into this hole and shake it. Using an enclosed container like this will greatly reduce the quantity of pollen lost to wind and "fallout." The fact that you don't have to bend the cattail stalk over, combined with the convenience of holding the container in one hand, will greatly in-

This pollen was collected in a few minutes from several flower heads.

crease the ease and efficiency of your pollen collection. It is best to collect the pollen after several consecutive calm days, since gusts of wind will blow it away and rain will shake or wash it out. Under good conditions I can gather about a quart of pollen per hour.

The great thing about cattail pollen is that it requires very little processing once harvested; it is already in the form of powder and thus does not have to be ground for flour. You should shake it through a cheesecloth or screen, however, to sift out the insects and wooly fibers that always get mixed in, then dry it before storing it. The pollen is a beautiful golden color and has a pleasant flavor.

Cattail pollen makes wonderful muffins, breads, and other baked goods, but it must be mixed with wheat flour because it is not sticky by itself. It can also be used in hot cereal or mixed with many other foods, since the flavor is mild and pleasant.

Laterals: My favorite part of the cattail to eat is the lateral shoot of the rhizome, which I have come to call simply a *lateral*. Cattail laterals are white or cream-colored and smooth on the outside because they have not yet developed any roots. The laterals break very easily and have not yet differentiated into distinct layers of rind and core like the mature rhizomes. The tip of the lateral points sideways; it does not curve upwards or terminate in a leafy bud.

Although the lateral differs greatly from the mature rhizome in appearance, texture, culinary use, flavor, and season of harvest, I know of no wild food author

Cattail laterals. Note the light color and the absence of roots. The darkening portions on the right are maturing into rhizomes but have not completely toughened yet.

who has made the distinction between these two vegetables. The accounts of cattail rhizome in some books refer to the mature rhizome, while those in other books clearly pertain to the laterals. I believe that this explains much of the discrepancy between the various literary accounts of cattail rhizomes and their use.

You can collect laterals from late summer into early fall – generally, any time after the plants have flowered but before they begin to die and turn brown. They are easiest to collect at the deep edge of a cattail mat growing in soft mud; however, they are found throughout the cattail stand.

To harvest laterals, reach into the muck at the base of a stalk and feel for the rhizomes. When you find one that heads toward an area where there are no stalks, follow it with your hands. If it ends abruptly in a pointed tip *that does not turn upwards*, you are in luck. Feel along the lateral back toward the parent plant; at about the point where you feel the first roots, pull upwards until the lateral breaks off. (Very likely it will have already broken off from you feeling it.) Then grab the lateral and try to pull it out of the mud without breaking it. It sounds complicated, but once you know what you are doing these vegetables can be gathered quickly.

The laterals are about an inch (2.5 cm) thick and may be anywhere from 3–14 inches (8–36 cm) long. They are easy to clean by simply rinsing, cutting off the dirty ends, and removing the few sheaths that are usually attached to their surface. Laterals can be stored in a refrigerator for several days if kept wrapped so they do not dry out.

Sweet, mild, and soft with no objectionable flavor, cattail laterals are delicious just to snack on raw. They can be sliced into salads or cooked in many vegetable dishes. In soup they are fabulous. Almost everybody will find them palatable when boiled or steamed and served with butter and seasonings. Laterals are large, easy to work with, and are the most pleasing of all the cattail vegetables in both flavor and texture. They are definitely worth getting muddy for.

Buds: At the tip of the mature cattail rhizomes, large buds that point skyward will form in the fall. They consist of a bundle of several layers of tightly packed young leaves, two to eight inches long. This part has also been variously called the "shoot" or (erroneously) "corm." Cattail buds lie dormant from autumn to the middle of spring and can be collected during that whole season by simply breaking or cutting them from the rhizome.

Take the larger buds, cut off the ends, and peel away the outer layer or two of leaves, as these parts will be too tough to eat. The interior of the bud is soft and whitish-yellow. Like other cattail parts, the bud has a mild and pleasant flavor and is an excellent cooked vegetable. However, in my opinion its tender interior is usually too small to be worth the trouble of collecting. I rarely go out of my way to gather the buds but sometimes harvest them incidentally when I am collecting rhizomes to make flour.

Leaf Hearts or Shoot Cores: These are the interior of the cluster of growing leaves in spring and early summer. This part is called the heart, shoot, core, or "Cossack asparagus," and is probably the best known vegetable to come from the cattail plant. The hearts can be collected from the time the cattail buds

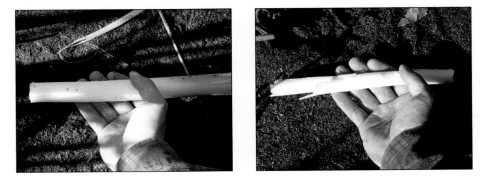

The base of a cattail shoot or leaf cluster in early summer (left) and the same cluster after peeling to show the edible core (right).

begin to grow in spring until about the middle of summer. The best time to get them is in late spring or early summer when the plants are one half to two-thirds grown and the flower stalks are not yet formed.

The way to collect cattail hearts is to grab the center leaves of a cluster (all but the outer two leaves, which form a sort of sheath around the others) and pull them firmly and steadily upward, with slowly increasing force, until they detach from the rhizome and come free from the sheath. As the leaf heart pulls out, it usually makes a distinctive, rubbery squeaking noise. I usually walk around in a cattail patch and pull these hearts out with my right hand while I cradle the pile of harvested ones in my left arm. Since they are totally clean when I get them, I try to keep them that way.

Sometimes the cores have a tendency to break off above the base, leaving the thickest and tenderest portion behind. You can avoid this by using a knife to cut the whole leaf cluster at the base and then peeling off the outer layer. However, this takes more time and usually gets the vegetable dirty, requiring that you wash it later.

The leaf core is a little bit annoying because the interior leaves are tender much higher up than the outer layers are. To deal with this, use a progressively smaller portion of the core as you go up the stalk. The bottom few inches of the leaf heart will be soft and light in color. You should be able to pinch through it with your fingernail; if not, remove the outer layer of leaves until the bottom of the core is tender. Cut the tender section off the bottom of the core (and keep it). Remove the outer layer of leaves from the rest of the core and again cut off the tender part thereby exposed. Repeat this process until you reach the innermost leaves, at which point you will have gotten all of the good edible core from that leaf cluster. There will be a lot of wasted leaf material, especially later in the season, but don't sweat it – cattails are prolific enough to handle the harvest.

I like to eat these cattail hearts cooked in a variety of dishes, especially soups. They have a mild, slightly sweet flavor that very few will object to. Many people say that they like to eat cattail hearts raw, but they give me an itchy, irritated feeling in the back of my throat. Others have reported the same experience. For this reason, I rarely eat them unless they are cooked.

Rhizomes: Anyone who has followed the advice of one of the multitude of authors who claim that the cattail "root" makes a potato-like vegetable has learned through experience that such literary analogies do not always accurately reflect reality. Cattail rhizomes are starchy, but that is about where their

Mature, healthy rhizomes of common cattail harvested in fall.

similarity to potatoes ends. Although many have said that the rootstock can be roasted or boiled like "young potatoes," note that they refrain from saying *eaten and enjoyed* like young potatoes. After having consumed hundreds of cattail rootstocks, I still have not managed to find any part that I would enjoy, or even be willing to eat except under dire circumstances, if it was prepared and served like new potatoes. Or old potatoes. The rootstocks contain much palatable and edible starch, but it is found between thick and tough dental floss-like fibers that most people simply would not eat.

Cattail rhizomes crisscross under every square foot of a cattail marsh, usually two to six inches under the surface of the mud. Each cattail shoot or plant will be connected to many others by means of these rhizomes. They run horizontally, are usually about an inch thick, and can be from a few inches to several feet long. Cattail rhizomes *do not branch between stalks*. They are a tan or reddish-brown color for most of their length, although the leading ends are sometimes lighter in color. All along the rootstock there are small wiry roots that are a few inches long. The rhizome consists of two distinct layers; a spongy rind and a dense, fibrous core that contains the starch. If you pinch a cattail rhizome you will feel the outer sponge layer compress under the force, but this compression will stop at the core. The outermost layer of the rhizome is smooth but is broken by rough rings every few inches, appearing to divide the rootstock into segments. The rhizomes of narrow-leaf cattail are much thinner than those of the common cattail and are therefore significantly more labor-intensive to use for food; I only gather them if the common cattail is unavailable.

The best time to gather cattail rhizomes is from fall to late spring – the dormant season. They can be used during the growing season also but contain significantly less starch at that time.

Rarely, where the mud is loose and the water is deep, it is possible to gather cattail rhizomes simply by pulling up gently on the aerial stalk. Alternately pulling on the plants and releasing them helps to loosen the mud and break the suction in these situations. Unfortunately, it is usually only possible to use this method to collect cattail rhizomes from isolated plants at the open-water edge of a colony. In normal circumstances you will have to dig for them. For greater efficiency and ease of collection while digging, you should still look for places where the cattails are growing sparsely and the mud is soft near the deep-water edge of a colony. I dig them with my bare hands to prevent breakage and so that I can feel what is going on better.

It is best to bring a knife to cut the rhizomes from their stalks rather than try to rip them. Torn rhizomes get tiny splits in them that let in mud, which is wicked along the fibers, ruining much of the starch. Furthermore, cutting them is just easier. Some rhizomes connect two plants and must be cut at each end; these rootstocks are far more likely to be spoiled than are those that end in a bud. A cattail rhizome that terminates in a bud should be severed from the parent plant and then pulled toward it.

If you find a floating cattail mat or "island," such as those that often break free from marshes after storms, you are in luck. If you can manage to turn one of these mats over, the bottom will generally be a solid mass of ready-rinsed rootstocks that can be collected with little effort. They tend to be smaller and more twisted than rhizomes dug from the mud, but overall these floating mats are a bargain for your labor.

However I end up collecting the rhizomes, I am always careful to cut them into manageable lengths that I will not have to bend to fit into a bag or bucket for carrying home. That's because when they bend, they crack open, letting mud get to the core – plus bent cores tend to fray and are harder to work with later when I make flour. I like to do as much of the washing as possible at the body of water where I collect the rhizomes, so that the sections that I pack to bring home need little or no further cleaning.

At the base of each stalk there is an enlarged fibrous mass that contains much starch and is densely covered by roots. This cluster of roots usually holds a lot of mud, so I try to trim them in the field if it is possible.

The two layers of the rhizome – a spongy rind and a hard inner core of starch supported by coarse fibers – are distinctly separate, and this distinction can be seen in cross section when the ends of the rhizomes are cut. Cutting off the dirty ends is the first step in the peeling process. The core and the rind are both almost white, but their textures are quite different. If your core is tainted by mud, cut off more. If it is an orange-brown color, then it is beginning to rot and should not be used.

In a survival situation, or just on a hungry hike such as I have experienced countless times, you can take the core and chew on it and suck out the starch. It is easy, requires no tools or cooking, and the starch actually tastes quite good. After a few minutes of chewing you will have a wad of fibers that you can spit out; then repeat the process with another piece of rootstock core. Because of cattail's long season of availability and great abundance, it is one of the best sources of energy available in the wilderness.

It is possible to boil the rhizome cores and eat them in the same way – which is certainly not like eating potatoes. Anyone who fails to mention the part about chewing and spitting out a wad of floss is being remiss. In *Stalking the Wild Asparagus*, Euell Gibbons writes about a "sizeable lump of tender starchy material" (SLOTSM) located just where a sprout or shoot joins the rootstock, which he recommends roasting with meat as one would do with potatoes. This has been variously misconstrued by many later authors to mean that some part of the rootstock is tender and can be used like a potato. This is simply untrue; all parts of the mature rootstock contain the tough fibers. The SLOTSM that Gibbons was talking about is a part of the shoot or bud's base where it connects to the rhizome; it is not a part of the rhizome itself. Although small and somewhat frustrating to extract, it is an excellent starchy vegetable.

Making Cattail Rhizome Flour

The main use of cattail rhizomes is in the production of flour. There are two main methods used to separate the starch from the fibers for flour making, each with its benefits and drawbacks. I call these simply the wet method and the dry method.

The first step of either method is to remove the spongy rind from the rhizomes. I do this by using my thumbnail like a chisel to push (not peel) strips of it off. Sometimes I use the chiseling motion to get a strip started, and then peel it the rest of the way. This is one of the most difficult things to explain in my classes and I fear that it will be even harder by way of the

Sections of cattail rhizome after peeling. One is left half-peeled to show the relative size of the rind and core. If the core is peeled properly it will be stiff with no loose fibers hanging off.

Cross section of rhizomes, showing the two distinct layers.

written word, but anybody will catch on after peeling enough rootstocks. A properly peeled core should have no loose fibers and a smooth, hard outer surface. The point of peeling this way is to avoid grabbing some of the inner fibers and peeling them away, thus wasting starch; most neophytes throw away about a third of the edible starch in this manner. To experienced hands, however, the less wasteful method of peeling is also the faster one.

Occasionally someone gets very upset that I discard the rind, which is a lot of the rhizome's volume. Perhaps these people also eat oat straw, nutshells, and chicken feathers. They will save the peeled spongy material, look at it hopefully, and ask, "Why don't we eat this part?" Some of them, no matter how much I insist that it will be fruitless, smuggle a bagful of rind home to try extracting something edible. Don't waste your time with it.

The Wet Method: This has also been called the "soak and settle" method; it was popularized by Euell Gibbons.

Once you have peeled your rhizomes, take the cores and break them up with your hands in a container of clean, cold water. Do this by grabbing the rhizome at two points about two inches apart and pushing each side towards the center while simultaneously twisting a little. When the fibers separate, rotate them vigorously to loosen the starch. Then move a little farther down the core and do the same again. After you have done this to many cores you can take the whole mass of fiber and rub it in your hands to loosen any remaining starch. Remove the fibers and let the starch settle to the bottom of the container over several hours; it will form a layer of light-colored sludge. Pour off the slimy water above the sludge – carefully so as not to lose any of the starch. Then pick out any remaining bits of fiber, or run the sludge through a screen to accomplish this.

Some people put the starch through multiple soakings as described to remove more impurities, but this is not necessary. You can take this soupy starch and use it as the base for pancake batter or bread dough – just add enough wheat flour to attain the proper consistency. Or you can use it to thicken a soup or casserole. If you want cattail rhizome flour you'll have to dehydrate this sludge, which is difficult in any substantial quantity, and herein lies, in my opinion, the greatest drawback to using the wet method of starch separation. It is almost a necessity to have your drying surface near a woodstove or heater to desiccate the starch quickly enough to avoid having it mold or spoil – as I had happen to a few of my early batches. Also, the slime that is poured off with the soaking water is digestible starch, so some of the food value of the rhizome is lost in the soak-and-settle process.

The Dry Method: As with the wet method, begin by peeling the rhizomes. After attaining a pile of peeled cores, cut them into sections of about a quarter to a third of an inch. Proper peeling becomes a factor here; those that have had part of the core peeled off, resulting in loose strings and starch, will stick to the knife and the cutting board. They will also be annoying and troublesome to cut because they are less rigid. Properly peeled cores, on the other hand, will cut cleanly and quickly.

The cut-up core pieces should then be dried. They dry pretty fast, since they are not very wet to begin with. I spread them on a baking tray that I place on my drying rack for one or two days.

It is also possible to dry the entire rhizomes *before* peeling them. First, clean the rhizomes and cut them into manageable lengths with no dirty ends. Then spread them on a surface to dry; they need not desiccate quickly because they are not prone to fast spoilage. Drying the rhizomes beforehand allows you to harvest many in the fall and then wait until winter to do the more time-consuming work of making flour. It also is somewhat easier to peel the dried rhizomes – as long as they are not bent up and damaged. These pre-dried cores are difficult to cut, however; I find it more practical to break them.

After drying, I grind the cut or broken rhizome pieces in my flourmill (with iron burrs) on a coarse setting. I end up with a mixture of fiber and flour.

Jelly bag suspended in jar for separating flour from fiber.

Now, here comes the cool part. I put a big handful of the flour and fiber mixture into a jelly bag. Then I hang the jelly bag inside of a glass gallon jar, with the top of the bag over the lip and outside of the jar. I keep it suspended there by screwing on the lid, which also keeps the flour from floating away as dust. Then I shake the jar vigorously. The flour will pass through the fine holes in the bag and settle to the bottom of the jar, while the fibers will stay inside the bag. The result is a refined flour that is extremely fine and resembles whole wheat flour in color.

Rhizome flour produced in this fashion has a slightly different flavor and a more mucilaginous quality than that produced by the wet method, but both are palatable and useful food products.

Cattail flour is not a substitute for wheat flour. There is absolutely no plant, wild or domestic, that can substitute for wheat flour, so don't expect to make fluffy bread from all-wild products. Cattail rhizome flour lacks gluten and will not rise by itself. I make pretty good tortillas from it, but they are more brittle than those made from wheat. I often use cattail flour to thicken soups or to help casseroles stick together better. It is superb for those purposes, both mechanically and in flavor. I also have a great recipe for pancake mix that includes cattail, acorn, and wheat flour, which produces a unique flavor and texture. I'm sure there are many great uses for this flour that need only to be discovered.

As you have seen, the cattail is a plant of incredibly varied culinary uses. Its products are not marginally edible – they are delicious. And surely there is much more to discover about this versatile plant: better harvest methods, preparation techniques, and recipes. Perhaps you will be the one to discover these.

Wapato, Arrowhead

Sagittaria spp.

The elusive tubers of *Sagittaria latifolia*, the broad-leaved arrowhead or wapato.

Wapato or arrowhead is a plant that many wild food enthusiasts have heard of but few have tried. Things that grow hidden deep in the muck do not catch one's eye. The literary accounts of Native women walking chest-deep in frigid water to harvest these tubers have done little to entice people into the marshes in search of them. Furthermore, most accounts of the use and harvest of wapato provide an insufficient description of the process. Thus one of North America's most exciting wild foods has been kept largely a secret.

I still remember the first wapato that I ever tasted. When I was ten years old my family lived beside a large, shallow, marshy lake. Sometime in the spring, as I was wading the shore, I found a floating vegetable about the size of a golf ball. I picked it up and examined it, breaking it open and smelling the inside. It smelled like something that I wanted to bite. I recognized it as a wapato, which I had recently read about, so I bit into it.

Today I don't even consider raw wapato worth eating, but back then its crispness and slightly sweet flavor was enough to get me very excited. I prowled the shore looking for more, but without any luck. Occasionally during the late spring, my siblings and I would find what we called "stink bombs" floating in the lake while we were swimming. We delighted in throwing these at each other or, worse yet, smashing them against each other's skin. The next time I found one, I realized that they were rotten wapatoes. I still regularly find stink bombs while I am harvesting wapato.

I never ate another wapato from that lake. I learned to identify the plant, however, and for more than a decade following that first experience, I would occasionally pull or dig them up without discovering any tubers. I began to doubt that the tuber that I had eaten long ago was actually a wapato. Admittedly, I was not trying very hard or very often, but I never found anything at all to encourage me.

I read about wapato in numerous books. I learned that in the East, certain tribes for whom it was an important food called it *katniss*, while in the Northwest, where it often formed one of the staples, it was called *wapato*. Merriweather Lewis recorded that at the mouth of the Willamette River, it was an important sustenance of the Natives. The tubers, described as "potato-like," invariably came highly recommended. I have since discovered that a species of wapato, *Sagittaria sagittifolia*, has been domesticated in China. But I never seemed to be able to find any of those elusive tubers.

Then I met Jon Wheeler. Jon was hard-core. He wasn't afraid to get muddy or to do something that the average person would consider dangerous or foolish. He didn't mind getting into cold water, either. Not only was Jon a pretty experienced forager and somebody who loved the outdoors, but he assured me that he had found arrowhead tubers.

One day, he came back from a foray with about half a dozen large wapatoes that he had gathered from the edge of the Bad River in northern Wisconsin. When I saw them, I felt reassured that what I had eaten so many years ago was truly a wapato. Jon explained how he had collected these tubers: "I saw a spot where there were some arrowhead plants at the edge of the river and I just got in and started feeling around in the muck."

The next year, I located a spot with lots of wapato plants. It was deeper water with a softer bottom and larger plants than any place that I'd tried before. I returned with a shovel. I got in and "started feeling around in the muck" and was quickly reminded that Jon's arms were much longer than mine. I found sticks, rocks, and broken glass, so I went out deeper where the mud was softer. It was too deep for me to reach very far into the muck without submerging my head, which I intended not to do, so I grabbed the shovel and began digging. It was several minutes before the first tuber floated to the surface, but a half hour later, I had enough for my first meal of wapato. Since then, I've gathered wapato every fall and spring, and I've gotten more efficient at it with each season. It is these experiences that I would like to share with you in this account.

Description

Arrowhead or wapato is an emergent aquatic plant of the family *Alismataceae*. (It is not the same thing as the "arrowroot" available commercially.) North America is home to numerous species in the genus *Sagittaria*, most of which produce edible tubers. However, some kinds are definitely more worth your time than others. The species that is most commonly harvested is the broad-leaved arrowhead, *S. latifolia*, which is the largest of the species that I am familiar with. *S. cuneata* is another common species, smaller than the former. Its tubers, being smaller, are more difficult to gather. Another common wapato of the northern U.S. and Canada is *S. rigida*, which can grow quite large but always has small tubers. There may be other excellent species of wapato in other areas of the country.

All wapato species have long-stalked basal leaves. These range greatly in shape, but the classic form is pointed at the tip with two long, pointed lobes projecting in the opposite direction. This leaf shape (in botanical terms called *sagittate*) accounts for the name "arrowhead." These sagittate leaves vary from 3 inches (8 cm) to more than 3 feet (1 m) in length; they can be ribbon-like and only .5 inch (1 cm) wide, or they may be robust and as much as 1.5 feet (.5 m) wide. Immense variation in form can exist among plants growing only a few feet apart. Wapato also varies enormously in size; some leaves rise 5 feet (1.5 m) off the water, while others are no more than a few inches high.

Sagittaria rigida is unusual in that it does not have backward pointing lobes on its leaves; they are lanceolate or linear. One of our common species of wapato, *S. cuneata*, sometimes produces floating leaves. Most species also produce totally submerged, ribbon-like leaves. Despite the variability, wapato plants of any size look distinctive to the trained eye.

There are other water plants with sagittate leaves. Notable among them are arrow arum *Peltandra virginica* and pickerelweed *Pontederia cordata*.

Mature, full-figured leaf of *S. latifolia*.

103

Neither of these is difficult to distinguish from wapato, even by leaf characters alone. The lobes of pickerelweed leaves are rounded rather than pointed, and the veins reach the lobes by making a j-shaped route from the midvein of the leaf, then heading up toward the tip, while the veins in the lobes of an arrowhead leaf dead end there. The pickerelweed leaf is curled (while that of wapato is rather flat) and also has many more veins. The tips and lobes of arrow arum leaves are usually less pointed than those of wapato. Also, there is a distinct vein that runs around the arum leaf just inside the perimeter, and the veins radiating from the center of the leaf visibly stop there. Arrowhead distinctly lacks this feature.

There is an easy way to distinguish the leaves of the broad-leaved wapato at a glance: The backward pointing lobes are far larger than those of any other plant with a similar leaf shape. The two lobes combined usually cover about the same surface area as the main portion of the leaf, and often they cover more. Each lobe is about as long as the main section of the leaf as well. No other water plants have lobes like these.

Wapato's white, 3-petaled flowers bloom on a spike from mid summer through early autumn. The flowering stalk is separate from the leaves but rises about as high off the water. Later in summer, small green balls form in place of the flowers. These turn brown in fall and break apart to disperse tiny, flat, winged, floating seeds.

Leaf variations of *S. rigida.*

If you somehow misidentify the aerial portion of wapato, you might waste a lot of time digging in the wrong spot – but there is no excuse for misidentifying the tubers. They look about as much like the rhizomes of arrow arum or pickerelweed as giraffes look like trout.

While wapato is often described as "potato-like," this tuber is actually very distinct in appearance and has no particular resemblance to a potato. Unlike many tubers, those of wapato display surprising

Flowers of *S. latifolia.*

uniformity in shape. They range from the size of a pea to the size of a goose egg, with about 1.5 inch (4 cm) in diameter being typical in a good locality. Not surprisingly, larger plants produce larger tubers. The wapatoes are spherical or ovoid in shape, sometimes slightly flattened, especially in the largest specimens. The raw tubers and other parts of the plant are scented mildly like grapefruit peel.

Arrow arum *Peltandra virginica*, the plant most often confused with wapato. Note the proportionately smaller lobes, different venation, and tilted leaves. The rootstock looks nothing like wapato.

Mature wapato with seed balls.

Tubers of *S. rigida.*

Tubers of *S. cuneata.*

Tubers of *S. latifolia.*

Each tuber is borne singly at the end of a soft, spongy, unforked rhizome, and a plant typically produces 2–8 tubers. The rhizomes on medium to large plants (from which you will most likely be collecting) are .5–.75 inch (1.25–2 cm) thick and 2–6 feet (.5–2 m) long. Where the bottom is harder, the rhizomes will be shorter and shallower.

Each tuber has one pointed shoot sticking out of the end, usually curling slightly to give the whole thing the shape of a large comma. There are usually two distinct rings around the wapato, to which thin, leafy "veils" are attached. There are no roots attached to the tuber.

The color of wapato tubers varies greatly, not only between the various species, but within each species as well. In one marsh a certain color will predominate, while in another marsh the typical coloration will be drastically different. Small to medium sized tubers of *S. latifolia* and especially *S. cuneata* are often a brilliant purple, and this is the color that I typically associate with wapato, but in darker water they are often darker purplish or reddish-brown. The larger tubers of *S. latifolia* are sometimes white or cream-colored. Others have reported yellow, green, reddish, or orange hues. Tubers of *S. rigida* are more spherical than the other species, rarely as large as an inch in diameter, and all of them that I have seen were white or creamy in color.

When cut, arrowhead tubers exude a small amount of latex. A thin coating of this will sometimes stick to cooking utensils and your fingers, but it is not really a problem. The flesh of the tubers is whitish, often with a hint of yellow, and crisp like a very hard apple. It does not contain visible fibers, nor is it marbled or opaque.

The wapato's function in the life cycle of the plant differs from that of other tubers. In the spring it does not produce stalks or roots like a potato – all it does is send a single shoot upward to the surface of the mud, where a "knob" is formed. The leaves, roots, and flower stalk grow from this knob, and the tuber feeds them energy from deep in the mud through its "umbilical cord." As the tuber's energy is used up, it dies and withers. This system allows wapato to protect its starch reserves deep in the mud while still enjoying the benefits of growing on the surface. Novice wapato collectors sometimes mistakenly harvest this knob, but it is not edible and does not resemble the tuber.

Range and Habitat

Different species of wapato are found across North America wherever there are wetlands, except they are absent from the Far North. Wapato is also widespread in Europe and Asia.

Wapato of one species or another is present in most slow or stagnant warm-water wetlands within its range, but the species to seek, at least in most of North America, is *S. latifolia*, the broad-leaved arrowhead. This species comes to dominate large areas in nearly pure stands where five important conditions are met: there are large areas of shallow standing water, 4–18 inches (10–46 cm) above the mud line; the mud is moderately soft (hard enough to hold the wapato tuber in place despite the fact that it is buoyant, but soft enough for the rhizomes to penetrate the mud easily); the mud is not shallowly deposited over a hard substrate (otherwise bulrushes tend to take over); there is great fluctuation of water level; and there is ample sunlight. Cattail, bur reed, wild rice, and pickerelweed are the plants most commonly found alongside large wapato stands.

The proper conditions for large stands of wapato occur along sloughs and backwaters of rivers and streams (where water levels fluctuate rapidly with rainfall) and in marshes where streams enter the Great Lakes or the Ocean. Pothole ponds that fill up with each downpour and then slowly dry out until the next rainfall are sometimes lined with dense stands of wapato. Most lakeshores and marshes have at least a few scattered clumps of arrowhead, and these can be productive places to harvest the tubers if the plants are large. Look for such clumps especially where streams flow into larger bodies of water.

There are places scattered across the continent where wapato can be gathered in enormous quantities. I have seen nearly pure stands that covered hundreds of acres. Once you learn to recognize this plant there is a high likelihood that you will be able to locate a nice colony reasonably close to your home.

All wapato patches were not created equal. In a sandy lakeshore where the plants are dainty, trying to harvest wapato can be as frustrating as trying to milk aphids. But don't get discouraged; think big. Seek large colonies of large plants with large leaves, for these will produce larger tubers, which accumulate faster and are easier to clean and peel. Look specifically for wide leaves with a large surface area as opposed to leaves with long and narrow lobes. Until you find such a place, keep playing with the small and frustrating stuff from time to time so that you are ready to appreciate the miracle of a good wapato patch when you find it.

Harvest

Wapato can be harvested beginning in late summer, but most of the tubers will not be fully grown until the plants begin to turn brown and die. I prefer

Pickerelweed *Pontederia cordata.* Unlike wapato, the lobes are rounded and the leaves are concave. Note also the different venation and fruit.

to harvest mine in late September and early October, when the tubers have attained their full size but the water is not yet exceedingly cold. In areas where the water does not freeze, wapato can be harvested all winter long. The tubers are excellent in spring, but the water is usually colder and deeper then than in the fall. After the shoots have grown substantially, the tubers will shrink and die; this occurs in late spring or early summer, marking the end of the collecting season.

Effectively collecting wapato takes some practice; in the beginning, it also takes faith that there is really something worth your time down there in the muck. Trust me, there is.

This is a narrow-leaved specimen of *S. latifolia*. Note the extreme range of variation between this and the broad-leaved form. Photo by Clayton Oslund.

If you just try to pull up arrowhead plants and hope that the tubers will be somehow attached to the base, your chances of procuring a meal are slimmer than a starving eel. Wapato unfortunately does not make itself available through such half-hearted efforts. After a number of unsuccessful attempts along these lines when I was younger, I knew that I didn't know enough about harvesting wapato. Euell Gibbons to the rescue.

Wapato is the subject of the fourth chapter in Euell's first foraging book, *Stalking the Wild Asparagus*. Here he recommends using waders and, while standing in the shallow water, raking back and forth in the muck with a potato hook (which is a long-handled garden implement with four tines bent at a right angle). I got myself a potato hook with a five-foot handle as well as a similar three-tined garden rake with a three and a half foot handle and headed to the marsh where I harvest wapato. It worked. I harvested a lot of wapato that year, and almost all of it with one of these tools. Sometimes I was standing in the water getting soaked, and other times I was kneeling in a canoe getting less wapato.

When Euell said, "Rake back and forth through the mud, stirring it vigorously," he made it sound a little easier than it actually is. The mud can be pretty dense, and usually you have to really put some muscle into getting the rake to move through it. More elaborately explained, you scrape away the top layers of muck in a small area between several wapato plants, then work your way deeper and deeper, swishing the muck away from your excavation in the water. Often I have to remove several dead wapato plants from the area before proceeding, otherwise they will get tangled in the tines of the rake. One drawback of this method is that the rake tines damage many tubers.

It is important not to get discouraged at first, for it will probably be a few minutes before you get any tubers. In fact, when I bring people out to collect wapato, with any method, the experienced gatherers usually start getting tubers after thirty seconds to a minute, while few of the rookie participants get a tuber in less than ten minutes. It's just the necessary breaking-in period. My advice is to keep the rake moving, keep going deeper, and don't be afraid to churn up a lot of muck.

Eventually, a wapato will appear floating somewhere in or near your work area. This means that you have reached the top of the "tuber zone." Expect to see more shortly, as long as you keep working. The arrowhead plant deposits most of its tubers at least six inches (15 cm) deep in the mud. (At least, this is the case in good harvesting areas. Areas with smaller plants and harder bottoms will have the tubers closer to the surface.) It wants them to be safe from scouring floods (which could remove the softer mud at the surface and allow the tubers to be swept away) and from various animals that eat them. The smaller tubers are generally closer to the surface, while the big monsters are at about two to three feet (60–90 cm) under the surface of the mud.

In an area of four feet by four feet (1.2 m by 1.2 m), in a good patch of wapato, you might get twenty or thirty tubers. When you are down pretty deep and you haven't gotten any for a while, you have probably worked past the tuber zone; it's time to either move to a new place or expand your excavation to one side.

Sometimes I collect wapato with my hands. This is a wet and muddy affair, and when I'm in the right mood, I love it. I feel in the muck around the base of a wapato plant for the rhizomes radiating from it. Each one terminates in a single tuber, unless it runs horizontally (in which case it connects to another plant). Larger rhizomes produce proportionately larger tubers. Usually they run at about a 35-degree angle downward, although some are oriented almost straight down. By feeling in this way, I can quickly determine how many tubers a plant will have, and approximately how large they will be. Unlike other harvest methods, this one allows me to be selective and collect only the largest tubers, which saves time later.

I feel along the rhizome *all the way to the end, careful not to pull or break it* because the tuber will easily detach. If the rhizome detaches by accident, keep feeling a little past the detached end; the wapato is there somewhere. Usually the tubers are two to five feet from the parent plant, but on small plants they will be closer.

I used these two methods to harvest the tubers before I talked to John Kallas in September of 2000. In *The Wild Food Adventurer,* Vol. 1 No. 4, John provides an excellent account of wapato harvest. He describes wading into a patch of wapato and stomping and working the mud in one area very thoroughly to loosen the tubers and allow them to float to the surface.

Many foragers have ignored wapato because they disdain getting wet and muddy, acting as if one must endure virtual torture to partake of this food.

A few hundred acres of wapato along the Mississippi River.

That is an unfortunate attitude. Duck hunters do not complain about wading for their sport, nor do smelt netters. They eagerly await the chance to do so, year after year, and daydream about it in the off-season. Many drive hundreds of miles and spend thousands of dollars for the privilege of wading waist-deep in frigid water while reveling in the bounty of Nature as they harvest food. Why can't foragers love their outdoor pursuit with as much passion? Harvesting wapato is great fun.

Since learning the "stomping" technique I have used it to harvest hundreds of pounds of wapato. I like to go on a warm autumn day. I enter the marsh wearing tennis shoes, shorts, and a T-shirt. When I find a promising locality, I begin running in place while turning in a slow circle, working my feet deeper and deeper into the mud. Usually when the water is at about mid-thigh I start to get tubers. I pick them up and toss them at a plastic bag (which I set nearby in some vegetation to keep it from floating away). As I work my way deeper, several tubers will usually appear each minute. They will float to the surface of their own accord; all your feet have to do is break up the mud, freeing the tubers.

After the water level reaches my navel, I'm generally to the bottom of the tuber zone. (Again, this depth will vary greatly with growing conditions.) Then I start expanding my hole by stomping chunks of mud from the side into the hole. Periodically I'll kick or flail my legs vigorously in the hole where the chunks have accumulated to create a current, which washes away the mud and releases the tubers imbedded in it. (I call this *fanning*.) Often the tubers wait several minutes to surface, for the water has to dissolve the heavy mud that clings to them and prevents them from floating.

Stomping and fanning has proven to be by far the most efficient method I've employed for harvesting wapato. With this method I usually gather about five pounds per hour, and in the best locations I manage ten to fifteen.

The vigorous movement of harvesting wapato keeps me warm for quite a while, but I always make sure to get out before I become chilled. Some people get cold much more easily than others; to avoid hypothermia, be aware of your limits and don't push beyond them. Have a warm place and dry clothes available when you are finished, as well as a place to shower or at least rinse off.

I have read several accounts claiming that Native Americans gathered wapato by raiding muskrat lodges. The muskrats in my area generally don't build lodges, so I've never had the opportunity to try this. It sounds mean, but it could save a lot of time.

Canada geese also love wapato. One April, just as the ice was receding from one of my favorite wapato patches, I sat for 45 minutes and watched these birds feeding on the tubers. They bobbed repeatedly, craning their long necks deep into the water and paddling vigorously with their hind feet to maintain their upside-down position. They did this repeatedly before finally coming up with a wapato. After repositioning the tubers in their beaks, they would swallow them whole. Between dunkings, the geese even paddled away the mud by kicking their legs furiously while right-side up, fanning just like I do.

It is difficult to overharvest wapato. When the tubers are thinned out, the remaining plants simply grow bigger and produce eight or ten tubers per plant as opposed to the usual two to five. The spaced-out plants grow longer rhizomes, so any empty spots in the muck are soon filled. Add to this the enormous quantity of seed that is produced annually by wapato plants and you can see that they are extremely prolific. It would take careless industrial exploitation to eliminate a large colony of wapato, but you should be cautious of overcollection in smaller colonies. One year several people collected heavily in an area of about 40 by 70 feet (12 by 20 m), and the patch was notably thinner there the next year; it took it a few seasons to recover. Harvest areas no more than 6 feet (2 m) wide (or 3 feet at the edge of the colony) so that nearby plants can easily reclaim the stomped area.

Preparation

Once you bring some of these tubers home you will have the well deserved privilege of eating them. Wapato is not just edible; it is a delicacy – so invite some friends. Perhaps it will prompt them to come with you on the next collecting foray.

First, clean the tubers by removing the leafy skirts with your fingers and rinsing the tubers. Cut off the end with the shoot as well as the opposite end, where the tuber was attached to the rhizome. Then peel the tuber with a sharp knife or a carrot peeler. Try not to waste a lot of the tuber's flesh while peeling it.

There is some debate about whether or not the tubers need peeling. This is understandable, since it is work. They will not hurt you if left unpeeled, but the bitter flavor seems to be more concentrated in the skin. An important reason to peel them, however, is to make it easier to identify tubers that are beginning to spoil. Most books say to boil them and then peel them. I think it's better to peel them first, otherwise one ends up boiling some of the skin flavor into the flesh. Besides, I don't find it any easier to peel them after they are cooked. If

Wapatoes peeled and ready for boiling.

you find that yours don't need peeling, don't peel them.

I've often been accused of being too picky about my food. What I think it boils down to is that if you eat something once or twice, and you're very excited about it, you're going to like it unless it's terrible. When you eat it regularly, however, the excitement loses its power to override the taste buds. So I expect my wapato to be not just edible, but something that I want to eat on a daily basis. Peeling the tubers makes the final product taste and look better, so I do it.

After the tubers have been peeled, you can use them in many of the same ways that you would use potatoes. They are reminiscent of potatoes, but you will immediately recognize a difference. Wapato has a faint bitterness and a flavor reminiscent of sweet corn; many people prefer it to potatoes.

I most commonly boil wapatoes for about half an hour, drain the water, and then mash them. They are drier than potatoes, so I usually add a little bit of water or milk to the mashed wapatoes along with butter, salt, and pepper. They are excellent in this fashion. Top them in the same way you would serve mashed or baked potatoes. (However, I find that I dislike wapato seasoned with garlic.)

I also eat wapato as a hot cereal. I dry the boiled and mashed wapato

Harvested immature flower stalk shoots of wapato.

by placing it on a tray near my woodstove, then grind it coarsely in a flour mill. When I want a bowl, I just pour some of this ground wapato into boiling water and stir, and it reconstitutes in about a minute. The wapato expands considerably in the water, creating a texture like Malto-Meal™. Served with maple syrup, hickory nuts, and crushed strawberries, it is heavenly.

Occasionally I use wapato in stew, but sparingly due to the dry texture and faint grapefruit-peel flavor. You can use the cooked tubers to make dishes similar to potato salad or scalloped potatoes, or put them in casseroles, stir-fries, or any other place you feel they would work.

Other Edible Parts

Although the tuber is the main food provided by the wapato plant, it also produces some other notable vegetables. In late summer, when the plants are vigorously growing, the **tender tips of the rhizomes** (laterals) are a fairly good vegetable both raw and cooked. The flavor is reminiscent of the tubers, but it is a little sweeter and has less bitterness than the raw tubers.

Young, tender wapato leaves make an excellent cooked green and are available from late spring until late summer. These stand out from the older leaves by their lighter green color, extreme glossiness, and the fact that the edges of them are curled up. The new leaves are also much thinner, softer, and have a sort of rubbery elasticity to them. The grapefruit-peel scent is noticeable on the young **leaves and leafstalks**, but boiling them gets rid of all but a trace of this flavor, rendering them delicious. They are very tender and I consider

Young wapato leaf with edges still curled, at the perfect stage to collect for greens.

them one of the best cooked greens of late summer; their prolific nature makes them extremely easy to collect. In fact, wapato is well worth learning for its greens alone.

The last vegetable produced by wapato is the **shoot of the flower stalk**, when it is still young and tender, long before the flowers have opened. These appear in midsummer and are available for a generous season several weeks long. Like the leaves, they should be boiled to rid them of their grapefruit-peel flavor; after this they are tender and delectable.

Storage

Cold storage works well for wapato, but if you plan to keep the tubers for more than a month or two, sort them carefully shortly after harvest. Separate any that are damaged in any way (including having broken shoots) and use them first. Only those wapatoes that remain in perfect condition should be stored for long periods. They should stay very moist but should not be left in standing water, and they should not be piled too deeply.

Wapato tubers will show no visible signs of deterioration during the first stages of spoilage; they will simply begin to taste bad. (They will begin to taste bad long before they can make you sick.) Since one or two bad tubers can ruin a dish, improperly stored tubers can be a culinary disaster. If you peel a tuber and find that it looks different in any way from the rest of the batch, smell for an off odor. If there is none, taste a bite of it raw to see if there is anything unusual about the flavor. If there is any question, do not use the tuber. Tubers that do not float are often spoiled or spoiling. To avoid this dilemma, use wapatoes within several weeks of harvest, dry them, or be very attentive to proper cold storage procedures. Wapato that is sliced and dried without being cooked first develops an unpleasant flavor.

I have not experimented with baking using wapato flour, but that is another possible avenue of exploration.

I have never stored any parts of this plant besides the tuber, although presumably the leaves could be dried, canned, or frozen and the flower stalks could be frozen.

When you sit down to a meal of wapato, you'll understand why so many hunting and gathering groups around the world made them a staff of life. You'll look at the marshes in a new light, while experiencing a delicacy that few have partaken of. After all, good things come to those who wade.

Wild Rice

Zizania aquatica, Z. palustris

Wild rice is among the few wild food plants that are almost universally known. It is widely regarded as a delicacy and is often served around the holidays. Although farm-grown "wild" rice is available in grocery stores across the country, few people realize that this gourmet grain can be harvested from the wild over much of the continent. And what's more, the truly wild stuff tastes far better than the commercial "wild" rice.

Although the tradition of harvesting wild rice remains strong in some regions, in most areas it is virtually unknown. Even in the areas where the use of wild rice has persisted, the practice is gradually diminishing, like other aspects of traditional Native American culture. There are a number of people who desire to participate in this activity but don't know where or how to begin. In this chapter I hope to provide the basic knowledge that will make wild rice harvesting possible. Through all of this I will attempt to maintain and convey the traditional reverence for wild rice, for a novice who disregards the many conservation considerations during harvest can damage both the resource and the experience for others.

Fully grown wild rice plants standing about 6 ft. above the water. The kernels are just beginning to ripen and male flowers can be seen hanging from some of the lower branches.

History of the Use of Wild Rice

Native Americans used wild rice at least as early as the Late Archaic Period 1500 years ago, and probably considerably earlier. At the time of contact with Europeans it was known to be harvested by the Seminole in Florida, the Seneca in New York, the Omaha and Ponca on the Great Plains, and the Ojibwa,

Assiniboin, Dakota, Fox, Sauk, Ho-Chunk, Menominee, Potawatomi, and Ottawa in the Great Lakes Region (Vennum, 1988). Of course, it must have also been harvested in places of which we do not have record.

Although the Menominee are named for the plant, the Ojibwa are by far the most famous users of wild rice. For many groups of Ojibwa, especially in the southwestern part of their territory, wild rice was *the* staple food. It was usually stored in large quantity and eaten year-round.

Wild rice became an important article of commerce between the Ojibwa and white traders, but the Europeans considered it to be of low desirability. For example, at Sandy Lake, Minnesota, in 1833, wheat flour was valued 20 times more than wild rice in trade (Vennum, 1988).

The white settlers called this grain by many names, including *folle avoine* (fool oats), *riz sauvage* (wild rice), water oats, and water rye. *Folle avoine* was the dominant name while the French controlled the area, but the term eventually gave way to *wild rice*. The Ojibwa word for this food is *manoomin*; the Dakota, *psin*. These epithets are reflected in many place names across the region.

Aspects of European technology were slowly incorporated into Native American harvest and processing of manoomin. Early on, steel kettles and pots were adopted for parching the rice. In the early 1900s, wooden skiffs began replacing birch bark canoes for harvesting, and later came aluminum canoes. Over the last sixty years, small-scale machinery has been increasingly employed in the various stages of rice processing. Harvest methods for the individual ricer have changed little, however, and a pair of knocking sticks used today would not look out-of-place in a rice camp of 100 years ago.

There is no record of white people harvesting wild rice before about 1900, although many (and at first, nearly all) who resided in the rice regions relied heavily on it as a food source and obtained it through trade. However, by the 1920s some white people began to take a keen interest in this grain. At first, they purchased it from traditional Ojibwa ricers and resold it in urban markets. Soon they were buying green (unprocessed) rice directly from the harvesters and processing it themselves with machinery. Then mechanical harvesters were invented, and the resulting overharvest devastated some rice beds. In the 1960s, non-Indians began growing "wild" rice in artificial paddies in California and Minnesota, and every step of the process was mechanized. Today, the vast majority of wild rice for sale is not wild at all; it is just as much a product of fossil fuels, heavy machinery, pesticides, fertilizers, and agribusiness as the white rice in the grocery store.

The competition from cultivated wild rice has harmed the market for real manoomin to the extent that today there are few traditional harvesters and the number is steadily decreasing. But the rice remains, offering the same rich nourishment every year to those who desire to participate in this ancient craft.

Food Value of Wild Rice

Wild rice compares favorably with domestic grains in terms of its nutrition. At about 11% protein, it has slightly less than wheat and oats, but has more than white rice or corn. The easily digestible kernels are about 80% carbohydrate and 1% fat. Wild rice is low in iron but fairly high in calcium. Amazingly, it ranks higher than white rice, corn, or oats in levels of magnesium, phosphorus, sodium, zinc, potassium, copper, thiamin, riboflavin, niacin, vitamin B6, and folic acid – usually by a wide margin. (Statistics from Vennum, 1988, pg. 40)

It is no surprise, then, that as a staple food wild rice kept an active population in good health. Like all cereal grains, wild rice does not provide a complete protein unless combined with a legume.

Description

Wild rice *Zizania* spp. is an aquatic grass, and despite the resemblance of the seeds, it is not in the same genus as the domestic rice *Oryza sativa*. It does, however, have a close relative in North America, Texas wild rice *Zizania texana*, which has a very limited range on the Gulf Coast. This species is reported to be edible, but I have not read any accounts of its use. Texas wild rice is now endangered.

Wild rice is quite easy to recognize when it is mature. It is a large grass that grows in the water. In fact, it appears surprisingly like overgrown reed-canary grass or rye that is trying to drown itself. Like most grasses, wild rice grows in clumps of several stems. Unlike marsh plants that grow in shallow water or at the water's edge, wild rice typically grows *in* the water, forming fields (rice beds) covering large areas of what would otherwise be open lake or river.

The only grass that I know of that attains a comparable size and occasionally grows in the water is great manna grass *Glyceria grandis*. But the seeds of great manna grass are tiny, perhaps only a fiftieth of the size of a wild rice kernel, and manna grass usually does not form vast colonies.

Typical height for wild rice is 3–7 feet (1–2 m) above the water, but it ranges from 1.5–12.5 feet (.5–4 m) tall when mature. On the largest plants,

Average-sized wild rice plants. Although the panicle branches are held tight to the stalk, these are at their peak of ripeness. Note in this and other wild rice photos that when the grain is ripe, the plants are still green. By the time the leaves and stalks are brown, it is too late to harvest.

the stalks are as massive as small cornstalks. That makes wild rice perhaps the largest annual grass growing wild in North America.

There is a great deal of confusion regarding the taxonomy of wild rice. Some authorities recognize a single species of wild rice with two or three sub-species or varieties: *Z. aquatica aquatica, Z. a. angustifolia,* and *Z. a. interior.* My own observations and experiences, however, lead me to agree with those botanists who recognize two similar but entirely separate species. In this case they are called *Z. palustris* (northern wild rice) and *Z. aquatica* (southern wild rice). The southern wild rice tends to be a taller and more robust plant, but its kernels are much smaller than those of the northern wild rice, and the chaff enclosing the kernel is more bristly.

While both species are edible, the northern wild rice is presumably more practical to harvest and process due to the smaller stature of the plants and the larger seeds. I say "presumably" because, although I have seen southern wild rice on many occasions and have collected small amounts, I have never seriously harvested it.

Experienced ricers make a distinction between river rice and lake rice. River rice generally has shorter, thicker kernels than lake rice. The plants tend to be shorter as well, and the grain usually ripens five to fourteen days earlier than that of lakes. During their good years, lakes can be incredibly productive, but rivers seem to be more consistent in their crop.

Range and Habitat

The natural range of wild rice extends from the Great Plains to the East Coast, and from the Gulf of Mexico north into Canada. In parts of this broad range, the plant was always sparsely distributed due to the scarcity of suitable waterways; in other areas it was quite abundant. In places like the Potomac and Connecticut Rivers and Chesapeake Bay, extensive stands once existed which today are gone. Human activity has unfortunately eliminated or greatly reduced populations of this plant over most of its range.

Wild rice grows in water up to 5 feet (1.5 m) deep – another unique trait among emergent aquatic plants. Typically, it is found in water 1–3 feet (.3–1 m) deep, with a bottom of very soft muck. In some places the muck may be thinly laid over sand or gravel, but in other places it may be many feet thick.

Manoomin also has a preference for water that is not stagnant. Small, isolated lakes or marshes with no inlet or outlet rarely support rice. Spring fed lakes or those on stream or river systems are suitable, as are sloughs, backwaters, and slow current areas of clean rivers. Clear water is important because the rice seed has little stored energy compared to the rhizomes or tubers of aquatic perennials, and the seedling therefore needs to receive enough sunlight on the lakebed to photosynthesize.

Clearing land for agriculture causes an increase in the severity of floods, which scour away the mud, uproot the young rice plants, and wash them away in the current. Pollutants from farm runoff and industry also have adverse effects on the plants. Siltation from agricultural runoff clouds the water, preventing the rice seedlings from receiving the light necessary for growth. Motorized watercraft create severe wakes that uproot the plants in their more fragile floating stage. Thus, wild rice has disappeared from thousands of waterways across the continent.

Another strike against *Zizania* is that it tends to form the largest colonies on large, shallow, fertile lakes and in places where rivers flow into large lakes. These places also happen to be where human beings form their largest colonies. Duluth and Green Bay, two of the largest cities in the Upper Great Lakes Region, have dredged and destroyed two of the largest wild rice beds in the region. The city of Rice Lake, Wisconsin, is situated on the shore of a very fertile body of water that now contains not a single stalk of wild rice.

Fortunately, the soils of much of Wisconsin, Minnesota, Michigan, Ontario, and Manitoba are unsuitable for agriculture, and these areas also contain tens of thousands of lakes and rivers. Many of them still contain prolific beds of wild rice. A ricing tradition survives in some of these areas, but there are healthy stands still scattered across the rest of the plant's range, and this resource goes largely neglected. Responsible harvest of the wild rice will in no way adversely affect these populations.

The Life Cycle of Wild Rice

Wild rice is probably the only annual plant in North America that forms a kind of "climax" community, dominating the same areas for hundreds of years. It has achieved this remarkable feat by adapting superbly to a unique and specific environment where few other plants have any chance of competing with it. The specialized adaptations of wild rice are manifested in every aspect of its growth and reproduction.

A rice kernel falls from its parent plant at the end of summer, knocked loose by the wind, a raindrop, a blackbird, or a ricer's stick. It plummets through the air and water like a tiny spear, guided by the long, barbed awn attached to its top. It sinks immediately until it reaches the bed of the lake or slough and gently impales the soft muck, stopping out of sight or barely visible. If it survives the feasting of waterfowl and is not washed away by a flood, the seed will rest all winter in the frigid water.

The following spring, the grain may begin to send tiny roots into the mud. (Some of the seeds will wait another year or even longer to germinate.

Wild rice in the floating stage, early July. A few of the plants are beginning to emerge and stand erect.

The delayed germination of a portion of the seed allows the rice population to recover after a year of complete crop failure or other disaster.) First, the seedling produces thin, ribbon-like underwater leaves. This is known as the submerged stage of growth. These leaves elongate until they reach the surface of the water. Sometime in June, the leaves begin to form a floating mat on the water's surface to increase their exposure to light. The floating section of each leaf eventually reaches two to three feet in length. This is known appropriately as the floating stage. The emergent stage begins in July, when the plant first produces its upright stalk. The stalk grows quickly until, about four or five weeks later, it reaches its full height of 3–9 feet (1–3 m).

During the submerged and floating stages, wild rice can be easily uprooted or damaged by floods or heavy wakes. High water levels can also deprive the plants of light and have serious effects on the stand density and yield of grain. Therefore, rice often does very well in years of low water levels.

In August the stalk produces a panicle or flower spike that can be as much as two feet long. The female flowers are borne at the top of the panicle, close to the stem, while the male flowers are produced near the bottom on delicate branches that hang out several inches. The female blossoms ripen a few days before their male counterparts on the same plant, decreasing the likelihood of self-pollination. A few weeks later, the seeds begin to ripen, with those at the top of the plant maturing first. The peak of ripening is in late summer, from about August 25–September 10.

Wild rice is an amazing asset to the ecology of a wetland. In terms of biomass, the annual production of a stand is astounding. Muskrats find the stalks delicious. Small fish thrive in the thick growth. Muskellunge and northern pike lurk in the rice beds in great numbers. Rice worms, the hairless caterpillar of a moth, *Apamea apamiformis*, that feeds on milkweed nectar in its adult stage, are usually found by the millions in the beds. While rice worms can severely damage rice crops, they feed fish, frogs, turtles, other insects, and birds. Waterfowl come in droves to glean fallen grain from the water. Recognizing its importance, many conservation groups and agencies are trying to reestablish wild rice in some of its former haunts. We wish them success.

Ricing

Our paddles plunge silently into the tea-tinted water, guiding the canoe downstream in the narrow ribbon of open river. Flanked on both sides by cattails and bulrushes that quiver in the current, we thrust off the sandy bottom to hasten our trip downstream. Our canoe passes a lone, stunted rice stalk, and our disturbance causes it to drop a handful of yellow-green flowers onto the glassy surface. The current slows, and the excitement builds. Around the next bend lies the first rice bed.

I reach out to feel a tuft of the scattered rice heads before we reach the thicker stand. At the touch of my hand, a few kernels plummet into the water.

"It's falling."

We turn the canoe around. The paddles are laid upon the tarp in the center. I grab the cedar sticks and anxiously knock a little rice into the canoe to test it, although we haven't really started yet. The sound of the first kernels hitting the tarp sends adrenaline through me. Let's go!

My partner positions her feet in the trailing end of the craft and stands up, then adjusts them for balance. She slowly swings the pole into position and begins to push the canoe forward. All without a word, what we have done so many times before. Off we go.

I reach out with one stick and gently pull in a clump of stalks, then swipe along them with the other stick, sending a spray of kernels into the canoe. They rain rhythmically upon the tarp. She speeds up and so do I. The sticks whir and the rice pours in. Every now and then a kernel hits her thigh. Pull, swipe. Pull, swipe. Pull, swipe. Pull, swipe.

She stops. "Nice. . . Nice! It's falling good!" The paddles are covered in rice – only the handles are visible. All the kernels have landed with the awns facing up, making the tarp look like the coarse fur of some green beast. She guzzles water; I flip the paddle over and ruin our handiwork because I like to watch it slowly disappear again under a layer of rice. Off we go again, the rhythm even better. Stroke SWIPE, stroke SWIPE, stroke SWIPE.

I give it full concentration, absolute commitment: I will stroke with fluid gentleness and swipe with speed and accuracy, using both arms in one unbroken motion. I will not break stalks. I will not miss rice. I watch the stalks come up behind me and tailor each stroke to their height, thickness, and lean. I focus, and the kernels pile deep.

We stop and drink. I pull a rice worm from my neck and then kneel down on the mass of green and hunch over. She climbs over me and we switch places.

Push, jitter, change the angle, push, thrust, retrieve the pole as fast as I can, begin pushing again before the canoe comes to a stop. Steer the craft; put her in good rice. Don't hit the same rice twice, and don't crisscross trails. Keep it moving at her speed. Not too fast, but don't let it stop. Slow down a little when the crop is heavy, speed up when the crop is light.

The sun darkens my bare skin and shines on the clustered birches; a breeze ruffles their leaves. Spiders, worms, and moths clamber over the rice in the canoe. Painted turtles bask on piles of rice stalks where they have been stacked by feeding muskrats, and muskellunge lurk in openings amidst the plants. Blue-winged teals occasionally explode from the marsh, their whirring wings taking them to hide somewhere in the next bed upstream. The manoomin accumulates. It is August 27 on paper somewhere, but the rice beds are timeless. It could be this year, or seven hundred years ago. I see the peninsula where the ricers used to camp in the old days; it is where I would camp, too. The spirits there smile on us as we keep the old ways alive. Every year we come for our rice, and the rice grows on.

I will never forget my first experience with wild rice. It was in early September of 1992. I awoke early and paddled out on the small flowage where I was camped to go fishing. A tall grass in the lake near the shore caught my eye, so I paddled over to investigate. "Could this be," I wondered, "wild rice? It must be. What else?" I grabbed a seedhead and stared in amazement at a handful of purple-brown rice grains enclosed in husks. I peeled the chaff off of one and tasted a kernel. I peered down the shoreline and gazed at the narrow band of rice that extended as far as I could see. My heart started pounding.

"How do you gather wild rice? How do you gather wild rice!?" was all I could think as I paddled back to camp. I grabbed a garbage bag and a stick. "You hit it with a stick – I remember reading that much."

Harvesting wild rice.

When I got back out there, I leaned the plants over the canoe and tried to hit the kernels into the bag. I got a quart of rice and just as many worms, for it was too late in the season. I brought that rice home and peeled kernels individually by hand for my first taste of real wild rice. It was a small helping, but a giant step towards realizing my lifelong dream of living on the bounty of the wild.

When and Where to Rice

In my home state there are hundreds of sites where rice grows, and I doubt that even half of them are visited by human harvesters each year. Outside of the upper Great Lakes Region, wild rice is rarely harvested. When you find a spot, you'll probably have it to yourself or perhaps have to share with a few others.

If you don't know of a rice water in your area, call your natural resources agency. If they can't help, look for interconnected lake chains on a river system. Especially keep an eye out for names like "Rice Lake." Drive to such areas with binoculars in July or early August and look for rice beds from boat landings or other vantage points. If you see something that looks like a floating field of rye, you're in luck. If you still can't find any rice, talk to duck hunters.

Starting in early or middle August, canoe out to the rice and check the grainheads for developing kernels. In some places you'll find almost all of the husks empty; elsewhere a good portion of them will be full. The grains you are looking for will be small and green, in the soft "milk stage." If you can find a place where there are several kernels per spike, come back later when the rice is ripe. It's a good idea to have several places in mind in case some of them don't pan out.

Whether or not a place is good for ricing is determined by the quantity of rice *kernels* that can be harvested there, not by how tall, thick, or abundant the plants are. The most significant and frequent mistake that I see inexperienced (and some experienced) ricers make is that they insist on ricing in a locality with many stalks but few kernels. Some rice waters, in some years, just aren't worth your time – yet many people waste a day, a weekend, or an entire season in one of these unproductive beds.

I prefer plants of medium stature that are in thick but not impenetrable stands. Anyplace is worth a try, though – especially if it's close to home. Experienced ricers test out a place for a minute or so before deciding whether to stay or find another spot. Of course, in the beginning you won't know what to expect, but if you start to feel like milking aphids would be more productive, it's time to move on.

The second most common mistake of the beginning ricer is attempting to harvest the grain at the wrong time. If it isn't ready, you can't beat it into ripening. Once it is ripe, it waits for nobody; it falls, and if you're not there, too bad. The season is fairly short: 10–14 days on a particular body of water.

Most people think of wild rice as something harvested in the fall. In fact, it is impossible to convince many folks that wild rice ripens as early as it actually does. I am commonly admonished by ignorant fishermen who claim that I am harvesting rice "too early." But wild rice really is more characteristic of late summer than of fall.

The majority of wild rice ripens between August 25 and September 10. The time of ripening varies greatly according to several factors: warm water, current, thin muck, and short plants all seem to favor early ripening; while cold water, lack of current, thick mud, and tall plants all seem to favor later ripening. At the extremes, there are places in Wisconsin where the rice is ripe in the first week of August, and others where enough kernels remain to warrant harvest through the end of September. Wide variation will exist among waters only a few miles apart. Rice generally falls about a week to a week and a half earlier on rivers than on lakes.

When wild rice is ripe it is not necessarily brown; it may be, but often this is difficult to notice from a distance. River rice tends to be greener than lake rice when it is ripe. A tap or swipe of the seedhead will cause ripe kernels to readily fall from the spike. Take a few test strokes with your sticks, or just hit a few seedheads with your hand. If no rice falls, there are no kernels or the kernels are not yet ripe – move on to someplace else or wait and return later. It is silly and destructive to beat up the plants when the grain is not yet falling.

There is no special or mysterious skill to getting "only the ripe rice to fall" as one often reads in the accounts given by observers who have never harvested rice themselves. Unless you beat the heck out of it, only the ripe rice falls. You give it a single fast but not violent stroke with

Nils Pearson with a nice pair of knocking sticks.

your sticks (as will soon be explained in detail). That's the trick. In fact, to a ricer, "ripe" means "that which falls."

Rice kernels that fall into your canoe will be a mixture of grayish-green, tawny, brown, and purple. All of these colors are acceptable – part of what makes real manoomin taste so good is the mixture of different levels of ripeness. Don't expect the kernels to be uniformly black like the cultivated stuff sold at the store.

With trial and error you'll come to know when you're ricing in the right place at the right time. Until then, keep trying.

Ricing Equipment

If you wish to harvest wild rice with a tolerable level of effectiveness, you'll need these things: a canoe, a paddle, a pole, a pair of knocking sticks, a tarp, and gunnysacks. You can do without the pole if you rice alone (see the section on solo ricing) and you can do without the paddle if the rice bed is very close to the site from which you will launch your canoe. You can do without the tarp if you keep your canoe perfectly clean.

Most any canoe will do. Mine is 15 feet (4.6 m) long. Sixteen would be perfect, in my opinion. Seventeen feet works but it just feels too big and is somewhat awkward to maneuver. Since you will be standing up, a canoe that is too small or too narrow can be difficult, as these are less stable. You want a craft 32–36 inches (81–91 cm) wide. Rather than a canoe, some people use a small, narrow, canoe-like skiff with a squared stern. Whatever watercraft you choose, keep in mind that some jurisdictions have regulations on the dimensions of craft that can be legally used to harvest wild rice. Check these laws out before you go.

If you use a tarp it should cover the entire bottom of the canoe from seat to seat and extend well up the sides. It should be absolutely, positively free of sand and dirt.

The pole is a beautiful tool. It should be at least ten feet long, and twelve to sixteen feet is typical. I like to use a pole that is about as long as the canoe. I have two poles. My favorite one is 14 feet, 3 inches (4.3 m) long. It is tailored to my favorite place to rice; in many other places I would use a longer pole. The pole should be made of a light wood and should be as near to perfectly straight as you can find, with as little taper as possible; my poles are made of balsam fir. Many people use cedar, which is light and doesn't crack as much, but it is hard to find cedar poles of the proper dimensions. I have used inferior poles of red pine, maple, and aspen that were cut on the spot. They were heavy,

Grain heads covered by dew at dawn. Some are spread, while on others the branches are pulled in tight.

awkward, rough on the hands, and sometimes broke – but I got rice with them. However, you don't want to waste precious hours of ricing time searching out and fashioning a pole. Do that long before the season.

In an ideal world, your pole would season for a year with the bark on before you peel it – that way it won't get so many lateral checks in it as it dries. In the real world you'll probably cut your pole a few months before ricing and peel it immediately to hasten drying. It will get some cracks in it, but that's OK. After the pole is dry and peeled, rasp or plane off any nicks or bumps so that they don't tear up your hands later on.

You'll probably want to get a duckbill attachment for your pole to help provide purchase when you push off the mud. The duckbill is a near necessity in about two thirds of ricing waters: wherever the muck is too deep for your pole to hit bottom. You can buy one of these at many sporting goods stores (duck hunters use them) and easily attach it to your pole with a nail or screw in the hole provided.

After the canoe, the knocking sticks are probably the most important piece of equipment. When I started ricing I would often just cut my sticks from saplings near the boat landing – usually heavy wood like hazel. They were serviceable, but my hands got very sore after a few hours of knocking. When I finally whittled myself a nice pair of sticks from dry white cedar, I was amazed

This rice bed near my house covers well over 100 acres.

at the difference. Using these sticks was easy, graceful, comfortable, and much more effective than what I had been doing. Now I have three pairs. Do yourself a favor and start off with a good set of sticks.

Your finished sticks should be 26–32 inches (66–81 cm) long; a good measure is roughly the distance from your armpit to your fingertips. My favorite set of sticks is 29 inches (74 cm) long. The handle area is 4.5 inches (11.5 cm) long and 1.25 inches (3.2 cm) thick. Make sure that the handles are comfortable. Past the handle the sticks should narrow abruptly to about ⅞ of an inch (2.25 cm). From there they should taper gently to the tips, which are about ⅜ of an inch (1 cm) thick. The sticks should be light but still sturdy enough to do the job effectively. Cedar is an ideal wood because it is easy to work, light, strong for its weight, and doesn't warp much with repeated wetting and drying. Avoid making sticks from crooked or knotty wood. Use shorter sticks for tall, thick rice and longer, heavier sticks for short, thin rice.

Unless you're planning for failure, you'll want some gunnysacks. These are usually sold cheap at feed mills. Bring about ten one-bushel bags, or the equivalent, just to be safe. If there's not too much rice, you can also just fold the tarp over it and use it as a bag – but be careful not to get sand in the rice.

Keeping the Rice Clean

A friend of mine once gave me a jar of wild rice: beautiful, long-grained lake rice. I cooked some, but got no further than two bites into eating it. "CRUNCH . . . OWW. Ooh, did I break a tooth? No. Good. Thanks for the rice."

I found out the history of that rice. The friend who had given it to me had it given to her by someone who received it from someone else who harvested it somewhere in northern Minnesota. What's the moral of this anecdote? *Nobody wants to eat sand!* I eventually fed that rice to the birds.

I cannot overemphasize this: avoid getting sand or gravel in the rice! Religiously clean any dirt or sand out of the canoe. If you put a tarp on the bottom, make sure that, too, is absolutely free of sand or dirt. When you step into the canoe, carefully rinse each foot. Do not push the pole into a gravel or sand bottom and then let the butt end drip into the canoe. With every part of the process you should think about keeping the rice free of grit.

Setting up for Ricing

The canoe is reversed for ricing; the seat that is normally the stern (back) becomes the bow (front). The knocker sits in the front but faces rearward, while the poler stands in the back and faces to the side. That arrangement is so that the rice plants don't get pushed so far away by the sides of the canoe as it passes the knocker, which makes it harder for the sticks to reach them; and to give the poler a better place to stand. Some ricers successfully use other arrangements, such as having the knocker kneel directly in front of the poler, both facing the same direction. However, the arrangement I recommend is most common and is highly preferable for canoes of typical dimensions.

Ricing is, or should be, an exercise in teamwork. The poler's job is to keep the canoe moving at the steadiest pace possible, matching his speed to the rice conditions and the knocker's skill or energy level. The knocker is the one actually bringing rice into the canoe, and she should adjust her methods continually to the height, thickness, and ripeness of the rice, as well as to the speed of the craft and many other factors. Most longtime ricing partners are couples. Usually, the woman is the knocker. I like to do both and switch with my partner about every hour and a half.

Poling

The poler must stand in the canoe. This makes some people uncomfortable, but it is a necessity. ***If you can't swim, it is unsafe to be ricing.*** When I am coaching a person poling for the first time, I have them stand up and rock the canoe with their feet to get comfortable with their balance. When I pole, I stand with my right foot near the seat (towards the front) and my left foot towards the back, legs spread slightly for balance. Do not face forward, as you will probably be tempted to do; stand with your head and body facing to the left if you are right handed, or vice-versa.

Most of the mechanics of poling cannot be explained — it can only be learned by watching and by experience. But I'll give you a few tips now, some of which won't mean anything until you've tried it.

Here are the basics: you place the thick end of the pole into the mud close to the canoe somewhere in front of your body and push the canoe forward, working your hands to the tip of the pole as if you were climbing a rope. When you get to the tip of the pole, turn towards the back of the canoe and thrust, then retrieve the pole to begin another stroke. Of course, it's not that simple.

When the pole first enters the mud it is almost vertical, but as you work your way to the tip the angle decreases to about 25 to 35 degrees. This change in angle forces the pole to bend in the mud, and the tension thus created makes it difficult to pull the pole back out. For this reason, about halfway through the pole stroke I do what I call a jitter: I very quickly pull the pole out about a foot and shake it to break the suction, then change the angle all at once. This little trick makes poling smoother by making it easier to retrieve the pole at the end of the stroke. You don't need to do it if the mud is thin and the bottom solid, or if you are using a duckbill and only pushing off root clumps near the surface.

When you retrieve the pole for a new stroke, do so as fast as you can so that the canoe doesn't come to a halt between strokes; this is the key to being a good poler. In fact, I actually throw the pole forward and catch it, which is the fastest way to move it, but don't worry over this detail until later. Sometimes, however, conditions are such that it is simply impossible to keep the canoe moving steadily.

While poling you can steer the canoe effectively in either direction without changing sides. To turn left (if poling on the left side, as would be the case for a right-handed person) thrust the pole alongside the canoe and slightly underneath it. When the butt of the pole is imbedded in the mud pull the top of the pole in toward you; this will push the back end of the canoe to the right and steer the front end to the left. To turn right, you must get the butt end of the pole imbedded in the mud some distance away from the canoe and then pull the canoe towards the pole. Steering is easiest when done gradually; it should be part of almost every pole stroke. You should always be planning ahead where you want the canoe to go.

Don't go fast just because the poling is easy or slow just because the poling is difficult. Match your effort to the task appropriately. You are the engine that propels the knocker, and it is your partner's needs that should dictate your speed.

Knocking

They gave such a clumsy word to such a graceful art. The Ojibwa term must be much more eloquent. The word "knocking" also misleads many as to how the sticks are really used. I read with amusement the accounts in so many wild food books that tell us to lean the plants over and beat them with a stick to dislodge the grain. (Perhaps this violence is triggered by the frustration of trying to harvest the grain in the fall when there is none left.)

When knocking, you are sitting down and the un-knocked rice stalks are beside you, sometimes slightly in front of you or slightly behind. You move into the un-knocked rice backwards. On your right side, reach out with your right stick first and pull some rice stalks toward the canoe. Be sure to make contact with the stalks well below the seedhead – usually around the middle of the stalk or lower – or you will prematurely dislodge much of the grain. Imagine bending the rice toward the middle of the canoe in front of you. The first stick should gently slide toward the seedhead as the plants lean toward the canoe. Now follow up with your left stick; its contact with the rice stalks should begin only moments after that of the right stick. The second (left) stick accelerates in speed so that it passes the first (right) stick before it reaches the seedhead. The second stick dislodges the grain but it does not tap, rap, beat, or hit the stalk. Instead, it slides along the leaning stalk with gradually increasing speed and force, applying pressure at an angle that gradually increases from about 20–60 degrees. This essentially sends a wave through the stalk, which causes the seedhead to throw its loose grain in the direction of the wave at the end of the knock, in the same way that water is thrown when you spray someone by snapping a wet towel. Imagine aiming the second stick toward the left front of the canoe, and follow through at the end, speeding up rather than slowing down.

This complex motion, involving both arms and both sticks working in unison, is called a "knock." You'll have to get the rhythm down, but in typical ricing a knock takes about one second. As the canoe moves, keep knocking on alternate sides; resist the temptation to knock repeatedly on one side.

Very tall rice (over 6.5 feet or 2 m) must be pulled in more slowly and carefully and leaned forward more because you cannot reach the seedheads as easily. Grab tall rice from as far behind you as is reasonably possible so the tops are closer to you as they lean over; each knock requires more time and care but will yield more grain.

When you begin knocking you may have a tendency to lead your knocking on both sides with the same hand (whichever is dominant). Train your body not to do this, even if it feels natural at first. Always start with your right hand on the right side and with your left hand on the left side.

The knocking motion is fast and assertive but not violent. You should not be breaking rice stalks; that's what happens when you hit, beat, rap, or tap the stalks at a right angle. If you are breaking stalks, reassess what you are doing.

Beginners often want to keep knocking the same rice over and over to see if they can get more kernels from it. Don't do this; the ripe grains should all shatter from the heads the first time. Within two days, however, you can knock the same rice again, because many new kernels will have ripened.

Sit down with a pair of sticks and practice the knocking motion before ricing so that it feels natural; you can even practice on reed-canary or some terrestrial grass of similar size. You don't need to master it to be successful at ricing; as long as you try, it will work out. However, when you do master it, you will be much more efficient. Learning to knock is just like learning a new dance, and if you treat it as such it will be much easier.

Besides being certain to rice at a good place at the proper time, the best advice that I can give to beginners to improve their effectiveness is to keep the boat and the sticks moving. Get into a rhythm and don't stop. It is dancing. Let the motion flow until it is done without a thought. That's the difference between a little rice and a lot of rice in the canoe at the end of the day.

So, how much rice will you get? My partner and I expect to harvest an average of about a bushel of green (unfinished) rice per hour. We've done as well as 2 bushels per hour. Each bushel yields 6–18 lbs (3–8 kg) of finished, dried rice, equivalent to 1–3 gallons (4–11 liters). On the other hand, I know of people who have gone out for an entire weekend and come home with three pounds of rice. Don't expect a bushel per hour until you become proficient, but if you can't get a bushel in a day your technique, timing, or locality is wrong.

Solo Ricing

If you're serious about ricing, there's a good chance that you'll have to do it alone before you find a serious partner. Solo ricing can be very effective but it is less comfortable, more demanding, and more problematic than ricing with a partner. Nevertheless, some claim that solo ricing is more labor efficient. Certainly, a solo ricer in a prime locality can outdo a pair in average conditions, and the prime benefit of ricing alone is that you don't have to worry about another person's schedule – you can put yourself in the right place at the right time.

For this you do not always need a pole. Kneel in the canoe just in front of the back seat. Propel the canoe by putting one arm over each side, holding

Canoe at the end of a typical good day of ricing, containing 6 bushels totaling 140 lbs (64 kg) of green rice. This pile is what we call the "green fuzzy monster."

a stick in each hand, and thrusting backward with both sticks at once. Try to push against something that gives a little bit of purchase, like rice plants, roots, or hard mud. After moving forward a bit, knock the rice plants on one side, then the other, using the same motions described above in the knocking section. Then move the canoe forward again for the next round. Keep your paddle handy in case you get to a tough spot. Sometimes you can propel yourself through thin rice using only your paddle. In this case you get to sit on the seat when you knock.

In other places where the rice is very dense or the water shallow you will find it virtually impossible to move the canoe using the sticks. Under such conditions you will need to push with a paddle or pole to rice solo. When doing so I push a few feet with the pole and drop it outside the canoe, then I knock the rice on both sides of the boat.

Solo ricing is generally effective; its main drawbacks being that people find it lonely, and that it is difficult to get into a rhythm due to the constant switching from pushing to knocking.

Binding Rice

Long ago, when wild rice was a staple, the grain was not always harvested in the fashion just described; a method called *binding* was often employed. A short time before the rice ripened the plants were bound together in bundles or sheaves while they were still growing. This prevented the kernels from falling as they ripened. At the end of the season, when all of the rice was ripe, the bundles were leaned over a canoe and carefully untied. The grains then were easily knocked out by beating with a single stick (accounting for the origin of our present misconception that the rice knocker beats the grain from the plant). Sometimes all of the rice was tied and other times just a few bundles were made to mark a certain family's harvest area. Tying increased the proportion of the rice that could be harvested and was probably done more where rice was a scarce commodity. Handfuls of rice were intentionally broadcast to reseed the plants in intensively bound and harvested beds.

Because they remain on the plant for a longer time, tied kernels are riper than those harvested by poling and knocking, turning nearly as dark as the farm-grown, "blackened" wild rice sold in grocery stores. They also develop a thicker seedcoat and thus take longer to cook. Such rice was kept separately by the Indians and was used for different purposes.

Harvesting rice by binding is not legal today in most areas. In fact, those who harvest wild rice should check with their local natural resources agency to find out if there are licensing requirements, seasons, or other regulations governing the harvest of wild rice, as there are in Wisconsin and Minnesota.

Finishing the Rice

Unfortunately, wild rice does not fall off the plant ready-to-eat or even ready-to-cook. As with all wild grasses, wild rice grains are protected by an armor that makes them difficult for large mammals – especially humans – to chew and digest. This armor, which technically consists of a palea and lemma with barbed awn, is collectively known as chaff – and it must be removed before the rice is eaten.

Processing of the grain from green wild rice to a product that is ready for cooking is commonly known as "finishing." To finish wild rice it must be dried, parched to harden the kernels and make the chaff brittle, rubbed or "jigged" to loosen the chaff from the kernel, and winnowed to remove the chaff. To ease the monotony of the work, to increase labor efficiency, and to celebrate the bounty of Nature's gift, the Ojibwa made a great social event out of finishing their manoomin.

Finishing wild rice is significantly more labor-intensive than harvesting, and one should expect some troubleshooting the first few times. Machines have been invented which drastically reduce the labor involved in finishing rice. You can't buy these machines, but if you live in an area where ricing is popular you can bring your harvest to a local processor who has designed and made his own equipment. For a fee or a portion of the rice, these processors will finish the rice for you. This is convenient, but it precludes the feeling of accomplishment that comes with finishing the rice yourself, and it is not available in all areas. The bulk of my rice is finished with machinery but I like to keep a little of it to do the old-fashioned way.

In this section I will talk about the methods and equipment traditionally used by the Ojibwa for finishing rice as well as how those methods have changed with the introduction of new technology. I'll tell you what I do with my rice and try to give you an idea what modern rice harvesters generally do.

Once you understand the process, feel free to improvise, but I recommend that your first efforts follow these instructions closely. These methods have been developed by thousands of people through many years of trial and error. I have seen way too many hours wasted by people attempting to finish wild rice with chintzy, Mickey-Mouse methods (such as rolling pins). Many such methods seem obvious and easy, but are truthfully so unproductive and frustrating that they subtly discourage one from harvesting or eating wild rice. The extra effort required upfront to set up for finishing manoomin in a time-tested fashion will save you greatly in the long run.

Drying and Parching

When harvested, green rice contains a lot of moisture that makes it prone to spoilage if left at room temperature. Wet rice left in a sack out in the sun will get very moldy in just one day, and rice worms will eat more of the grain every day until it is dry. I dry my rice as soon as possible after harvest by spreading it out on a tarp in the sun. If you cannot dry the rice immediately, put it in the coolest place possible. Take it out of the gunnysacks and spread it out loosely, especially if there is no cool place to put it, for tightly packed rice molds more quickly.

Two full days in the sun is usually sufficient to dry the rice adequately, but that depends on the air temperature, how thickly the rice is spread on the tarp (I try to keep mine less than an inch deep), and how large the kernels are. Try to mix it up once a day so that it dries more evenly. Sand or gravel can stick to your feet, hands, knees, or the underside of the tarp and find its way into the rice, so be careful when you are spreading it out. The surest way to avoid sand is to lay your drying tarp on a nice grassy lawn. If you dry your rice indoors it will dry slowly – plus you will usually find rice worms crawling around your house for the next several days. But that is better than letting it spoil.

To see if your rice is thoroughly dried, remove the husk from a few kernels and break them. If the kernels are stiff and brittle, snapping without the slightest bend, then your rice is fully dried and can be stored as is for a long time before being finished. I recommend drying your rice to this degree unless you are going to parch it immediately. (If you are going to parch your rice right away, you don't have to dry it, but most people still do so for at least a day before parching.)

Parching is the process of heating the rice to completely desiccate it, which hardens the kernels and makes the chaff brittle enough to be rubbed off. It is also said to make the rice keep better. This process is commonly called "scorching" by the Ojibwa but in fact the rice is carefully tended during the process to prevent scorching. Most do-it-yourselfers that I know parch their rice in a galvanized steel washtub placed over a low fire. This allows them to parch about one quarter of a bushel at a time. I parch mine in a galvanized watering trough in batches of about a bushel at a time. There is no benefit to the galvanization – it just happens that most metal containers of appropriate size are galvanized. If you use a galvanized container for parching, be sure not to get it so hot that the coating burns; you don't want this toxin tainting your rice.

I build a medium-sized fire and let it burn down to coals, then place the trough over it, held 8–10 inches (20–25 cm) off the ground by concrete blocks on each end. I keep a supply of thin firewood pieces on hand so that I can control the level of heat with some accuracy.

Green lake rice.

Once the rice is placed over the flames it should be stirred constantly to keep it from burning. Make sure the fire is not too hot, as overparched rice becomes brittle and tends to break up into tiny pieces when hulled – plus it can get a scorched flavor. If you hear the rice crackling a lot, the flame is too high. In this case, stir the rice more vigorously until the flame dies down, quickly spread the coals out more, or remove some fuel. The rice is stirred with a long-handled paddle, which can be one specifically carved for the purpose or simply an old wooden canoe paddle.

A small batch of rice that is fully dried may need to be parched for only ten minutes, while larger batches and those that are moister might have to be parched for a over an hour. You'll know that it is done by examining a small handful of grains. The chaff should be brown and brittle, and rubbing it very hard between the palms of your hands should cause some of the kernels to

Harvested manoomin drying on tarps. On the far right is river rice (note the green color) while the other tarps contain lake rice.

come free of their hulls. The kernels should be hard and brittle, and most of them will show lengthwise corrugations resulting from shrinkage. If the rice is parched when it is still fairly moist, many of the kernels will be slightly puffed out and they will have a slightly lighter color than rice that was parched when fully dry. Beginners have a tendency to overparch their rice because they believe that they will eventually reach a magical point where the chaff will just slip right off of the grain. Unfortunately, that will never happen.

In the distant past, before the Native people had access to metal kettles, the processes of drying and parching were combined into one step: fire curing. A large scaffolding was built with a latticework of green sticks and fires were built underneath the platform. Upon this platform the rice was slowly dried for about three days. After the introduction of kettles fire curing died out – not because parching in kettles saved labor, since in fact fire curing took less labor and was sometimes resorted to in personnel shortages – but rather because people preferred the flavor of parched rice to smoked rice.

Manoomin cured over an open flame in this manner acquired a notably smoky flavor, as was reported by explorers and traders. Many wild food books still parrot that wild rice has a "smoky flavor" despite the fact that this method of curing has been largely discontinued for over a hundred years and is unheard of in the last fifty.

If you have a lot of rice, do not parch it all at once; only parch that quantity which you will have the opportunity to immediately hull. If you parch the rice and then let it sit for a few days, it will re-absorb moisture from the air, rendering the chaff more supple and the kernel more brittle – both of which will make it more difficult to separate the chaff. Rice that you let sit for long after parching may have to be briefly re-parched, and re-parched rice will usually break up very badly. So if it's your first time, set aside at least half a day to do the first batch, and don't make it too big. It will get easier after that.

Hulling

The process of removing the hull from the parched rice is the most labor-intensive and physically difficult part of dealing with wild rice. It is a two step process: breaking the hulls from the kernels followed by winnowing out the broken hulls.

To separate the hull from the grain it needs to be rubbed between two surfaces while the hull is brittle. One stationary surface "catches" one side of the hull, while a moving surface catches the other side, thereby ripping the hull apart. The Ojibwa traditionally did this by placing the rice in a pit lined with a thick hide and treading vigorously upon the grain. Other pits were lined with a *bootaagan* – which looks something like a giant wooden pail with a wide top tapering to a narrow bottom. The side of the bootaagan was made of wooden staves and a log section formed the bottom. The bootaagan stuck several inches above the ground and was surrounded by a canvas to catch any rice that spilled out, and also to keep the person treading in the bootaagan from getting his moccasins dirty if he stepped out of the rice for a break. Parched rice was poured into this vessel for treading. Later on, metal pails, barrels, and other such containers were adopted as ready-made bootaagans, and rubber pads were often used to line the containers. Treading was the only part of ricing that men were traditionally involved in. Occasionally, rather than by treading, the rice was hulled with long-handled softwood pestles. These were jabbed with moderate force along the sides of the hulling pit to rub the rice against it (rather than pounding the rice as some have surmised).

Because of the constant and rhythmic motion of one's feet in the bootaagan or pit, this step is often called "dancing" or "jigging" the rice. It is also variously called "threshing," "thrashing," "trashing," "treading," or "rubbing." (Reference to this step as "threshing," though common even in the literature, is simply wrong. Threshing is the separation of the grain from the plant; it is what one does in the canoe with rice knockers.)

Jigging is done wearing moccasins or, sometimes today, tennis shoes that have had all traces of dirt or sand cleaned from their soles. The object is to get some rice between one's footgear and the bottom or sides of the pit and, with a twisting motion of the feet, rub off the hull between the two surfaces. It is the lateral motion of the feet after making contact with the rice, not the downward impact of the feet, which loosens the hulls. One or two poles were usually driven in the ground near the bootaagan, or a sort of makeshift railing was built, so that the dancer could hold on for stability while treading.

How long the rice needs to be rubbed depends largely on the size of the batch. A bushel will probably need to be trodden for forty-five minutes to an hour, winnowed, and then trodden again for about as long. Small batches, on the other hand, might take only twenty minutes of rubbing. During the process some of the rice kernels will break; one tries to apply force in such a way that it is adequate and vigorous but minimizes breakage.

For treading rice, wear clothes that are tightly woven, like jeans: something which the rice barbs will not easily stick to or penetrate. Don't plan on wearing the same clothes around all day, for they will be itchy and uncomfortable. Treading rice is really boring to do alone. Try to get a bunch of friends to come over (preferably the same people who harvested the rice with you) and make a party out of it. When one person gets tired of treading, another can take his place to keep the process going at full throttle.

Winnowing

After the husks are loosened from the kernels they are removed by winnowing. The husks and other detritus are known as *chaff*. Winnowing is the process of separating materials using the different rates that they fall through the air due to their differing densities. In simpler terms, the heavy stuff falls into a container and the light stuff blows away. Winnowing is used all over the world to separate hundreds of different kinds of edible seeds from their chaff. In theory it is very simple, but in practice it sometimes takes much skill. Luckily, wild rice is one of the easiest things to winnow.

Close-up of ripe grain head, showing short, thick kernels ranging from green to tan to purple-brown. 18 of 26 kernels on this plant were ripe this day in late August.

141

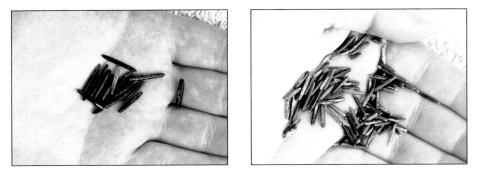

Finished kernels of lake rice (left) and river rice (right).

The Ojibwa traditionally winnowed their rice in a birchbark tray held in the hands. The tray was brought out away from the body and swung upward and outward, then the rice was suddenly thrown back toward the winnower. The tray would then be pulled quickly back in to catch the kernels. The lighter material would not be thrown as far and thus some of it would fall outside of the tray. The winnower does this repeatedly, hundreds and hundreds of times, making it look very easy, losing a little of the chaff each time until only (or mostly) hulled kernels remain.

The reason that this doesn't sound easy is because it is not. Before you get the knack, you will probably lose a few pounds of rice on the ground. This skill allowed the Ojibwa to winnow rice when it was calm out and was very efficient, but you don't have to do yours this way.

I often winnow rice simply by pouring it slowly from a dustpan into a bin in a breeze or in front of a fan. This accomplishes the same thing: the chaff is blown away and the kernels fall into the bin. Adjust the pouring height and position according to the strength of the wind so that you do not lose any kernels. Some of the chaff will always fall back in with the kernels, but just keep repeating the process until the rice is more or less clean.

Earlier I mentioned an intermediate winnowing before treading the rice a second time. This is very helpful, especially with larger batches, because the buildup of loose hulls in the rice being treaded reduces friction and causes the treading to take more effort. If your rice is fully dry, you can even winnow out the empty hulls before parching; this will generally be about a third of the volume. And I always quickly winnow my rice after parching but before treading to get rid of some more empties as well as bothersome dust and broken barbs that come off in parching. This also gives the hot rice a few minutes to cool down before somebody has to stand in it.

After the rice is winnowed you will be very excited; there is something magical about turning that green itchy mess into a finished grain product. Now, you are almost ready to cook the manoomin. First, however, spread it out on a flat surface and pick through it to remove unwanted debris and the last few kernels that still have their hulls.

One optional last step is to run the grain over some kind of screen or shake it in a strainer to separate the small, broken pieces from the larger kernels. The broken rice can be used in any way that whole or "fancy" rice is used, but it is most popularly used in soup. It will cook a lot more quickly than the whole kernel rice.

Cooking and Storage of Wild Rice

The rice will keep as long as it remains dry, but it tastes best the first month or so after processing, when it has a fresh-roasted flavor from parching. Make sure to store your rice in a container that is impervious to mice and insects, in an area that is not going to flood, and preferably not in a humid location.

Before cooking the rice, rinse it several times with cold water, stirring gently as you pour the liquid off. This will remove little bits of remaining chaff as well as the "rice dust." If a few kernels that you missed while hand-picking still have husks attached, they will usually float during the process of rinsing and stirring.

Wild rice should be mixed at a roughly one to two ratio with water when it is boiled. It generally takes 20–35 minutes to cook river rice and 30–45 minutes for lake rice. (Cultivated wild rice takes considerably longer to cook because the blackening process hardens the seedcoat.) When you have your own real wild rice, don't dilute it with white rice like Uncle Ben does; eat it straight so that you can get the full force of its wonderful flavor. And don't forget to savor the scent that rises from the cooking pot.

Seasoned wild rice makes an excellent side dish for dinner or lunch. It is enjoyed by many with nothing but butter and salt added after cooking. I like to mix it with hickory nuts and maple syrup for breakfast. You can use it in casserole, soup, or any other concoction in place of commercial rice or barley–only it is much better. There are literally thousands of wild rice recipes in gourmet cookbooks, waiting for somebody to do them justice with real manoomin. The Ojibwa generally ate their rice boiled in water or broth and served with meat. After a vigorous day outdoors, there's no dinner better than that.

Wild Leek, Ramp

Allium tricoccum

Healthy wild leek clump.

It was late in the month of May. I was nineteen years old, just married, and exhilarated to be exploring the wilds near the sixty-acre abandoned farm that I had just bought, where I had begun to attempt living my childhood dream of building a log cabin and living off the land. In those days I used to pass the winter poring over the pages of my collection of plant books, so that when spring came and the real things were at hand, I would recognize many of them at first sight, having already espied and collected them many times in my daydreams. This was one of those warm and carefree spring days in the outdoors when such fantasies are apt to become real. Through dense young stands of aspen and balsam fir, varied here and there by a large white spruce or red maple, I made my way toward a small river shown on my map, about two miles distant through the woods, to see what excitement it offered.

Descending a steep clay slope, focusing on my footing so as not to slip, I first heard the rushing water. In excitement my pace quickened, and the sound grew louder and louder until it began to muffle the bird songs that surrounded me. At last, I could see the water – not crystal clear as I had imagined such a wilderness stream, but brick red with the clay of the valley. Along the banks of the river the vegetation changed dramatically. The loggers had left this riparian strip alone during their last harvest of the area. Above the banks grew tall balsam poplars, black ash, and aspen, mixed with an occasional basswood or maple. Here and there skeletons of once magnificent elms reminded me that it is not only by means of the saw that men have touched and blighted the forest.

I walked along this stream, crossing when I could on fallen logs, excited to find that some of the plant life of this remote river valley was typical of the regions further south where I had thus far spent my whole life. I knew the foraging would be good here: nannyberries, highbush cranberries, cow parsnip, burdock, ostrich fern, and other edible plants abounded. Suddenly, struck by a strong and familiar scent, I stopped and examined the air. Onions! Onions? I knelt down and picked a large, lily-like leaf from a plant that was partially crushed under my foot, lifting it to my nose. Not quite onion, but close. A moment of scrutiny and I knew what treasure I had found: a wild leek. I grabbed a nearby stick and grubbed a few of the bulbs out of the ground, impressed at their size compared to the wild garlic with which I was acquainted from southern Wisconsin. I stood up and surveyed my surroundings; to my amazement, I was standing in an acre or more that was carpeted almost solidly with wild leeks! I ran to the bank and jumped down to the river's edge with my handful of leeks and rubbed them in the ruddy current, then took a nibble. It was a strong flavor indeed, but one that I knew I would find delightful and useful.

Description

This plant is usually called "wild leek" in the northern part of its range and "ramp" in the southern and central Appalachians, but the names can be used interchangeably. It belongs to that large, diverse, and useful genus *Allium*, which contains our domestic onion, leek, garlic, shallot, chive, and a huge number of wild onion species around the world. Despite its name, the wild leek is not some woodland counterpart of the domestic vegetable that goes by the same name; it is no more closely related to the cultivated leek than it is to the onion or chive.

This plant tends to form large clumps about four to ten inches wide, with bulbs packed tightly together in that area. Where many such clumps are side by side or run together, wild leeks may carpet large areas of the forest floor with a magical luxuriance. Each plant has two or three lanceolate, basal leaves, which are 8–12 inches (20–30 cm) long and 1–3 inches (2–7 cm) wide. These leaves are quite unonionlike; they are flat and wide, resembling lily leaves.

Wild leek flower umbel.

Dead flower stalks and seedheads of wild leek. For much of the year these are the most visible indicator of the presence of wild leeks.

The narrow base of the leaf is channeled. This part is often maroon in color, which is sometimes cited as an identifying characteristic of wild leek – but almost as often the base of the leaf is pure green. I have been unable to figure out what factor causes the color variation. Smooth and rather flimsy, ramp leaves have a rubbery feel. In hot weather they often droop like the ears of a puppy. They have a groove down the center of the leaf and sometimes show ripples running lengthwise, but lack a distinct midvein.

In late spring a flower stalk with a small, pointed bud appears on some of the plants. As this flower stalk grows the foliage of the ramp begins to die. First, yellow spots and wilted edges appear, and soon afterward the entire leaf turns yellow and then brown. By the time that the plant is flowering a few weeks later, in early to mid summer, the leaves have completely withered away.

The narrow, straight, unbranching flower stalk reaches 8–20 inches (20–50 cm) in height, terminating in a tight, almost hemispherical umbel of small, white, three-petaled flowers. Later on, a cluster of hard, BB-like black seeds is borne; this persists through the summer, fall, and often the winter. It is very helpful to learn to recognize these seed clusters because for most of the year they are the best indicator of where patches of wild leeks are located.

Ramp bulbs have an elongated teardrop shape. They are white and smooth on the outside. Their maximum size is about 2 inches (5 cm) in length and .75 inch (2 cm) thick, although typical mature bulbs are about two-thirds of that size. At the bottom of the bulb is a cluster of small fibrous roots, so that if you turn the leek upside down and draw a face on the bulb it looks like a doll with dreadlocks. A small, knobby projection sticks out of the bottom of the bulb, and it gets a tiny bit longer each year (and it is actually to this knob that the roots are attached). You can use this knob to determine the relative age of leek plants.

Range and Habitat

Wild leeks are found from northern Minnesota east across southern Ontario and Quebec to Nova Scotia and New Brunswick, south in the Appalachians to Tennessee and Georgia, and west to eastern Missouri and Iowa. In the south-ernmost part of their range they are confined to higher elevations.

These plants inhabit areas of rich, moist, neutral soil in mesic hardwood forests and the floodplains of small rivers. They are strongly associated with sugar maple and are found throughout the Eastern Woodlands almost every-where that this tree is predominant, especially if it is growing along with beech, basswood, yellow birch, and elm. In drier, hotter regions ramps are especially abundant in cool ravines and on north-facing slopes.

Wild leeks are spring ephemerals; they appear very early in the growing sea-son and accomplish most of their growth before the leaves of the canopy trees are fully formed, then die back in early summer soon after heavy shade is cast on the forest floor. This special adaptation allows them to take advantage of brief but excellent growing conditions found on the floor of the mesic forest. They are very closely associated with other species of spring ephemerals such as spring beauty, toothwort, Dutchman's breeches, squirrel corn, and trout lily – being rarely found where these species are absent. Ramps are often found in amazing abundance; I know of places where one could walk for miles and never be more than a few steps from one of these plants. They often dominate the forest floor in springtime, forming thick colonies covering several acres.

Harvest

Both the leaves and the bulbs of wild leeks are edible, and it is a shameful waste when people discard the tops and eat only the bulbs. The best time to gather wild leeks, in my opinion, is when the leaves have attained about two thirds of their full size. This falls somewhere in the middle part of spring. At this time both the greens and bulbs will be tender, flavorful, and fairly large. Earlier, the flavor is just as good, but you must invest more labor and kill more plants for the same amount of food. After the plants reach full size the leaves begin to toughen and the flavor changes – although all ramp greens are good as long as they are green. I also feel that the fully grown bulbs do not taste quite as good as the young ones, but they are still excellent. Plants with flower stalks, however, tend to have poorly-flavored and tougher bulbs. If you can locate patches of leeks, whether by the dead seedheads, by memory, or by noticing the tiny,

A harvested and cleaned bunch of ramps, at the size when I prefer to gather them.

Full-sized, cleaned wild leek bulbs, harvested just as the tops are beginning to die back.

tooth-like tips of the dormant bulbs, you can collect the bulbs throughout the summer and fall.

The dense clumps that make ramps convenient to harvest are the result of a single founder plant reproducing itself vegetatively and spreading slowly in all directions. One of these clumps may be several decades old. Even where ramps are exceedingly abundant, they are slow to reproduce and susceptible to overharvest. Many patches of wild leeks have been decimated or destroyed by wanton collection, especially for the market. When you collect leeks, always leave a part of each clump undisturbed to keep growing; treat the patch as if it were your garden, even if you plan on never coming back. Take a shovel-scoop here and there around the colony rather than collecting heavily in a small area.

I unearth large bunches of ramps at once, leaving behind about a quarter of the clump. The bulbs will often be stuck together, making them easier to handle. I like to clean the leeks outside in a stream or lake, separating the individual plants and rinsing off the excess dirt. Convenient for the final cleaning, there is a thin sheath covering the bulb. This sheath can be peeled off from the top down, taking any remaining dirt off with it. The last step is to cut or break off the root knob at the base of the bulb.

Preparation

With a taste that suggests both onions and garlic, ramps have a great variety of uses. I toss the raw greens or bulbs into salads or use them on sandwiches, and I use cooked leeks in almost any dish that would call for onions.

Since ramps are so abundant and can be gathered quickly, I like to collect a fairly large quantity of them each spring and store them for year-round consumption. They are one of the more important wild foods in my diet. Some of them I preserve by pressure canning, especially in a mixture with wood nettle and ostrich fern, so that I can open up a jar at any time of the winter to use as the base for a soup or other concoction. I also cut some bulbs into very thin slices and roast them until dry above my woodstove.

Ramps are truly one of the forager's most useful plants. They are abundant, easy to collect, simple to prepare, and delicious. It is no surprise that wild leeks are served in many fine restaurants in the East. Learn to recognize them yourself and you can have that fine dining in your own home for free.

This hardwood forest is carpeted with luxuriant growth of wild leeks in mid-spring.

Smilax, Carrion Flower

Smilax herbacea. S. ecirrata, S. illinoensis, S. lasioneura

Smilax vine in summer.

Sometimes the best things get the worst names. So it is with carrion flower, a plant whose name is so utterly unappealing that the beginning forager is likely to pass it up – unless it comes highly recommended. I intend to give the carrion flower just such an accolade.

In my edible wild plant classes I insist on calling the carrion flower "smilax" because its other name is cumbersome, repulsive, and mostly inappropriate. I use the two terms interchangeably in this account. This is admittedly somewhat confusing, however, because not all species of the genus *Smilax* are called "carrion flower" – the genus also contains many woody vines known as greenbriers. Although most wild food books lump the greenbriers and carrion flowers together for discussion, they are truly very different vegetables. When referring to those species generally called "carrion flower," I use the common name "smilax" without capitals or italics. The capitalized and italicized version, *Smilax*, refers to the scientific name of the genus.

The unfortunate name "carrion flower" comes from the putrid scent of the blossoms of one species, but I like to tell people that this plant is called "carry-on flower" because those who know the plant carry on and on about how good it tastes.

Range, Habitat, and Description

The various species of carrion flower range from northern Georgia to the eastern Rockies, north to southern Manitoba, and east to Maine. They are found primarily in river bottoms, along fencerows, at the edges of swamps and fields, and in other rich-soiled places that receive partial to full sun.

Carrion flowers are perennials but the above-ground portion of the plant dies back completely every fall. This habit and the lack of thorns or spines are the most important characteristics that separate these choice edibles from the persistent and usually heavily-armored stems of greenbriers.

Smilax leaves.

Although it is commonly said that carrion flowers are herbaceous vines, this is something of an exaggeration; I call them "lazy vines." They grow erect until they become too heavy for their stems to support their own weight, then they slowly fall over sideways until they come to rest on other vegetation, which they grab for support. This is actually an excellent adaptation. The plant grows incredibly fast when it emerges in spring (not uncommonly six feet in two weeks) and takes advantage of the abundant available light. As the foliage of the overhead trees and shrubs unfurls in late spring, casting shadows on the smilax plant, it leans over and spreads its leaves across a greater horizontal area to gather more sunlight in the intensifying shade.

Smilax vines typically grow from 6–10 feet (2–3 m) in length and their stems are as much as one inch (2.5 cm) thick; no other North American herbaceous vine is this hefty. The stems are round and smooth, sometimes with faint ridges running lengthwise. Some species have tendrils arising from the leaf axils and others do not; when these are present they serve to support the plant in its reclining state. Carrion flower forms large branches, an unusual trait among herbaceous vines. The stems of the early growth are green, darkening and often becoming reddish-brown by late summer, and persisting through the winter as tough, reddish-brown or straw-colored dead material.

Carrion flower leaves are broadly ovate to rounded or heart-shaped, with net-patterned veins between distinct parallel ribs. They are borne alternately on relatively long petioles. Glabrous on both sides with entire margins, the leaves are typically 3–5 inches (8–13 cm) in length. The young foliage is light green, slightly shiny, and remarkably soft, but later in the season it becomes much darker green, developing wavy edges and a tough, leathery texture.

The dull, greenish-white flowers appear in early summer, borne in tight, rounded umbels at the end of long stems that arise from the upper leaf axils. Each flower has 6 petals and stamens, but these are so small that they are difficult to observe. It is often said that these flowers produce a terrible smell resembling rotting flesh, but I believe this characteristic is confined to *S. herbacea*; the other species have little or no scent but still go by the same stinking name. Smilax flower clusters develop into distinctive balls of blue-black fruits, each containing several seeds, that ripen in late summer and fall and often persist into the winter. The fruits are usually a little less than a half-inch in diameter and are often coated with a heavy bloom.

Smilax fruit.

Cluster of smilax flowers.

Carrion flower shoot about 7 feet (2 m) tall, the top 2 feet (60 cm) perfect for eating.

Smilax is a distant relative of asparagus, and similarities are evident when the shoots first appear and the leaves are still nothing more than tiny scales pressed against the thick, juicy, and tender stem. The stalk will snap easily when bent and will be solid all the way through with an opaque green color on the interior. Toward the top of the stalk one sees embryonic flower clusters, making the whole plant at this stage look something like a cross between asparagus and broccoli. These tiny flower clusters will be mixed among minute, soft, needle-like leaves and sometimes whisker-like tendrils.

Harvest

There is only a brief period in mid to late spring when carrion flower shoots are at their best; this corresponds to the period when most canopy trees are forming their leaves, which is the height of the season for wild greens in general. Where I live in northern Wisconsin this occurs from about May 10 to May 25. However, larger smilax vines, especially those growing in the open, often send up their shoots much later than this, extending the season for collection into early June.

Small carrion flower shoots, such as those that are only a quarter of an inch thick, might get tough by the time they are 18 inches (46 cm) tall and should be picked when they are only half that height. On the other hand, if

Tender, growing tips of two species of carrion flower.

you see carrion flower shoots that are 8–10 inches (20–25 cm) in length but .75 inch (2 cm) thick, you might as well wait until they are larger to harvest them. Some of the stems are perfectly tender at the height of three feet (1 m) – which makes for one whopping shoot vegetable!

A little later in spring the top 1–2 feet (30–60 cm) of the shoot may still be nice and tender despite the fact that the base of the stalk has become tough. To harvest these tops, sever them wherever they break easily. After you break the top off, the vine will not die back to the base but rather will produce several branches radiating from the point of breakage. Into early summer, after the carrion flower stalks topple sideways and begin to act like vines, you can still harvest their tender, growing tips for greens, but this will provide a much smaller volume of food than the thick shoots.

Carrion flower tends not to grow in colonies; the individual plants are spread out in their habitat, and each produces one to five stems. For this reason it is not common to find enough to warrant storing by canning or freezing. However, if you are familiar with smilax it is by no means difficult to find enough for a large meal, and a single stalk provides a considerable trailside snack. Carrion flower is a long-lived perennial, and the rhizome stores enough energy to withstand having the top occasionally harvested; however, repeated picking of the stalks of the same plant year after year will eventually deplete the rootstock, shrinking and finally killing the plant. For the sake of conservation, please be kind to these generous vines and employ reasonable moderation in your collection.

Preparation

I can't tell you how well carrion flower shoots last in the refrigerator because I always eat mine within a day – they're lucky to even make it home intact. Certainly they must have a longer shelf life than leafy greens, and probably they keep as well as asparagus – but unless you have a big pile of them, why wait? Since they are not hairy and grow so fast they tend to be very clean; I have never felt the need to wash my smilax shoots.

Carrion flower shoots are probably the closest wild vegetable to asparagus in both flavor and texture (excluding, of course, wild asparagus). When raw they are crunchy, succulent, slightly mucilaginous, and slightly sweet with no objectionable taste. Their flavor is milder than that of asparagus and they are also more tender, so they work well in salads. They are one of my favorite greens to nibble on as I walk through the springtime woods. Carrion flower shoots cook into a very soft vegetable that is hard to beat in stir-fry or stew. Just boiled or steamed and eaten with a touch of salt or butter they are fabulous.

So don't let the name scare you away; this plant is far more delicious than rotting flesh. Give it a try and you'll carry on about it too.

Butternut

Juglans cinerea

A cluster of ripe butternuts in late August.

The only edible wild plant that my father ever taught me was the butternut. One of these trees grew in the yard across the street from our house, and when I was around five years old he pointed out a couple of the nuts lying on the sidewalk, noting how they looked like little green footballs. It was something that he just mentioned in passing, unaware of my fascination with plants, but I never forgot it. Shortly thereafter, that butternut tree was cut down, and for many years I searched in vain for another. It seemed that whenever I spotted one of these nuts, whether in town or in the woods, the parent tree was nowhere to be found.

Perhaps it is those early memories that have made me so fond of butternut trees today. Perhaps each time I find one I am consummating a dozen child-hood searches with long-delayed success. Or maybe I feel indebted to them for the time that a truck mechanic told me to look for morels near dead butternut

157

Healthy, open-grown butternut tree.

trees; I followed his advice that spring and found a lot of mushrooms. I grew even more fond of butternuts during my first winter in the Northwoods – so long, bitterly cold, and snowy that I wondered if my translocation had been a mistake. I went out with skis upon the crusted, belly-deep snow one day in late March, looking for some hope of spring, and was shocked to find four butternut trees standing tall among the hemlocks and maples, further north than I had imagined they would grow. If these woods had butternuts, I decided, then I could live here too.

Description

The butternut is a medium-sized tree, usually attaining 40–80 feet (12–25 m) in height. Open-grown trees are often as broad as they are tall, with a spreading, flat-topped crown, while forest-grown specimens usually have small crowns and no branches for the first two-thirds of their trunk. Butternut trees are frequently found growing in clumps of 2–3 trees emanating from the same spot, probably because squirrels usually bury multiple nuts in a cache. The bark is smooth, on older trees becoming divided by fissures into separate, wavy ridges. The bark pattern is quite distinctive, and the trained eye can instantly recognize the butternut by this characteristic alone. The twigs are very thick with dark-brown, chambered pith, bearing prominent leaf scars that are often described as "monkey faces." The terminal buds of butternut are also very distinctive. They are large and elongated with a slightly convoluted surface (as opposed to the smooth or scaly surface of the buds of most trees) that reminds me of a hand with all of the fingers extended and pressed together.

The leaves of butternut, borne alternately, are pinnately compound with 11–17 ovate leaflets, each of which is 3–4 inches (8–10 cm) long. The entire leaf may exceed 2 feet (.6 m) in length. The leaflets are very thin, sessile, finely pubescent, with slightly rough or very finely serrated edges, and often have a light yellow-green color on the upper surface which makes this tree easy to spot from a distance. The side leaflets get notably longer

Butternut's distinctive bark.

Winter twig of butternut. Note the naked bud, which looks like a compressed leaf, and the "monkey face" leaf scar.

Butternut foliage.

toward the end of the leaf, and the terminal leaflet is well-developed. This trait, along with thinner, broader, larger, and lighter-colored leaflets, helps to differentiate the butternut from its close relative the black walnut, which bears its largest leaflets in the middle of the leaf and has its terminal leaflet shrunken or absent. Butternut is one of the last trees to acquire leaves in the spring and among the first to drop them in autumn.

Butternut blooms in very late spring when the leaves appear. As with all nut trees, the weather at this time is the most important factor influencing the nut crop for the year. The unshowy male and female flowers are borne separately on the same twigs. The former occur as a drooping, green catkin, while the latter are small reddish flowers with two long appendages, occurring in a small cluster. Pollination is by wind.

The fruit is a large nut, 2–3.5 inches (5–9 cm) long, egg or football-shaped with the terminal end more pointed. The outer hull is dark green, moist, and fleshy with sticky, reddish-brown hairs. It emits a strong aroma reminiscent of citrus. The nutshell beneath this rind has a jagged surface with lengthwise ridges and a very sharp, pointed tip. Butternuts are usually produced in clusters of 3–7, but they may hang singly and I have seen clusters containing as many as 16 nuts.

Range and Habitat

Butternut grows throughout most of the Eastern Woodlands of the United States except for the Southern Atlantic and Gulf Coastal Plains. It is also present in the southern parts of Quebec and Ontario. The butternut ranges farther north than any other member of the walnut/hickory family in North America.

The butternut is a fast-growing, sun-loving species that rarely lives more than 150 years. It is found in rich mixed hardwood forests, especially those which have been disturbed by logging or windstorms. It seems to prefer dry limestone ridges, rich loamy sand, and river valleys just above the floodplain. The butternut is usually no more than a minor component of the forests where it is found. In part due to its large seed, this tree is an effective colonizer of fields and is often prevalent in abandoned farmland and along forest edges and fencerows. It bears nuts most heavily in open, sunny situations where it grows a wide, spreading crown.

Harvest and Preparation

Butternuts ripen and fall from late August to late September. Sometimes the branches will bend many feet towards the ground under their load of nuts, and a kick or a shake will send dozens, maybe hundreds, plummeting earthward. In heavy mast years, a few bushels of nuts may be produced by a single tree; in other years the trees may be barren. Nut production is partly cyclical and

Green butternuts being hulled, with a few having softened and turned black.

If all goes well, the butternut kernel is shelled out as two "paddles" like these.

partly determined by the weather.

When the butternut crop is heavy I gather large quantities of them. The task is simple: just pick them up off the ground and fill a bag or bucket. Often it is possible to gather a bushel in fifteen minutes.

After harvest comes the more difficult part; removing the fleshy hull or rind. I like to do this as soon as possible after collection, by standing the nut on its end on a chopping block and hitting the other end lightly with a hammer. This loosens the rind, which can then be pulled off with the fingers. After removing the rind, let the nuts dry to prevent molding. You may want to wear glasses for hulling green butternuts, since the impact of the hammer often causes liquid to squirt from the rind, and this really stings if it gets in your eyes. Also, if you handle butternut husks without gloves, your hands will stain brown for a week or more.

If you do not remove the hulls within a week or two, they will begin to turn black and soften, oozing inky liquid. Butternut maggots will appear, eating the rinds, but they will not penetrate the nutshell. You can let a pile of butternuts decompose for several weeks or more – even all winter. When spring comes, gather up the messy nuts (there shouldn't be too much left of the hulls) and place them somewhere to dry. When the nuts are dry, what is left of the hulls will be brittle and crumbly. At this point I take the sack and beat it against the ground or stomp on it, which will cause what is left of the hulls to just kind of disintegrate, leaving cleaned nuts that are ready to crack. This sounds complicated, but it is actually not much work at all, and I know of no more labor-efficient way to remove the hulls.

However, there is one enormous drawback to this mass-production method of removing butternut hulls: it is detrimental to the flavor of the kernels. The inky liquid that seeps from the disintegrating rinds will bleed through the shells and give the nuts a slight bitter taste, making them more reminiscent of black walnuts. I like black walnuts, so I still use butternuts hulled like this. However, those that are hulled promptly when green are much, much better; they hardly taste like the same kind of nut. When I gather butternuts, then, I try to remove the rinds when they are still fresh and green, but if I don't have time to get to all of them, I let the rinds rot off of the remainder.

Some authors report a tendency for butternuts to go rancid. I've never had any trouble with this. However, if you remove the hulls by driving over the nuts with your car, as many people suggest, you are probably going to get hairline cracks in the nuts and have some of them go rancid. Butternuts with intact shells can be stored for years with minimal spoilage.

To crack butternuts, I hold them vertically on a chopping block, either end up, and give them a sharp, controlled blow on the tip with a hammer. I usually wear a glove on the hand holding the nut, for the ridges on the shell are hard on the fingers. When butternuts crack, pieces tend to fly everywhere. For this reason it's important to keep holding the shell with one hand even while you strike it. You may want to wear safety glasses. Soaking the nuts in water for a week or so before cracking reduces the splintering and usually makes the nuts a little easier to crack, but it is certainly not necessary. Butternuts are tough, and it takes a lot of force to crack them, but with practice one learns to crack them quickly and efficiently with the method described.

After cracking some nuts I sort the nutmeats from the shells by hand, using a nut pick to coax out the fugitive pieces hiding in shell crevices. If all goes well, I end up with two paddle-shaped pieces from each nut. You may at first be disappointed by the small amount of edible product obtained from such a large heap of whole nuts, but don't despair – just collect more next time. They're easy to gather and worth the effort.

Butternuts that have had the hulls peeled while green are a delicacy. Their sweet flavor hints at bananas and vanilla ice cream, and they are very soft. Those that have had their hulls blackened taste much like walnuts and are suitable for baking.

I most often consume butternuts in hot cereal. A simple recipe, fit for the gods, is cooked wild rice with uncooked butternuts, served hot, sweetened with maple syrup. Another marvelous hot cereal is acorn grits with butternuts and maple syrup. I also like to snack on butternuts all by themselves or put them on ice cream.

Butternuts are wonderful in soup; I sometimes include them as a major ingredient. After boiling, they taste something like beans, but they add their own oils to the soup broth. Ground-up butternuts have a multitude of uses. I like to mix them half-and-half with cold-leached acorns and add spices to make a kind of falafel. You can mix them with wild rice, seasonings, egg, and flour, and then fry or bake them as "veggie burgers." Use your imagination; there are hundreds of good recipes that would benefit from butternuts.

The butternut tree produces another, little-known product: syrup. One spring, several years ago, I was able to try making this. I tapped four large butternut trees in late April, around the peak of sap flow in the maples that year. At first the sap dripped quickly from the butternut taps, but within a few days the tap holes seemed to heal up, for their flow stopped even as the maples kept on. I drilled a few more tap holes, which flowed for a day or two and then stopped again. This is where I stopped the experiment, for I didn't want to riddle the trees with holes and kill them. The sap that I did procure boiled down into a very delicious syrup, very similar to that of maples.

Quite often I've seen recipes for butternut pickles, made from the unripe nuts, as long as one can still "easily push a pin through them." I tried this one summer and it was a disaster. The boiling water, which I was supposed to change until it no longer darkened, got darker with each water change. The nuts themselves turned black, and when I tried one, after several hours of boiling and more than half a dozen water changes, I deemed it among the most unpleasant objects to ever find its way into my mouth. Someday I will try making butternut pickles again, using even younger, smaller nuts, that can have a needle pushed through them even more easily.

Unfortunately, this wonderful tree is dying off over most of its range due to a disease called butternut canker. The formidable-sounding scientific name for this fungal disease is *Sirococcus clavigignenti-juglandacearum*. Large black lesions develop on the bark of the tree as the inner bark dies, beginning on branches and working its way to the trunk and roots. This eventually girdles the tree and kills it. In many areas there are very few butternuts left – except in the open, since trees with sunlight on their bark are apparently less susceptible to the disease.

There is some promise, however, in that certain trees appear to be largely resistant to the blight. If you find a thriving butternut tree today, it might be just such an individual. When you fill a basket of the bounty that this food-bearer so generously gives, take the time to plant a few nuts where the land seems to be asking for a tree. The world will appreciate it. At least, the squirrels and I will.

Siberian Elm

Ulmus pumila

A few years ago a student in one of my classes went into a rant about the horrible, useless, invasive, and ugly Siberian elm that was taking over the old fields and young woods around Minneapolis and St. Paul. It is unusual to hear such disdain for a tree – even a so-called weed tree – and I was taken aback.

So many of my childhood adventures took place in urban waste areas that the typical trees of these neglected lots – cottonwood, boxelder, and Siberian elm – became dear to me. I chased opossums, tracked rabbits, and observed woodchucks in these tiny, garbage-strewn woodlots. I found the nests of red-tailed hawks and great-horned owls, the dens of red foxes, the burdock clumps where pheasants hid, and the piles of concrete rubble where garter snakes hibernated. Granted, these woods did not have the diversity nor the beauty of a native forest, but for a Nature-lover stuck in the city, they were the next best thing: a plant and animal community all its own, hiding in the midst of a city ignorant of its existence, with much to teach. Not the least of its lessons was that wherever the scarring hand of man has left its mark, Nature is there to cover the wound and bring forth the miracle of life.

Note the blocky bark and rugged, spreading form of the Siberian elm.

Description

Siberian elm is a rugged-looking tree with a crooked trunk and widely spreading crown, more squat in appearance than our tall and elegant native elms. This fast-growing tree rarely exceeds 60 feet (18 m) in height and 2 feet (60 cm) in diameter. Open-grown Siberian elms produce a dome-shaped rather than vase-shaped crown. The bark is dark gray, thick, and blocky, again contrasting with the intertwined ridges of soft bark characteristic of its native cousins.

Like other elms, this species bears alternate, ovate leaves with serrated margins, but these are more symmetrical than the leaves of our native elms and much smaller, usually only 1.5 to 2.5 inches (4–6 cm) in length. Siberian elm leaves are tough and nearly glabrous, dark green above and slightly paler on the underside, with extremely short petioles of about .25 inches (.5 cm) in length. The slender twigs bear short, blunt buds that are more squat than those of our other elms. The flower buds are much larger than the leaf buds and are globose; these can be noticed very easily in the winter and are a helpful distinguishing feature. The short-stalked, clustered flowers, though numerous in early spring before the leaves appear, are very small and rather inconspicuous. The fruit is a disc-shaped, one-seeded samara that varies from .3–.6 inch (.8–1.5 cm) in diameter. These are borne in tight clusters in mid-spring, about the time the leaves are coming out.

Siberian elm leaves are smaller and less lopsided than those of our native elms.

Range and Habitat

This tree was brought to North America in the 1860s from northeastern Asia, where it inhabited river floodplains in semi-arid regions. Ecologically, it seems to be the Asian equivalent of the boxelder. In its new home it has become a weed tree in urban areas across the continent, except in the warmest and wettest regions. Often planted for shade, the Siberian elm is common in yards and along city streets, especially in the Midwest and Great Plains. It does well on dry soil and has spread to many roadsides, empty lots, and fencerows near places where it was planted ornamentally. In some regions, particularly where the prairies of the Heartland meet with the woodlands of the East, the Siberian elm has invaded native forest communities and is a regular sight in rural wood-lots. The hardiness of the Siberian elm allows it to thrive where none of our native elms would survive, thus it has been planted as an ornamental through much of the Rockies and well up into Canada in the Prairie Provinces. It is considered a nuisance in and around many major cities, including Albuquer-que, Denver, Kansas City, Minneapolis, Winnipeg, and Salt Lake.

Siberian elm is fast-growing, sun-loving, and thrives where the summers are hot and the winters cold, as in its original homeland. It is generally smaller and shorter-lived than our native elms but is more resistant to the Dutch elm disease. It tolerates a wide range of soil types.

Other species of elm produce edible samaras. Those of American elm *Ulmus americana* are small, hairy, and rather dry but not altogether bad, although two reports of people developing an allergic reaction to these seeds have been brought to my attention. However, the samaras of slippery elm *Ulmus rubra* are equal to those of the Siberian elm in palatability.

Clusters of young Siberian elm samaras, as you want them for eating.

167

Harvest and Preparation

The part of the Siberian elm that one eats is the samara. These dime-sized, light green wafers hang from the twigs in handful-sized clusters in spring. As soon as the samaras appear they are ready to eat – and as long as their papery wings are light green and tender, showing no signs of drying or browning, they are absolutely delicious. In the center of the wafer is a small seed that is sweet, soft, and nutty. It is very easy to pull handfuls of these fruits from the lower branches of open-grown elms in as vast a quantity as one might desire, as the trees produce them profusely.

The time to get Siberian elm samaras is in the middle of spring, just as the leaf buds are beginning to open. In two weeks the leaves will be fully formed

Dry, ripe Siberian elm seeds, before (top) and after (bottom) being rubbed and winnowed. Finished seeds are about the size of lentils.

and the samaras will have become tough, so the season for collecting them is short. You don't want to miss it.

Elm samaras are simply gourmet. Their size, unique appearance, and pleasant texture make them fun to eat, which I see fit to do several times per day during the brief blessing of their availability. While Siberian elm samaras are in season, they are tops on my list of salad ingredients.

Winter twig of Siberian elm, with small, blunt buds.

You don't have to eat them raw, however. Embellish any soup or cooked vegetable dish by throwing a handful of elm samaras into it. Use them to garnish pasta dishes or to make rice pilaf colorful and interesting. Omelets, lasagna, tacos: Siberian elm samaras have such a mild and agreeable manner that they belong almost everywhere you could put them (OK, not quite everywhere, but I even think they're good in oatmeal).

Once the seeds of the Siberian elm ripen, the samaras become dry and brown. They flutter from the tree in the breeze, littering the ground below and sometimes getting blown into convenient piles. They can often be collected very easily. After they are thoroughly dried, you can rub and winnow them to procure rather soft, lentil-like seeds. The ripe seeds are delicious raw or cooked. The flavor reminds me of a cross between sunflower seeds and oats. They can be added to hot cereal or used in many ways like other whole grains, but their texture seems too soft or oily to make good flour. I have only begun to experiment with the ripe seeds of Siberian elm, but they show immense promise as a versatile, delicious, wholesome, and easily stored wild grain, ripening at a time when others are not available.

Call this tree an obnoxious invasive if you must; cut it for firewood just to get it out of your woods; curse the rows of it that shade the roadside – but isn't it nice to see its defiant form growing through the cracked foundation of some factory razed long ago, its roots pushing up the broken concrete to let sunlight reach the long-imprisoned soil beneath, where the wind will scatter seeds to plant a new generation of unconquerable weeds? Personally, I'm glad that I don't have to go to Siberia to get my elm samaras.

Stinging Nettle

Urtica dioica

Summer leaves of stinging nettle.

I have heard a great many people list the stinging nettle as their favorite wild edible. There are few reputable foraging guides that fail to mention this popular weed. Not surprisingly, then, *Urtica dioica* was among the first edible greens that I learned as a child. In fact, it was instrumental in my development as a forager.

Like too many mothers, mine wasn't pleased that her son ate "weeds," partly due to her fear that I would misidentify the plants in question. Yet somehow I convinced her that I could accurately identify the stinging nettle. Then I showed her a number of books that proclaimed them perfectly wholesome when cooked. I was thereby granted permission to eat nettles. From then on, I no longer had to prepare wild greens in secret – as long as I could pass them off as "nettles" to my mother's undiscriminating eye.

I did honestly eat a lot of stinging nettles. There was a patch across some railroad tracks and a small field from our house, and I visited it several times a week in the spring and early summer. On camping trips I would always search for a patch of stinging nettles to add to my fare. I ate the greens with a little salt and drank the cooking water as tea with sugar or honey. Stinging nettle became one of my favorite wild edibles, too.

When the only other wild potherbs that I'd tried were dandelion, plantain, common mallow, burdock, winter cress, and black mustard, I was quite impressed with stinging nettles – I could actually eat a whole serving of them. Over the years, however, as I learned more and more edible wild plants, I ate fewer and fewer stinging nettle greens. In my opinion, the ecstatic descriptions of their flavor found in so many books is overwrought, and the occasional comparison to asparagus is both cliché and unrealistic. Although the flavor of stinging nettle greens is good, their coarse texture leaves many people disappointed. They are always rather stringy, no matter how early the plants are harvested. This doesn't mean that you shouldn't eat stinging nettle greens; I still do several times a year. They are still highly nutritious and readily available. But if you get burned-out or discouraged by stinging nettles, don't give up on wild greens.

Description

Stinging nettle is a tall and elegant perennial herb that grows in dense colonies connected by a network of narrow rhizomes. The stalks rarely exceed .4 inch (1 cm) in diameter. They are hollow and squarish with four deep grooves running their length, and rarely branch except where the plants have been injured. The stalks are typically 5–8 feet (1.5–2.5 m) tall at maturity. The bark of the stem is composed of strong fibers, which can easily be noted when the plant is broken. The main stem, petioles, and leaf surface bear stinging hairs, although these are generally absent from lower parts of the main stem after the plants reach full size.

The leaves, 2–5 inches (5–13 cm) long and coarsely toothed, are found in opposite pairs every few inches along the upper half of the stalk. They are ovate or lanceolate with a pointed tip and usually a heart-shaped base. The veins are depressed, giving them a rough appearance. The petioles are relatively long, as much as 2.5 inches (6.5 cm), and tend to be shorter towards the top of the plant.

Flowers are produced in small, branching clusters, usually less than 3 inches (8 cm) long, which spread from the leaf axils. Each flower is tiny, inconspicuous, and greenish; the small fruits are hidden in the remains of the flowering parts.

I have just described stinging nettle as I know it; in warmer climates this plant grows progressively larger and has larger, more dangerous stingers. A friend who recently spent a year in Nepal doing botany work told me that the *U. dioica* there grows like bamboo, 12–20 feet (4–6 m) tall and 1 inch (2.5 cm) thick, producing frightful stingers that will cause intense pain lasting for days. Be careful around such monster nettles.

Range and Habitat

Stinging nettles are found almost anywhere in North America where there is proper habitat, although they are uncommon or absent in the high mountains of the West, the dry plains, and the far north.

There is widespread confusion about the history of this plant on our continent. *Urtica dioica* is native to Europe and was brought here by colonists, but there were already stinging nettles present in North America. Some authorities recognize two species of native stinging nettle: *U. gracilis* and *U. lyallii*, while

Stinging nettle *U. gracilis* in flower.

other botanists consider the European and the North American forms to be of one species. Without getting into that debate, we will consider them all together in this account for the sake of convenience. Their food uses are identical, the plants look very similar, and they are believed to hybridize regularly, so there is little purpose discriminating between the native and imported stock.

The natural habitat of the stinging nettle is sunny openings in rich soil along rivers, streams, and lakes. This is where one finds the smaller, sparser, more narrow-leaved plants with fewer and smaller stingers that supposedly represent our native stock. Stinging nettle also does very well in areas disturbed by humans, as long as there is sufficient sunlight, very rich soil, and ample moisture.

Vigorous stinging nettle colonies grow along ditches, fencerows, and the lower edges of cultivated fields, and in abandoned farm fields and empty lots. This plant thrives on old, rotten piles of manure or hay around barns and the like, because it has a high nitrogen requirement. In many regions the stinging nettle is an abundant weed.

Harvest and Preparation

The first thing on the mind of those who ponder a culinary experiment with stinging nettles is invariably the sting. Most foraging guides recommend wearing gloves when gathering nettles. This is a good idea, but I do it bare-handed, as do most people I know. Occasionally I get stung. It's no big deal. I find that the hindrance of getting stung is not nearly as great as the hindrance of having to find and carry gloves, or the simple displeasure of wearing them. Whether or not you want protection is up to you and will depend greatly upon the potency of your local nettles. In my area the plants have few stingers, and these inflict mild stings.

I don't want you to think that I'm some macho woodsman who pretends not to feel nettle stings. I don't like them either. This isn't about being tough; it's about practicality. Needing gloves is a hindrance, and most of the time that I gather stinging nettles I do not get stung at all. There is a methodology to picking them that will greatly reduce the frequency of stings.

Young stinging nettle *U. dioica* plants at a good size for harvesting.

First, you only let the thick-skinned tips of your fingers touch the plants. (Inadvertently brushing the delicate skin of the wrist on a plant next to the one from which you are picking is the most common way to get stung while collecting.) The stinging hairs on the stem generally lean toward the top of the plant, and if pressed toward the stem in the direction of their lean rather than against it, they rarely prick you. Also, stings that you get from swiping across the stingers are generally much less severe than those that occur from pressing directly down on them. The thickness and toughness of the skin on your fingers will greatly affect how this method works for you (men generally have a much easier time than women), but most people find it not to be very difficult. With practice you can learn to pluck nettle shoots and greens carefully, respectfully, and precisely, while getting stung only rarely – and you will be able to outstrip any glove-encumbered collector beside you.

Young stinging nettle plants can be collected in the early spring soon after the ground thaws. You can find them at this time by the dead stalks of last year's plants, for they will appear in the same place each season. I pick the upper two or three pairs of leaves – which usually ends up being 4–6 inches (10–15 cm) of growth.

Stinging nettle leaves often have a musky, hemp-like scent when raw,

Young stinging nettle *U. gracilis* plants. Photo by Glenn Schmukler.

especially the young ones. This smell can be rather unappealing, but it disappears with cooking. The greens are at their prime for the first few weeks after they come up, during which time the leaves often have a purple tint that makes them darker than those of the adult plant. At this time they also have a more ruffled appearance than the mature leaves. As they grow the plants will get progressively more fibrous – especially the stalks. When they exceed about a foot in height I will take only the top two pairs of leaves for greens, and by early summer, when the nettle stalks are above my waist, they are tough enough that I generally do not collect them for use as greens.

Cooking nettles, even briefly, destroys their stinging property and renders them completely safe for consumption. After steaming or boiling, nettle greens can be employed in almost any recipe as one would use spinach. Their flavor is hearty and wholesome, with no bitterness or other strong taste; few who like green vegetables will find objection to them. I most often eat them served with a little salt, as a side to meat or fish along with wild rice or a starchy vegetable. I also like to chop nettle leaves fine and use them in soup, for they make a richly-flavored and filling vegetable broth.

The leaves can be used for tea, even long after they are too tough to enjoy as greens. Nettle tea is produced by boiling the leaves; it is yellow-green when freshly brewed but turns to a dark green if it is allowed to sit, or when made from dried leaves. This tea is a rich brew of nettle essence; hearty, filling, and very nutritious, it feels more like a food than a beverage. It is excellent unadulterated, but I prefer it with a little bit of honey or maple syrup. Adding salt turns it into soup broth.

I like to dry nettle leaves for making tea or soup during the winter. Made from dehydrated greens these taste almost as good as when prepared from the fresh plant. Drying nettles, like cooking them, destroys their stinging capacity. I take the dry leaves and rub them between the palms of my hands to get a green powder, which can easily be mixed with almost any dish to add color, flavor, and nourishment.

Nettles are extremely nutritious. They are high in vitamin C, very high in vitamin A, and according to some sources are higher in protein than any other known green vegetable. They are also high in calcium, potassium, magnesium, and iron (Brill, 1994). Nettles are so eminently nutritious that without their chemical protection, they would be quickly annihilated by hungry herbivores. Deer will scour nettle patches and pluck off those occasional leaves, branches, or even plants that are devoid of stingers. If the deer ever figure out how to cook, the nettles are going to be in big trouble.

Wood Nettle *Laportea canadensis*	**Stinging Nettle** *Urtica dioica*
Likes shade or partial shade	Likes full sun
Primarily inhabits river bottom forests and mesic hardwoods	Inhabits ditches, rich moist fields, open streamsides
Associates include ostrich fern, hopniss, tall meadow rue	Associates include reed canary grass, American elder, giant sunflower
Mature leaves ovate, alternate	Mature leaves lanceolate, opposite
Mature plant has usually less than a dozen leaves, distinctly larger toward the top	Mature plant usually has two dozen or more leaves of roughly the same size
8 inch (20 cm) shoot has a few drooping leaves on top	Has no shoot; 8 inch (20 cm) plant has several pairs of upraised leaves
Shoot stem round, solid, juicy, strongly tapered	Young plant's stem grooved, hollow, not juicy, little taper
Shoots appear in late spring (mid May)	Leafy plants appear in early spring (early April)
Plants very frost-sensitive	Plants persist after several frosts
Male flowers in clusters from leaf axils, female flowers in a large, flat, branching cluster on top	Flowers in small, strand-like clusters in leaf axils; no large cluster on top
Seeds dark brown, flattened, a little smaller than flax seeds	Seeds are very small, imbedded in flowering parts, not easily visible
3 to 5 feet (1–1.5 m) tall when mature	5 to 8 feet (1.5–2.5 m) tall when mature
New shoots and autumn plants have few active stingers; summer plants sting worse than stinging nettle	Stings as soon as it comes up in spring and well into the fall, but generally milder than the sting of wood nettle
Shoots make delicious, tender vegetable	Young plants good but slightly tough
Excellent greens, very nutritious	Good greens, very nutritious
Makes a delicious, hearty tea	Makes a delicious, hearty tea

Wood Nettle

Laportea canadensis

Young wood nettle shoots.

Wood nettle doesn't get even one-tenth the coverage of stinging nettle in the wild food literature, despite the fact that, in the opinions of most who have tried both plants, it is the superior vegetable by a wide margin. One must ask why the wood nettle is usually relegated to a brief acknowledgement in the "related edible plants" section of a stinging nettle account. Certainly the fact that stinging nettle is a European plant accounts for much of its fame; folklore and knowledge of its use came to the new world with the settlers, who knew nothing of the wood nettle that was endemic to the new continent. But that isn't the whole answer.

Many people collect wood nettle and call it "stinging nettle." Although both plants sting, some people erroneously assume that any nettle that stings is "stinging nettle." The two species are quite easy to differentiate, but even naturalists who should know better confuse them. Elias and Dykeman's *Field Guide to North American Edible Wild Plants*, one of the best-selling and most trusted references on the subject, shows a photograph on page 78 that is captioned "Stinging nettle: young plants," which actually shows a cluster of wood nettle shoots. Line drawings of "stinging nettle" in many books display a mixture of characteristics from both plants, resembling wood nettle at least as much as its cousin. The confusion must be widespread; I often hear stinging nettle shoots compared to asparagus, despite the fact that, besides being green plant matter, these two vegetables have virtually nothing in common. Wood nettle shoots, on the other hand, are notably reminiscent of asparagus in both flavor and texture; they are most likely the vegetable truly being esteemed in these comparisons.

If you like stinging nettles, you'll probably like wood nettles even more. If you've been let down because the young stinging nettles that you've tried did not live up to the raving reports that led you to do so, give wood nettle a shot. It just might live up to those original expectations. In my case, it exceeded them.

Description

Wood nettles grow from 2–5 feet (.6–1.5 m) tall, forming dense and often very extensive colonies by means of its creeping rhizomes. The stems are rounded in cross section and the bark is composed of very strong fibers. The unbranching stalks zigzag between alternate leaves that are widely spaced on the upper third or so of the plant. The stalk, petioles, and leaves are protected by long, stinging hairs.

Wood nettle leaves are broadly ovate, 3–7 inches (8–18 cm) long, and grow on petioles as much as 4 inches (10 cm) long. The coarsely-toothed leaves are thin and delicate with a soft look to them, somewhat resembling basswood leaves.

Wood nettle flowers grow in branching clusters from the leaf axils; the

Large, flat seed cluster atop a wood nettle plant in late summer. The seeds are hidden, dangling from the underside of this odd structure.

lower clusters are small, but those on the top of the plant are large and spread out over the upper leaves in a flattened panicle. The flowers are very small, inconspicuous, and a drab greenish color. The dark-brown, disc-like seeds are borne in late summer and fall.

Range and Habitat

The wood nettle is distributed across most of North America east of the Plains, except for the far north. Its primary habitat is river floodplain forests, where it often forms enormous colonies that cover many acres in a nearly pure stand. Smaller colonies of it grow along streams or ponds, or in moist depressions, ravines, or steep slopes in rich hardwood forests. In shady places the plants tend to be much smaller. Common associates include ostrich fern and tall meadow rue.

Harvest and Preparation

Wood nettle shoots come up in the middle of spring, about a month later than those of stinging nettle. They are totally different from the shoots of its relative in appearance and culinary application. When they first emerge they are mostly stem, with just a small tuft of leaves on the top. Such stems have yet to fully develop their stinging capability and can be harvested without gloves. Collect them by pinching or cutting a little bit above ground level. (The very bottom of the shoots will often be reddish and will usually be tough.) Try to collect them where the plants are clean, for the hairy stems can hold dirt.

Wood nettle in mid summer.

Wood nettle shoots differ from those of stinging nettle in that most of their volume is in the stem rather than the leaves (and in that they don't feel like boiled alfalfa in your mouth). These shoots are tender, juicy, and solid all the way through; after boiling they are soft and delicious. Wood nettle shoots are one of my favorite cooked green vegetables; their flavor is mild, slightly sweet, and thoroughly likeable. I love to eat them simply served with a little salt and butter, like asparagus. They combine delectably with mashed wapato and are one of my favorite soup ingredients. You can also rub all of the stingers off of wood nettle shoots (the stem part only, NOT the leaves), or peel off the skin (which takes the stingers with it) and eat them raw. They are juicy, slightly crunchy, and delicious.

After the plants get a little taller and the leaves unfurl, the stingers will become more formidable. At this time you will need to exercise extreme caution or use gloves when collecting the shoots or leafy tops. Despite names which imply the opposite, wood nettle generally has larger, longer, and more potent stingers than the stinging nettle, and it is armed with more of them.

From slightly larger (but still young and fast-growing) wood nettle plants with fully formed leaves, I pluck the top 4–6 inches (10–15 cm). The tops are good for greens if they bend and break easily and do not yet have tough, stringy skin. These cooked stems and greens will be much more tender than those of stinging nettle, but with an almost identical flavor. I use the tender topmost leaves of wood nettle as greens until early summer. At any time during the growing season I will use the leaves for making nettle tea; there is virtually no difference between wood and stinging nettles in this regard.

Wood nettle shoots and greens are an important component of my diet. Since they are found in such immense quantities and can be easily gathered, I store a fairly large amount every year by canning. They can also be frozen. While the canned shoots or greens are not nearly as good as fresh ones, they make a nice addition to soup, casserole, wild rice, or mashed wapato. Wood nettle leaves toughen as they dry and do not crumble well like those of stinging nettle.

The wood nettle produces another excellent food product: the seeds. These are surprisingly similar to flax seeds in size, shape, texture, and flavor, becoming mucilaginous when cooked. Wood nettle seeds ripen in late summer and fall. I harvest them (wearing gloves – the stems are well armed!) by cutting off the entire seedheads. The individual seeds are naked and hang from the underside of the seed cluster. After drying, they detach from the heads, and any unwanted debris can be cleaned out by rubbing and winnowing. Use this wood nettle grain in hot cereal or breads as you would use flax seed.

Through many years of foraging I ignored the wood nettle as a food source because the literature ignored it. When curiosity finally got the best of me and I tried this plant, I was pleasantly surprised. Even though I felt betrayed by what no book had told me, I was excited to think that similar unheralded delicacies must be waiting in the woods to be rediscovered.

Sheep Sorrel

Rumex acetosella

Sheep sorrel leaves, perfect for harvest.

Children love sheep sorrel. Somehow, millions of youngsters across the continent have learned to eat this plant without adult instruction. Once they learn, they pass the information on to each other. It spreads like wildfire. Parents who grew up eating sheep sorrel just watch and smile, while those who never knew this plant as a child gasp in horror to see their green-tongued children merrily grazing on "sour grass" in the front yard. Fear not. Examine the plant: if it looks like sheep sorrel, and it tastes like sheep sorrel, and the kids say they've always eaten it, then it is sheep sorrel, and you ought to join the fun.

Description

Sheep sorrel is a small perennial classified in the same genus as the docks, but it is smaller and more delicate with foliage of a wholly different texture than typical docks. The basal leaves of sheep sorrel are rather succulent but not thick, borne on slightly grooved petioles, and are usually 1.5–3 inches (4–8 cm) in length. Widening towards the tip, they are typically lopsided with two lobes or flares at the base. The leaves of young plants usually do not have the flares at the base; instead, they are simply spoon-shaped. The surface of sheep sorrel's leaf is covered with numerous structures that reflect sunlight, so that when one holds it up in the light and looks closely, it sparkles.

Sheep sorrel's flowering stalks rarely exceed 14 inches (36 cm) in height. These have a few small leaves borne alternately upon the stem, clasping it with a papery sheath. The upper part of the stalk bears a loosely branched spike of tiny green and reddish flowers. In early summer one often sees entire fields or roadsides colored in a rusty hue from millions of these flowers.

There are other species of edible sorrel found growing wild in North America. None are as widespread or common as sheep sorrel, but they may be as good or better for eating. The cultivated garden sorrel *R. acetosa*, is a much larger cousin that has escaped and grows wild in some parts of the Northeast. Wild sorrel, *R. hastatulus*, found in the southeastern United States, is very similar to sheep sorrel but somewhat larger.

Mature, flowering
sheep sorrel plant.

Range and Habitat

Sheep sorrel is one of the most accessible wild edibles in North America. Growing from coast to coast and from Canada to Mexico, it is equally at home in the wilderness or the front yard.

Sheep sorrel likes sunny sites that are sparsely vegetated, especially where the soil consists of sand or gravel. Although this herb needs well-drained soil, its moisture requirements prevent it from growing in arid areas. The best places to find sheep sorrel are old fields on sandy soil, roadsides, gravel and sand pits, and naturally bare sites such as steep slopes, beaches, and banks. This plant is often abundant in dry, sunny, pine-oak barrens or woodlands. I have seen large, healthy patches of it in gardens, agricultural fields, and yards, as well as in places far from recent disturbance. It spreads by rhizome as well as by seed and is considered a pesky weed by many.

Harvest and Preparation

The part of sheep sorrel that is used for food is the leaf; the stems and leaf stalks are too tough, and the flowering parts are small and bitter. Sheep sorrel leaves can be gathered from spring to fall. Look for the largest, most succulent leaves, and avoid those that have any red coloring, as these will be bitter. Leaves from flowering plants are tougher and more bitter than those from nonflowering specimens; I carefully avoid these when gathering sheep sorrel greens.

When you cook sheep sorrel, it shrinks to an almost absurd degree, so gather *a lot* – and that still might not be enough. You don't have to cook it, however; sheep sorrel is excellent on sandwiches, in salads, or just to nibble while you're out walking.

Sheep sorrel is very sour. Most people are a little shocked the first time they taste this plant because it packs an unexpected punch. The sour taste is due to a high concentration of oxalic acid, the same chemical that makes rhubarb sour.

You may have heard warnings about the danger of consuming too much oxalic acid. Although such warnings are repeated endlessly in the gossip-research of wild food literature, they are unwarranted. There is simply no evidence that plants containing this chemical are unsafe for humans – unless consumed in quantities that no human being would ever voluntarily eat (Kallas, 2001). I have found no documented cases of such poisonings in humans. There are many foods containing oxalic acid, yet one does not find such warnings accompanying recipes for cultivated plants blessed with this chemical. And I did say *blessed*, because there are few flavors that are as universally liked as that of oxalic acid.

Although sheep sorrel is not likely to be the main course in anybody's dinner, it has a wide range of culinary applications due to its pleasing sourness. Most of us douse our salads with vinegar to give it an acid flavor; sheep sorrel leaves can be used to replace some or all of this vinegar – although the flavor will not be the same. Dishes based on rice or couscous can be bland and boring without a touch of sour. Tradition-ally we might employ dried

Sheep sorrel seedlings, lacking flares.

tomatoes or a vinegar-based sauce to add the desired flavor, but sheep sorrel leaves will work marvelously in this capacity.

In my own kitchen the most important use of sheep sorrel is as an ingredient in soup. It is amazing what a handful or two of sheep sorrel greens does for a soup that is lacking that certain *je ne sais quoi*.

I have not tried drying or canning sheep sorrel greens because they are so small that they are difficult to collect in quantity. I suspect that either procedure would significantly reduce the sourness, but would still result in a good product.

It would be nice to have some sheep sorrel stored for the winter, but when it finds its way into my kitchen, it seems to quickly proceed to my stomach. The garden sorrel, considered a gourmet vegetable, is served only in the finest restaurants. Sheep sorrel, though smaller, is just as gourmet. Learn to identify this ubiquitous weed and you can have it throughout the growing season for free.

Goosefoot, Lamb's Quarters

Chenopodium spp.

Young maple-leaved goosefoot plants.

Current science tends to trickle down to the public fifty years or so after the fact – if it ever gets there. Thus today it is still widely believed that North American agriculture originated in Mexico, working its way slowly to the United States and reaching the Eastern Woodlands thousands of years later. Today, however, experts agree that agriculture originated in the Central Mississippi Valley independent of the happenings in Mexico, at a time roughly concurrent or only slightly later (Smith, 1999). The plants cultivated in this independent hearth of domestication were native to the United States and included only two that are significant crops today: sunflowers and squash. Also grown for their seeds were plants called sumpweed or marsh-elder *Iva annua* and goosefoot *Chenopodium berlandieri* (Smith, 1992). Thousands of years before Europeans set foot on this continent, Native Americans were growing luxuriant gardens of goosefoot for its easily-stored seeds and nutritious, tender greens.

While the domesticated form of goosefoot eventually died out in North America after the introduction of maize and beans, the species cultivated in the highlands of South America, quinoa *Chenopodium quinoa*, is still grown there, and its grain is available today in our health food stores. Archeologists have found remains of goosefoot thousands of years old in excavations around the world. Obviously, these plants were of great importance to people who hunted and gathered for a living, as well as to many early, and some modern, agriculturalists. For those who wish to reap where they did not sow, they are still among the most useful plants to know.

Description

There are several similar edible species in the genus *Chenopodium*, the best known and perhaps most abundant being *C. album*, commonly called lamb's quarters, goosefoot, or pigweed. This annual herb may grow to be 7 feet (2 m) tall, but 3–5 feet (1–1.5 m) is typical.

It is usually branched but tends to be taller than it is wide. The stems are grooved and often tinted red, especially near the leaf joints.

Leaves, up to 4 inches (10 cm) long, are borne alternately on petioles about half their length. Roughly diamond-shaped when mature, the leaves are irregularly toothed or shallowly lobed. They are dark bluish-green above but are often coated with a thick, whitish-gray powder on the underside, especially near the tips of vigorously growing plants. The small leaves near the top of the mature plants are linear or lanceolate in shape and lack teeth on their margins.

The flowers of goosefoot are tiny, green, and inconspicuous, clustered on spikes in the upper leaf axils and at the plant's tip. They appear at any time from early summer until autumn. Later the plant produces thousands of tiny, round, dark brown or black seeds,

Mature lamb's quarters plant.

187

each one enclosed in a persistent calyx. The fruiting heads appear as lumpy masses of green at the top of the plant; these turn to reddish and then to brown as they mature and dry in the fall.

Another common species of the East, growing up to 7 feet (2 m) tall, is the maple-leaved goosefoot *C. hybridum* (sometimes also known as *C. simplex*). This plant has larger leaves than lamb's quarters; they have very large teeth separated by shallow lobes, and the tip of the leaf is long and tapering. Usually darker green than that of lamb's quarters, maple-leaved goosefoot's foliage lacks the whitish powder on the undersurface. The flowers and seeds of this plant are spread out more loosely on their spikes than are those of lamb's quarters. When young, maple-leaved goosefoot often has a strong musky smell, yet its flavor is pleasant and nearly identical to that of other goosefoots.

Other edible members of this genus include *C. capitatum* of the northern part of the continent and the Rocky Mountains, *C. fremontii* of the West, and *C. berlandieri* of the central United States, plus many others.

Two members of this genus should not be considered part of this discussion: Mexican tea *C. ambrosioides*, and Jerusalem-oak or epazote *C. botrys*. Both of these plants have very strong, aromatic odors and may be unsafe to eat in quantity; they appear quite different from typical goosefoots.

Range and Habitat

At least one species of goosefoot is found in every part of North America, except perhaps the Arctic. The most widespread is probably lamb's quarters, which has followed humans almost everywhere that they have gone. (There is some confusion about the classification of these plants, hinging on the typical disagreements between those who prefer to lump plants together and those who prefer to divide them into separate species. I am using the term "lamb's quarters" here in its more inclusive sense, as some botanists do, covering several similar forms. Even though I recognize more than one kind of "lamb's quarters" when I am collecting, there is no difference in how I would treat these different types as food.)

It is commonly believed that lamb's quarters is not native to our continent, but archeologists have found *Chenopodium* seeds dating back thousands of years (Smith, 1992). Depending on classification, these seeds may or may not represent *C. album*; but some of them certainly represent plants that would commonly be called "lamb's quarters." Apparently, like stinging nettle, black nightshade, human beings, and many other cosmopolitan weeds, this species

Young lamb's
quarters plants.

was indeed brought from Europe – but to a continent that already had its own indigenous strain.

Lamb's quarters and similar goosefoot species are abundant weeds of agricultural fields, gardens, yards, roadsides, construction sites, empty urban lots, sunny slopes, beaches, or any other place where the soil is bare or disturbed. In the wild areas of the East they are largely confined to river bottoms, which regularly have areas of soil exposed or deposited by floods. In the West these plants are often found in desert or semi-arid regions, where there is bare soil upon which they can complete their life cycle quickly when moisture is supplied. In any of these cases the seeds can remain viable for long periods of time, waiting for the opportunity to germinate.

Maple-leaved goosefoot is primarily a plant of hardwood forests, where its seeds persist for decades in the soil. When proper conditions for germination present themselves, such as happens after blowdowns, fires, logging, or the construction of roads, these plants pop up all over the place. They are more tolerant of shade than most other species of *Chenopodium*.

Harvest and Preparation: Greens

Goosefoot is a warm-weather plant, not appearing until late spring after the danger of frost has passed. You can pick the young plants as soon as they appear. Some people use garden shears to cut them, but I just pinch off the succulent stalks near the base. Until they are six to twelve inches tall (depending on growing conditions) you can use the whole plant as a potherb. As they get taller you will have to use your discretion and collect only the tender top parts of the shoot. Usually, as long as they do not yet have flowers, the top few inches are good to eat. Many savvy gardeners who have learned to recognize goosefoot combine the tasks of weeding and harvesting – eating the succulent shoots before they get tall enough to shade the cultivated vegetables. Even after the plants have matured and the stems have toughened, the individual leaves will be reasonably tender. Thus goosefoot provides readily available greens through early autumn.

Goosefoot is closely related to spinach and has a similar flavor. The greens taste mild but hearty and can be used in any recipe that calls for cooked spinach, such as quiche, omelets, or lasagna, with fine results. They are excellent raw in salads or sandwiches. Most often, however, I eat my goosefoot greens just steamed or boiled in a very small amount of water and served with a little salt, as a side to the main course of a meal. If the tops are heavily coated with the gritty whitish powder that characterizes these plants, you will probably want to rub and rinse it off before cooking or eating the greens.

Unfortunately, goosefoot has a quality that irritates the tongues of some people, myself included, when it is eaten in quantity. If you have this problem with spinach, as I do, you will also have it with goosefoot. This does not stop me from eating the greens many times each year – it just means that I have

Lamb's quarters seeds
in early October,
mature but not dry.

to eat them in small servings or mixed with other foods. (But that's how one would normally consume a green vegetable anyway.)

One fall when I was working at an apple orchard we burned some brush, creating a big, bare, charred patch of ground. Lamb's quarters came up thick as dog's hair in that little burnt circle a week or so later, and I enjoyed it every day for a while, happy to have tender greens so late in the year. One clear, cool October day, however, I knew that frost would come with nightfall, so after work I harvested the whole patch of goosefoot greens, brought them home, and stayed up into the wee hours tending my pressure canner. If you aren't into pressure canning, you can store them by drying, or blanching and freezing.

Goosefoot Grain

Large goosefoot plants bear thousands of tiny seeds surrounded by a fine chaffy covering. These can be collected from late summer through the winter by stripping the seed-fruit clusters into a container by hand. I prefer to do this when the clusters have turned brown and dried in late fall or even early winter. Moist clusters need to be dried promptly after collection or they will mold or spoil. These seed clusters can be collected at a fairly fast rate of more than a gallon per hour – sometimes much more. Avoid harvesting them near bare, dry agricultural fields, for high winds in such places will often blow dirt and grit into the seed clusters, where it lodges and gets mixed in with the grain.

The seed clusters will appear as a lumpy brown mass, but if you rub the material firmly between the palms of your hands it will loosen the chaff to reveal small, round seeds that are dark brown or black. If the seeds are light brown or shrunken, your material was probably collected before it had time to mature.

Removing the chaff from goosefoot seeds is a chore; I would like to see how Native Americans of bygone years performed this task. I do it by rubbing firmly between my hands or two pieces of rubber and then winnowing away the trash. This reduces the volume dramatically, and it takes a lot more labor than simply harvesting the seeds. And while winnowing, the seeds themselves are so light that it is hard to keep them from blowing away with the chaff.

Some people that I have talked to do not separate the chaff from the seeds, but these are people who don't eat much goosefoot grain, either. The chaff is mostly indigestible and it comprises most of the bulk of the seed material; I think you could eat all the unseparated goosefoot grain you want and still starve. Plus the chaff does not taste as good as the grain itself. If you really

Dry seedhead of maple-leaved goosefoot in midwinter, still loaded with seeds.

want to eat goosefoot seeds, you should plan on separating them.

In my experience, the maple-leaved goosefoot is the best species to harvest for grain. Its seeds are much larger than those of other goosefoots, so they do not blow aside so easily during winnowing. (In fact, the North American *C. hybridum* is sometimes classified as *C. gigantospermum*, meaning "giant-seeded goosefoot.") Each seed has a proportionately smaller, more loosely attached calyx than other goosefoots, so there is less trash to get rid of and what there is separates more easily from the grain. Maple-leaf goosefoot seeds are more time-consuming to collect than those of other species, but the fact that they are *much* easier to rub and winnow more than makes up for this initial hindrance.

The grain can be boiled and eaten as a hot cereal, but it doesn't soften very well because of the hard seedcoat. I like the taste, which is quite like quinoa, but the texture and appearance gives me the odd feeling that I am eating black sand. To change the texture and allow them to soften more easily, you can grind the seeds coarsely and cook the meal as mush. You can also grind them more finely into flour to use mixed with other flours. *Chenopodium* seeds are high in protein, have some oil, and are a good source of starch.

It is no wonder that hunting and gathering people the world over chose to harvest and sometimes cultivate this superb dual-purpose food plant. In fact, what is strange is that we ever stopped.

Spring Beauty

Claytonia spp.

Flowers of *C. virginica.*

There are many who say that we should not eat spring beauty because it is such a beautiful spring wildflower. They are right about one thing: it is quite pretty. But I'm not yet convinced that there is any merit in limiting my diet to ugly things. If that were the case, I wouldn't be foraging at all, as there is not a single wild plant that I find unattractive. And while I must admit that subjectively some plants really do please the eye more than others, spring beauty (no disrespect intended) is not near the top of my list.

Would this hands-off attitude be so widely espoused if the plant happened to go by a less elegant sobriquet, like hepatica, ramp, baneberry, or hagar? I think not. So why should we let the same bygone consortium of incompetent name-manglers who gave us such gems as *bastard toadflax* and *lesser broomrape* decide what we can and cannot eat?

In virtually every wild food book that covers this plant you will find an advisory not to harvest it "except where abundant" or "in times of desperate need" because it is "a beautiful wildflower." I wholeheartedly agree that we need to employ sensible restraint while foraging, never forgetting ecological considerations and never threatening the populations of the plants we harvest, but I object to this special and irrational treatment lavished upon one plant for no reason other than its name or its physical appearance.

One *never* finds such admonitions to refrain from harvesting ramps in the wild food literature. Ramps, like spring beauty, are slowly-reproducing, long-lived woodland ephemerals; the two plants have the same habitat requirements in the eastern U.S. and Canada. While spring beauty is collected very rarely and I have never heard of problems caused by its overharvest, ramps are among the most popular wild vegetables on the continent and have been exterminated from many woodlands by collectors. Ramps are in fact more susceptible to overharvest than spring beauty, but apparently they are simply too ugly to be concerned about.

Spring beauty is an abundant plant in much of eastern North America. In the woods where I live, if you blindly tossed a hula hoop, it would land encircling a spring beauty plant nearly every time. The plant abounds over millions of acres in Wisconsin alone, and it is not unusually common here. So give the gathering of spring beauty the same careful consideration you give to any other plant that is killed when harvested, but don't feel guilty about eating it. Feel joyful.

Description

Spring beauties are in the purslane family along with several other edibles such as bitterroot, purslane, and miner's lettuce. (A few botanists even classify miner's lettuce in the same genus.) There are about a dozen species of spring beauty in North America, with most of that diversity in the West. All spring beauties are small, fleshy perennials, less than 10 inches (25 cm) tall. Because most of my experience is with *C. virginica* and *C. caroliniana*, the following discussion will focus on those species. While all the spring beauties are considered edible, readers will have to refer to other sources or their own experience to determine how the various kinds compare.

A typical spring beauty plant is composed of several short stems emanating from a single root. These stems are frail in appearance and can hardly support their own weight; often they lay prostrate on the ground. Typically there is a single pair of dark green leaves growing opposite each other about half way up the stalk; on *C. virginica* these are lanceolate or elongated and grass-like and lack petioles, while on *C. caroliniana* they are ovate and borne on short petioles. The leaves of spring beauty are soft, thick, and succulent, with little venation showing.

The flowers have five white or light pink petals with darker pink veins. They are about .5 to .7 inch (13–18 mm) wide, borne in a loose cluster at the apex of the plant. The blossoms open only in sunshine and usually turn to face the sun. One never finds a single, isolated spring beauty stem. Instead, they grow in colonies, and these colonies are often quite dense, containing many hundreds of stems.

Both *C. caroliniana* and *C. virginica* are spring ephemerals. Perhaps the perception that they are rare stems partly from their brief growing season of five to nine weeks. During the other ten months of the year, this beauty sleeps in the soil in the form of a "fairy spud," which is a roundish, slightly flattened, enlarged root ranging from .25 to 1.5 inches (.6–4cm) across. The root typically looks like a dark, puffed pita bread, but older specimens become more irregular in shape. The fairy spud is really the essence of what spring-beauty-hood is; the stems and blossoms are but short-lived effusions from it. Each root sends up multiple stalks. Year by year, the root gets larger and sends up more stalks; some produce over a dozen.

Virginia spring beauty *Claytonia virginica.*

There is disagreement in the literature as to whether the fairy spud is a tuber or a corm, with corm seeming to be the slightly more popular term. In fact, it is neither; it is a root.

Were it a corm, it would be an enlarged part of the upright stem, as with jack-in-the-pulpit or crocus. The upper stem would not easily detach from the enlarged base while growing. Corms are found *one per stalk*, because the corm is simply a part of the stalk, and it is usually more or less centered on it. (This is in fact how spring beauty "corms" are erroneously drawn in Peterson's *A Field Guide to Edible Wild Plants*, but the real ones don't look like that.) Corms also have a root crown *under them*, while spring beauty roots appear to have a distinct root crown *on top of them*. Since the multiple stems all emanate from this root crown, and the fairy spuds do not grow any buds or underground stems as tubers do, they should be considered roots. In fact, it is very easy to recognize the large taproot of the alpine spring beauty as such, and there has not been any debate about the matter; the smaller fairy spuds are just short, squat, unusually shaped versions of this taproot.

Range and Habitat

In the East, spring beauty is a plant of rich hardwood forests, especially those dominated by sugar maple. It is strongly associated with other mesic forest plants such as toothwort, jack-in-the-pulpit, maidenhair fern, blue cohosh, trout lily, wild leek, and Dutchman's breeches. It is widespread and often extremely abundant in such forests. Spring beauty is also found in river bottom woodlands.

Various western species inhabit different ecological niches. The western spring beauty *Claytonia lanceolata* grows in moist woods and openings in much of the mountainous West, often in great abundance. It produces lanceolate leaves that clasp the stem. Sierra spring beauty *C. nevadensis* has a more limited range confined to moist alpine slopes of the Sierra Nevada. This species has round leaves on short stalks. *C. acutifolia* grows in Alaska, as does the tundra species *C. tuberosa*. The two common spring beauties of the East are Virginia spring beauty *C. virginica*, and Carolina spring beauty *C. caroliniana*. Most of these species are commonly just called "spring beauty."

The most distinct spring beauty is the alpine spring beauty *C. megarrhiza*, which inhabits alpine meadows of the Rocky Mountains. It is unusual in that the plant has a rosette of rounded basal leaves as well as leaves upon the flower stalks. This plant also has an elongated taproot, which was reported by Euell

Gibbons (1973) to be quite large: about 1 inch (2.5 cm) thick at the top and up to 1 foot (30 cm) long. He considered both the roots and leaves to be delicious. Unfortunately, this plant is confined to alpine areas and is rather uncommon.

Refer to regional identification manuals to find out which species grow in your area, and find out if they are rare or protected. Foragers will have to study their local species and decide how much they can sustainably harvest, and if they are truly rare they should be left alone.

Harvest and Preparation

Spring beauty roots are usually located 2–4 inches (5–10 cm) below the surface of the soil. They can be dug rather easily with a small trowel or digging stick. Shovels work too, but they turn over so much soil that it just gets in the way, so I stick to the smaller implements.

The harvesting of fairy spuds poses a conundrum. The roots will be a little stiffer and more packed with starch both before and after their growing season, which is exactly when you usually cannot find them, because at this time there

Carolina
spring beauty
Claytonia
caroliniana.

197

is no trace of the plant above ground. Therefore, if it is practical, I dig mine up in early spring as soon as I can tell the plants are there, while they are still very small and the roots contain most of the energy – or in early summer after the stems have dried and turned yellow, sending nutrients back into the root. In real life, however, it rarely works out like that. I usually end up getting my spring beauty roots when the plants are in flower, because at that time it is easiest to notice the large colonies.

When collecting, look at the pattern of stems on the ground. After some experience, the seemingly random arrangement takes on meaning. A roughly circular or semi-circular clump of many stems suggests that a large root is somewhere in the middle of the ring. (All of those stems probably emanate from a single root.) A small tuft of four or five stems indicates a root of average size, while a carpet of seemingly unclumped stems denotes a colony of many small roots with only a few stems each. The stems might extend for three or four inches underground, confusing things a little, but you will get the hang of it.

To harvest spring beauty roots efficiently, selectively dig large ones here and there throughout a colony rather than turning over and thoroughly harvesting an area; the small roots are not worth your time. As with other wild plants, only harvest where they are well established – and do so in a sustainable fashion. Adopt the attitude of a caretaker, thinning the patch like a gardener and replanting small tubers rather than simply discarding them. Do not overestimate the fecundity of woodland perennials (wild ginseng, once a common forest plant, has been extirpated in almost all of its range in North America). Just because the spring beauty plants are abundant does not mean they can reproduce quickly; some of the large roots are probably decades old.

I will be the first to admit that gathering spring beauty roots is not very labor-efficient by modern standards. Tom Elpel of Pony, Montana, claims that he harvests about one cup of western spring beauty roots per hour (Elpel, 2002). That sounds comparable to my experience when not selectively harvesting the large roots (which is somewhat faster), and from his photos the roots appear similar in size to those that I find around here. This could help sustain a lost person, and it is fun to do it a few times a year whether you are lost or not, but I would not plan on putting up a big larder of these little guys.

That's a shame, because there are innumerable culinary possibilities for this vegetable. Fairy spuds are somewhat potato-like but softer and very mildly sweet. Just boiled they are wonderful – far superior to potatoes, in my opinion. Unlike potatoes, these roots are soft and pleasant raw as well.

Roots of spring beauty *C. virginica*, the larger one about 1.25 inches (3.2 cm) wide.

However, eating them raw sometimes leaves an unpleasant scratchy feeling in the back of my throat.

You don't have to peel spring beauty roots, but it is relatively easy to do so (especially with the large ones) when they are raw or cooked. In fact, I know of no other root or tuber that slips its skin so readily. With the skins on, they taste a little earthy, but are still quite good. With the skins removed, they really impress people. I usually peel mine because I like cuisine to be the best that it can be.

While not as well known as the fairy spuds, the greens of spring beauty are likewise an excellent food source. They are mild in flavor, thick, juicy, slightly crisp, and not stringy. I frequently use these greens in salads, and they are also good cooked. When speaking of the greens, I am referring to the entire portion of the plant that grows above ground: stems, leaves, and flowers. Spring beauty greens remind me of the closely related purslane, only the flavor of spring beauty is not so tangy; they are similar to miner's lettuce in flavor and texture.

You can easily gather the greens without destroying the plant; just don't pick all of the stems from one root. Avoid getting dirt in your collection, as the plants often lie limp directly on the soil.

Yes, spring beauty is an attractive plant, but it also tastes good. So admire it before sticking it in your mouth.

Marsh Marigold, Cowslip

Caltha palustris

Marsh marigold in the early stages of flowering, when the younger leaves are still fairly good to eat.

In the Northern United States and Canada, winter holds stubbornly to its grasp over the land. Though the snow may melt during a few warm days of March or April, the frost in the ground cannot be dispelled so lightly. As all who follow the cycle of the seasons in the wild know, that first melt and those first promising warm days are always cut short of releasing spring's splendor by a sudden return of frost. It is like the teasing peek of sunshine on an overcast afternoon. Another week or two or three of winter ensues, so that when the real thaw comes, we thank heaven and know that we deserve it.

Most of our garden plants are annuals misplaced from warmer climates and cannot handle even a light frost, but many of our native greens are endowed with an antifreeze in early spring – which colors them purple and allows them to grow even when the nighttime temperatures fall well below freezing. Even under a crust of snow, ever so slowly, skunk cabbage will begin to push its flower spathes up through the muck. Tiny purple tufts of stinging nettle, rigid and rough, hardly hint at what the plant will become in maturity. The maroon leaves of dock and swamp saxifrage spread flat over the frigid soil, and those of marsh marigold, paper-thin and glossy, curl up and huddle together above their mother-root in anxious patience. To the forager, these first greens are more precious than gems.

Identification

The marsh marigold *Caltha palustris* is a distinct and easily recognized plant. It has numerous leaves rising on long stalks from the base and a few short, branching flower stalks. The basal leaves, when mature, are ruffled and can

Marsh marigold in early spring, showing unopened flower buds. This plant is in the perfect stage to harvest from.

grow up to 7 inches (18 cm) across. At the time when they are gathered and the plants are in bloom, however, most leaves are 1–3 inches (2.5–8 cm) wide. As one moves up the flower stalk, the leaf stems get progressively shorter and the leaves smaller; the topmost leaf clasps the stalk with no stem at all. Cowslip leaves are very lightly toothed. They are kidney-shaped or round with a deep "cutout" where the stem attaches. They are very delicate and glossy when young.

The flower of this plant is well known and much appreciated as one of the first showy wildflowers of spring. Bright yellow and an inch or more across, cowslip blossoms look like giant, full-figured buttercups (to which they are related). They have 5–9 sepals that look like petals. The flowers are displayed in loose clusters. Later on they produce green, star-like fruits. Once you've identified marsh marigold in flower, you'll probably be able to spot it at any time of the growing season. Although this plant really has no dangerous look-similars, some violets do have a similar leaf shape.

Cowslip often grows side by side with the common and potently toxic water hemlock. Other than being green, the two plants look nothing alike, but a very careless forager who haphazardly mixed some of the latter herb with her cowslip greens could have serious trouble. But we're not careless, so don't sweat it.

Range and Habitat

As its name implies, this plant is an inhabitant of wet ground. It is generally found in shade or partial shade, and only rarely in full sun. Across the northeastern U.S. and almost all the wooded regions of Canada and Alaska, marsh marigold *Caltha palustris* is available to foragers. Where I live, and through much of its range, it is remarkably abundant. I have seen ash and alder swamps of many acres that looked like wildflower gardens, just brimming with the plant. Near my home there are scattered cowslip plants along every rill and drainage through the woods, and colonies surround every swamp, spring, and pond.

A closely related plant, *Caltha leptosepala,* is found in wet areas of mountain forests of the West. I have never eaten this species. H.D. Harrington (1967) often ate the flower buds and young leaves of this western marsh marigold raw in mixed salads or cooked as a potherb. Euell Gibbons (1973) reported similar uses. From these accounts it appears that this western species has a much milder and better flavor than its eastern counterpart. I have found no reports of the edibility of other North American *Caltha* species.

Mature marsh marigold, showing large leaves and star-like fruits. Photo by Glenn Schmukler.

Harvest and Preparation

Cowslip, as previously mentioned, is an early spring plant. While at certain sites one finds small leaves as soon as the snow melts, or even under it, more often the greens are unavailable until the ground thaws and spring is truly under way. Around here, that is generally early to mid April.

I prefer to gather marsh marigold when the plants are 3–7 inches (8–18 cm) high, before any flowers have opened. I gather basal leaves as well as the stalks. The small leaves and flower buds near the top of the stalk are my favorite part. I simply pinch off the cowslip greens or stalks with my thumbnail; at the proper time they are tender and easily broken. The stalks often have a dirty, papery sheath, which I remove. Marsh marigold leaves shrink considerably when they are cooked, so keep this in mind as you gather them. Later in the season, when the marsh marigold is in bloom, I am much more selective in my harvest, taking only the smaller, softer leaves. By the time the cowslips are done flowering, I am done harvesting them for the year.

Caltha palustris greens probably should not be eaten raw. The plant contains a poisonous constituent, known as protanemonin (Turner and Sczawinski, 1991), that is dispelled by boiling. The raw greens taste terribly acrid; on account of flavor alone I would not eat them. However, I know of people who have consumed small quantities of *C. palustris* raw and suffered no apparent ill effect, so the toxin is apparently rather mild.

The plant commonly called "cowslip" in England is *Primula veris*, an edible species of primrose very unlike *Caltha palustris*. This has led to much confusion over the identity of the two plants. The American cowslip or marsh marigold has been one of the most popular wild greens of the Northeast for hundreds of years. The same species also grows in England, mainland Europe, and across Asia.

The tried and true method for preparing cowslip as a potherb is to boil it for 20 to 40 minutes, discard the cooking water, and eat the greens. Many people change the water one or more times, as each change gives the greens a milder flavor. I use three waters, letting the final one boil for twenty to thirty minutes before draining and serving. When prepared this way, they are very soft in texture, forming a dark green mass after the water is drained.

Cooked cowslip greens make a unique, mushy-textured dish that some object to. I jokingly called this stuff "green pudding" once when serving the dish, and the name has stuck. I usually eat my green pudding with a little salt and butter. Some like it with cream or gravy, served on toast. I prefer the flavor of the flower buds to that of the leaves.

The problem with marsh marigold greens, however, is that they inherently taste bad. The more one boils them to leach the acrid principle out, the less bad they taste, but they never become truly good. Only by adding seasonings, cream, gravy, or other embellishments does cowslip become fit to serve to dinner guests.

The main attraction of marsh marigold is that it is abundant and easy to recognize, offering itself as a potherb over a month in advance of the earliest garden produce. There was a time when the springtime craving for wholesome fresh vegetables and dietary variety meant more to backcountry folk than the instant gratification of mere flavor. Perhaps it was this plant that prompted Robert Frost to pen the words, "Nature's first green is gold."

Swamp Saxifrage

Saxifraga pensylvanica

Swamp saxifrage stalk perfect for munching.

The swamp saxifrage is not a well-known wild edible, despite the fact that it is common throughout the northeastern United States and adjacent Canada. One finds very little said of this plant in wild food literature, so when I discovered that it was abundant in the swamps and brooksides near my home, I was excited to get to know more about it.

I first tried swamp saxifrage greens in late May some years ago and discovered that they were leathery and unpleasantly bitter. A subsequent spring I cooked the leaves about a half dozen times from late April to mid May to see if perhaps they might be more palatable earlier in the season. Although they weren't as tough and bitter at this time as the older leaves that I had tried before, they were still nothing that I would go out of my way for. Not even ten feet. Especially not in spring. I dismissed the swamp saxifrage as an inedible wild "edible."

Then one day while wandering the woods I espied a young swamp saxifrage flower stalk; it looked so succulent and appetizing that I decided to try it. I selected a large stalk, upon which the flowering parts of the top were still in a tight cluster. When I broke it off at the base, it made a sound that told me it was crisp like celery. Liquid poured out of the hollow stem. The shoot smelled inviting, but mild. I began to crunch at the base of the stem, and it was delicious. There was the same bitterness contained in the leaves, only it was faint and pleasant, as in lettuce, mixed with a light sweetness. The stem was crisp but juicier than any vegetable I had ever eaten. Since then I have been eating swamp saxifrage flower stalks whenever I get the chance; they are one of the wild treats that I covet most in spring.

Description

Swamp saxifrage is quite a distinct plant, and it is one of North America's largest species of saxifrage. It is a perennial rosette, with large leaves that grow from the base of the plant only, often hugging the ground. The blunt-tipped

Swamp saxifrage flowers.

oval or lance-shaped leaves grow as much as 10 inches (25 cm) long. The leaves are hairy, occasionally wavy, and toothed only slightly if at all. The midribs are light green and prominent, especially when viewed from underneath. Swamp saxifrage leaves grow on short, thick, flattened petioles that are often tinted red.

Individual swamp saxifrage plants do not bloom every year. When they do, the rosette sends up a single flower stalk in mid-spring. This stalk is stout, hollow, fragile, and covered with slightly sticky hairs. It grows rapidly, and while at first the flowers are clustered tightly at the top, soon the stalk branches widely into a loose panicle that may reach four feet in height. Swamp saxifrage blooms in late spring. The small, numerous flowers are about .25 inches (6 mm) wide, cream-colored to green, with five lanceolate petals. Later these produce a small, many-seeded capsule.

Range and Habitat

The northern edge of this plant's range extends roughly from northern Minnesota to Maine, and it is found as far south as Missouri and Virginia. Swamp saxifrage grows in wet meadows, brooksides, hardwood swamps, and along ponds and springs. It is most common in areas of partial shade.

There are numerous species of saxifrage in North America, especially in the west. I have heard of none in the genus *Saxifraga* that are known to be toxic, but certainly they vary greatly in their qualities. The leaves of lettuce saxifrage or deer tongue *S. micranthidifolia*, which grows along streams and brooks in the Appalachians from Pennsylvania to North Carolina, are reported to be a popular potherb and salad green in parts of that region (Medsger, 1929). The brook saxifrage *S. punctata*, which grows on brooksides at high elevations in the mountainous West, is said by Elpel (2000) to make a good, mild-flavored salad plant or cooked green.

Harvest and Preparation

There are two edible parts of the swamp saxifrage plant (if you consider them both edible). Chronologically, the first is the young leaves, which can be used as a boiled potherb, or sparingly in salads. The leaves are bitter and tough even when very young. I am not fond of them – in fact, I hardly consider them edible – but several people in my workshops have claimed to like them. If you insist on eating these greens, collect them in early in spring, before the flower stalk appears. Look for upright leaves with no reddish tint. Swamp saxifrage leaves, being rough and a little hairy, are good at clinging to sand; their habit of growing on stream edges often gives them sand to cling to. Carefully wash off this grit unless you want small teeth.

The only part of the swamp saxifrage plant that I consider worth collecting is the flower stalk. These are in the proper stage for collecting for only about two weeks in the middle of spring. The stalk can be picked between 8–20 inches (20–50 cm) tall – as long as the top has not yet begun to branch out and flower. All of the flower buds should be packed tightly at the apex of the stalk. If the stalks are harvested too late, they become tough and bitter. Even when the stalks are in their prime, the top third or so is usually less palatable.

Some people find the fuzzy texture of the flower stalks unpleasant, like peach skin. I don't have much to say about that except that it doesn't bother me at all. These shoots can be chopped up and added to salads or sandwiches, but most often I just crunch away at them while I am outdoors. Cooking makes them extremely soft, and their delicate flavor is mostly lost when they are boiled, but swamp saxifrage stalks are a good, neutral soup ingredient. I'm sure that an inventive cook could find many other uses for this interesting vegetable.

Swamp saxifrage is sometimes abundant; where it is rare or uncommon one should refrain from gathering it. Plucking a flower stalk does not kill the plant, but it eliminates its possibility for reproduction that year. Besides humans, black bears and deer feed on the flower stalks. Of course, it is wise to use moderation – never harvest the stalks heavily in one area, and never remove more than a few leaves from a single rosette. That way one can rest assured that there will be plenty of succulent stalks next year.

Early spring rosette of swamp saxifrage, when the greens are at their least bad.

Serviceberry, Juneberry, Saskatoon

Amelanchier spp.

Racemes of ripe serviceberries in mid-August.

O ver most of its range, the serviceberry gets little recognition for its excellence. In the area where I live it is probably the most abundant edible wild berry. Every year, local newspapers print articles about the wild blueberry crop, telling people when and where to pick and discussing the bounty of that particular season relative to others in recent history. Although the serviceberry ripens at about the same time and abounds in nearly all the same areas as blueberry, despite the fact that it is much easier to pick, found in greater quantities, and in my opinion tastes much better, it is never mentioned in these articles. I have had blueberry pickers stop along the backroads to ask me how the picking was, who, upon discovering that I was collecting serviceberries, looked at me in shock, confused as to why I would do such an outlandish thing. "Oh, you're picking *those*," they'd mutter before driving off.

But the native people of this continent knew better; many traditionally gathered serviceberries by the bushel, and dried huge quantities for the winter.

209

Today, growing serviceberries is a major industry in parts of Saskatchewan, but I think it's about time this plant gets its due recognition in the rest of North America.

Description

Serviceberry is among the earliest of our showy tree blossoms to appear in spring. Before the leaves have fully unfurled, its fragrant, star-like, five-petaled, white

Serviceberry flowers.

Smooth gray bark on a sinuous trunk characterizes the genus *Amelanchier*.

blossoms add beauty to many thickets and forest edges. These flowers, about 1 inch (2.5 cm) across, are produced in loose racemes of 3–11. The long, slender petals appear very spread-out and do not overlap at the base.

The leaves are small, usually about 1–2 inches (2.5–5 cm) long, and borne alternately on slender petioles that are about one third to one half the length of the leaf. They are round, elliptic, or ovate in shape, dark green on the upper surface, and have finely serrated margins. The twigs are very slender and smooth with small, pointed buds. One commonly sees these buds open "by mistake" in late autumn.

There are many different species of serviceberry in North America, ranging from knee-high shrubs to small trees. I have seen fruit on bushes 18 inches (45 cm) tall and on trees more than 1 foot (30 cm) in diameter and 40 feet (12 m) in height. Typically, however, serviceberry is a clump-forming large shrub or a small tree. Most that I collect fruit from are 1–3 inches (2.5–8 cm) in diameter and 12–20 feet (4–6 m) in height. The species can be very difficult to distinguish, and botanists

Another species of seviceberry, with small, sweet fruit and ovate leaves.

disagree as to their classification. The quality of the fruit varies from one species to the next, but all are edible and most are very good.

Serviceberry trees have a graceful appearance because their branching and growth patterns produce no sharp bends, only a wavy trunk and gently divergent branches. The light gray bark is extremely thin and smooth; only the largest trees develop grooves, and these are extremely shallow.

Serviceberries are borne in small racemes, each fruit being about .5 inch (1.25 cm) long and oval or globular. As the fruit ripens it turns from green to reddish to dark purple. Sometimes they are good to eat before attaining their darkest color, but they are always best when darkest. Ripe serviceberries are sweet, juicy, and extremely soft. Each one contains several chewy seeds with an almond-extract flavor. Some people dislike the seeds and try to spit them out, but I think they add an interesting flavor and texture without which the fruit is poorer.

The serviceberry goes by many names. The locals in my area call them juneberries, despite the fact that, even in the warmest years, few of them ripen during that month. The name "shadbush" refers to the tree's blossoming, which coincides with spawning runs of the shad in some areas. There is a fanciful story that this tree's blossoming also coincided with early spring funeral services that were delayed by snow and frozen ground until that time, accounting for the name "serviceberry." This legend was made up long after the name came into use. "Serviceberry" is actually a corruption of an older name for this or a similar fruit in England, "sarvissberry," and that name, or occasionally just "sarviss," can still be found in older American literature in reference to this fruit.

Range and Habitat

Serviceberries grow throughout most of North America, but they are more common in the northern parts of the continent and at higher altitudes. There are numerous species, and a few of them, admittedly, are not very tasteful. The downy serviceberry *Amelanchier arborea* in particular often has bland fruit; it is one of the more common species in the eastern states. Most kinds, however, are delicious, and the saskatoon *A. alnifolia* is a major crop in western Canada. (The city is named for the berry, not vice-versa.) At least five species grow near my house, but I don't try to differentiate them while picking. If the berries taste good, I collect them.

Serviceberry trees need ample sunlight to grow and they prefer well-drained sites, but they seem to thrive in any soil type. Pine barrens, lakeshores, bluffs, fencerows, field edges, abandoned farmlands, roadsides, and young or open woods are favored habitats. In many parts of the continent, this is the most common edible berry.

Harvest and Preparation

Where I live, the first serviceberries ripen in late June and the last ones are picked in early September. The season peaks from about July 20 to August 15, although the fruit is rarely ripe on any one tree for more than two weeks. The long season of harvest for this fruit is largely due to the presence of several species ripening at different times. The flavor varies quite a bit because there are multiple species, and this accounts for the conflicting reports of their palatability in the literature. I have found a few trees whose fruit was truly distasteful, but more commonly they bear what seems like a gift straight from heaven.

Picking serviceberries is serious business for me. I tie a blickey around my waist and use a berry hook with a foot-loop (see section on harvesting fruit, page 48) to hold the tree down so that both hands are free. On good trees I can do better than a gallon per hour, and I have picked as many as six gallons from a single tree.

Picking from a loaded serviceberry bush. This one yielded more than 6 gallons of fruit.

I store a lot of serviceberries and eat them year-round. If the weather is hot and sunny, I sun-dry them; if it is cloudy, I can them in a water-bath (see canning section, page 64). Dried serviceberries are absolutely wonderful, and I most commonly eat them alone as a snack. I often bring a small bag of them with me on day-trips into the woods. Mixed with hickory nuts they make a fulfilling, all-wild trail mix that seems too good to be true. The canned berries I spread on toast or acorn bread, mix with hot cereal, pour over pancakes or corn bread, or just dump into a bowl and eat as dessert. In my opinion, service-berries are not sour enough by themselves to make great pie, jam, or jelly – the results are better if some sour fruit or juice is added. For such products you can remove the serviceberry seeds with a strainer if you desire.

While serviceberries are in season I love to devour them fresh off the tree; I gorge myself and don't feel a bit guilty about it. The really good serviceberries are, in my opinion, one of the best fruits on Earth.

If you are among the fortunate people who live where choice serviceberries abound, don't fail to notice them this summer. Spend a day wandering in the brush, seeking what the bears seek. You just might decide to stay.

Chokecherry

Prunus virginiana

Black, over-ripened chokecherry fruit, perfect for harvest.

Most people refrain from eating any plant with the word "choke" in its name. Thus, the chokecherry is ignored by many who have access to its bountiful crop. That's a shame, for this fruit deserves much more attention than it receives.

The black bears know better. In late August when the chokecherries ripen, the bruins seek out the trees, pulling them to the ground and stripping off their succulent fruit. In their zeal they often tear the small trees limb from limb to get at the cherries. Raccoons similarly feast on chokecherries, only they tend to do far less damage in the process. Chipmunks and deer mice pick them, extract the stones, and leave the flesh behind, and many species of birds avidly consume the fruit.

The food value of this widespread native cherry was not lost on the Native Americans. For many tribes, particularly in the northern Rockies, northern Plains, and boreal forest region, chokecherry was a staple food item. The fruit was collected by the Pawnee, Omaha, Osage, Kiowa, Assiniboin, Dakota, Lakota, Comanche, Cree, Ponca, Arikara, Ute, Mandan, Crow, Cheyenne, Hidatsa, and Blackfoot (Kindscher, 1987). For many of these tribes, chokecherry was the most important fruit in the diet.

European settlers adopted the use of chokecherries in some areas – especially the northern Plains, where they have been traditionally used for jam, jelly, wine, and syrup. However, the chokecherry is mostly ignored today, and many people actually believe they are poisonous. Rarely are they eaten dried, as long was their primary use. In the literature on wild foods, chokecherries are often derided as second-rate to their cousin, the black cherry, and many authors wholly dismiss them as marginally edible. I disagree, and so did the many thousands of people for whom they were once a staple food. Today, as always, this wild cherry makes fine juice, jam, jelly, and syrup. Chokecherry leather is still a unique, convenient, healthy, and tasty snack. And every summer, across most of our continent, clusters of these opulent black fruits dangle from drooping branches, offering themselves to the first taker.

Identification

The chokecherry *Prunus virginiana* is a large shrub or small tree, usually found growing in small clonal clusters. The trunks of fruiting bushes are typically 1–3 inches (2.5–8 cm) in diameter and 8–15 feet (2.5–4.5 m) tall. Chokecherry bushes are completely thornless. Their bark is thin, dark gray or brown, and fairly smooth, showing only faint and scattered, paper-thin wavy ridges running roughly lengthwise. The bark also exhibits corky, oblong lenticels about .2 inches (5 mm) long.

Chokecherry leaves are simple, alternate, 1.5 to 2.5 inches (4–6 cm) long, and broadly ovate with finely serrated edges. The foliage is dull green above and lighter grayish green underneath. The petioles are usually .7 to 1.3 inches (18–33 mm) long and bear two glands near the base of the leaf.

Typical chokecherry bark.

215

Chokecherry leaves shading green, unripe fruit.

Chokecherry blooms in late spring when the leaves are almost fully grown. The five-petaled flowers, about .4 inch (1 cm) across, grow in rather tight, arched or drooping racemes, each flower on a stem about .25 inch (6 mm) long.

The mature fruit is spherical or oblong and dark purple to black when fully ripe. (It is reported that chokecherries in the eastern part of their range are red when ripe. If this is true, it may help to explain why this fruit has such a poor reputation in the East; I never collect chokecherries with a red tint because this normally means they are too astringent.) Each cherry is about .3 inch (8 mm) in diameter and contains one proportionately large oval stone. They are borne in drooping clusters 3–6 inches (8–15 cm) long, each containing 8–20 fruits.

Although chokecherry is easy to learn to recognize, it bears some resemblance to several common small trees. Many country dwellers do not differentiate between the chokecherry and smaller specimens of its close relative, the black cherry. Since I greatly prefer the flavor of the chokecherry, the distinction is important to me. Black cherry has much darker green, shinier, and more lanceolate leaves; larger fruit that grows on longer and more spaced-out racemes; and smaller, thinner, more numerous, and more distinct lenticels on its bark. Common buckthorn *Rhamnus cathartica*, a powerful cathartic, differs in the presence of thorns and in that its fruits each contain three to four seeds. From a distance the toxic glossy buckthorn *Rhamnus frangula* looks similar to the chokecherry. Its growth form and bark are nearly identical, but closer inspection shows that the leaves have smooth margins and the fruit, which grows in small clusters from the leaf axils, contains 2–3 seeds.

Range and Habitat

The chokecherry is thought by some to be the most widespread tree in North America. It is found from Newfoundland to British Colombia, through all but the most northern of our boreal forests. It ranges across the northern half of the United States, being found in the Appalachians south to Georgia and in the Rockies through southern Arizona and New Mexico. It is often a conspicuous feature of the vegetation. The chokecherries of the Southwest, said to be darker in color and less astringent, are classified by some as a separate species, *Prunus melanocarpa.*

Chokecherry is a riverside shrub. It tolerates wet or dry conditions and thrives upon disturbance. Like many other native riverside species, the chokecherry has been incredibly successful at colonizing old fields, roadsides, fencerows, railroad right-of-ways, and forest edges. The chokecherry is also found in open-canopy woodlands, pine barrens, cutovers, and swamps. It is tolerant of moderate shade but requires a generous dose of sunlight to bear fruit heavily.

Harvest

The greatest threat to the culinary reputation of the chokecherry comes from those who gather the fruit when it is under-ripe. Although a few varieties are red when fully ripe, chokecherries generally should not be picked until they have been dark purple-black for a few weeks. Such cherries will taste immensely better than those hastily collected as soon as they darken, as their astringency will be greatly reduced. Oftentimes the fruit appears ripe in late July or early August, but beware of the reddish tint – these early chokecherries are of inferior quality. In the Upper Midwest, the peak season for chokecherry picking coincides almost exactly with the harvest of wild rice: August 20 to September 10.

The flavor of fresh chokecherries varies quite a bit from one tree to the next; some are very astringent, most are somewhat astringent, and a few are hardly astringent at all and are wonderful to eat right off the bush. Some people never develop a liking for fresh chokecherries. The puckering mouth that they induce is a sensation, not a flavor. If you can learn to not let it scare you off you will be free to discover that the flavor behind the pucker is really pretty darn good.

Chokecherries often grow in profusion. They can be collected rather quickly by stripping one cluster at a time into your hand. Individual cherries should

Racemes of chokecherry flowers.

pop off the main stem easily; if they do not, they are insufficiently ripe. Certain thickets will yield several gallons of fruit, and in a good location you can gather two or three gallons per hour. When picking, keep an eye out for stinkbugs and conscientiously remove them from your pail.

I collect chokecherries with a blickey, which leaves both hands free for picking. Sometimes I use a berry hook to hold down the higher limbs, but if you do this be careful not to wantonly break branches like the bears do. Luckily, chokecherries are not as soft as most other fruits and therefore do not crush as easily in a big pail. Neither do they spoil as readily as some small fruits; you can keep them for perhaps a day at room temperature after collection, and in the refrigerator they might last for three days or more.

218

Preparation

Jelly is probably the most popular use of chokecherries. To make jelly, you must first extract the juice. After cleaning out the leaves, twigs, and invertebrates, place your chokecherries in a large pot. Add little less water than it would take to cover the cherries. Simmer until the cherries are soft and have released their juice, then take them out and strain through a jelly bag or a cheesecloth-lined colander. You will get around a quart and a half of juice for each gallon of cherries that you start with. You can drink this juice as is, can or freeze it for future use, or use it to make an excellent jelly.

Instead of boiling your chokecherries in plain water, you can start the jelly-making process by pouring the juice from boiled apples over them. This will tone down the potent flavor of slightly under-ripe chokecherries and, more importantly, add some pectin and malic acid to the jelly to improve its flavor and jelling. Instead of making juice, you can also puree the fruit through a

Chokecherry bushes loaded with ripe fruit in late August.

colander or food mill to strain out the seeds and use the pulp to make jam, preserves, or even pie. I do this with my Victorio strainer, but I need to remove the tension spring or the screen will clog with pits. Another traditional confection is chokecherry syrup, made by mixing the juice about half and half with sugar, perhaps with a little pectin to thicken it. This is eaten on pancakes, ice cream, or muffins.

All of these chokecherry products are delicious, and they are where I began my culinary experiments with this excellent fruit. Today, however, almost all of the chokecherries that I eat are in the form of dried fruit leather. This is convenient, delicious, and healthy since it is unadulterated by the addition of sugar. (For details on making fruit leather, see pages 67–70.) The secret to making really good chokecherry leather is to pick very ripe cherries and then let them sit in the refrigerator for a day or two before straining. This aging facilitates some chemical change that significantly reduces the astringency of the fruit's pulp.

I used to dry chokecherries with the pits in them simply because I didn't know of a good way to separate them. When I ate the cherries, I would just spit out the stones as I went. This tasted good, but the pits were very annoying. The Native Americans also lacked an effective way to separate the stones, but instead they pulverized the entire fruit, seeds included, before drying it in the sun. Though most of us today would find the seedshells in the traditionally prepared chokecherry patties unpleasant, the kernels contain significant quantities of oil and protein. The seeds contain prussic acid (a cyanide compound) and are toxic when raw. Crushing and drying the pits apparently breaks down this compound and renders the kernels edible. I like the flavor of the dried kernels but find them impractical to separate from the unpleasant shells.

After drying, the flavor of chokecherries mellows and becomes much less astringent, to the extent that almost everybody enjoys eating them. Throughout the winter I eat chokecherry leather as a snack and occasionally pour myself a cold glass of refreshing canned chokecherry juice. All told, there are few fruits that I will eat more of than this wonderful, neglected, and often maligned wild cherry. I sure hope that I don't choke on them.

Pin Cherry

Prunus pensylvanica

The house that I grew up in had a giant pin cherry tree growing beside it. The tree stood more than fifty feet tall and, although I'm afraid to hazard a guess as to its diameter, it was large enough that my older brother built a tree fort in it and we had a swing tied to one of its limbs. For a pin cherry, that's enormous. I came back one day to measure it, certain that it belonged in the record books, but the new owners of the house had just cut it down.

During my childhood I couldn't find anybody who knew this tree's identity, but my mother repeatedly warned my siblings and me that the berries were poisonous. Unfortunately, we believed her. We called it *the jelly tree* because wherever the tree was damaged (such as by the nails holding a tree-fort in place) it would exude thick gobs of translucent jelly to cover the

A pin cherry twig laden with succulent fruit.

wound. Today, however, I have learned of a far better reason to call the pin cherry *the jelly tree*.

I doubt that there is any individual tree that has been a more important part of my life than that pin cherry. My brother gave me climbing lessons up, down, and all around it. I spent hours at a time climbing and swinging in the tree. We had an "elevator swing," a zip-line, and a secret entrance to

221

the house that was accessed from the tree's upper limbs. The blooming of the jelly tree fascinated me every spring, for nothing else in our neighborhood was half as showy. When the thousands of tiny red fruits ripened in late July, the pin cherry became a mecca for local birds: orioles, robins, catbirds, cedar waxwings, and blackbirds. Nothing could have been more delightful to a budding urban ornithologist. Not once, however, did I eat the fruit of our giant pin cherry. My first taste did not come until years later.

Description

Pin cherry is a small tree that usually grows in loose clones. Fruiting specimens are usually 12–30 feet (4–9 m) tall and 2–6 inches (5–15 cm) in diameter with a prominent trunk extending well into the narrow, open crown. The bark is

Pin cherry bark. Note the large, horizontally-oriented and light-colored lenticels.

fairly smooth and thin, but on older trees it often peels into papery plates reminiscent of those on birches. It is dark reddish-brown to black and bears large, orange-brown lenticels. The thin twigs are red in their first year, darkening to brown. One distinctive feature of this tree is its habit of having several lateral buds clustered on the ends of its twigs.

Pin cherry's alternate leaves are typically only 1.5 to 3 inches (4–8 cm) long and very thin. Oblong or lanceolate in shape, the leaves are light green, glabrous on both sides, and have small, sharp, incurved teeth along their margins.

The five-petaled white flowers of pin cherry are less than .5 inch (13 mm) across. In mid-spring, before the leaves emerge, they hang from the twigs in small umbels of 3–5 flowers. The bright red cherries, borne on long individual stems, are generally less than .3 inch (8 mm) in diameter.

Range and Habitat

Pin cherry is found in the northeastern United States and upper Midwest, south through the Appalachians; skipping the Great Plains, it is also found in the eastern Rocky Mountains in Montana and Wyoming. It grows in all of the forested regions of Canada except for western British Columbia and the far north.

This small, short-lived tree is a classic pioneer species, only rarely found in mature woods. Pin cherry grows in well-drained sites exposed to full sun, often coming up in large numbers after heavy logging or fires. It prefers rock, sand, or gravel and can grow on sterile ground, such as heaps of mine waste or gravel pits. It inhabits roadsides, beaches, fencerows, ridges, steep banks or slopes, pine barrens, young woods, thickets, and abandoned fields.

Pin cherry leaves.

Harvest

Pin cherries ripen in mid to late summer, a few weeks before chokecherries and several weeks before black cherries. In my area, the first pin cherries turn red in mid to late July. During most years they can be collected throughout August, and occasionally they persist later. The prime collecting season for pin cherries averages about one week later than that for low-bush blueberries: July 25 to August 15. As pin cherries ripen they become moderately soft and juicy, normally turning bright red. Occasionally, however, one finds ripe fruit of a yellowish or orange color.

The flavor varies greatly from one tree to the next. Some pin cherries taste like cultivated sour cherries, only much more sour. I like to nibble these right off the tree. Other pin cherries have a bitter or sulphury taste and need to be sweetened or mixed with other fruit.

Pin cherry flowers.

I am not able to gather pin cherries nearly as fast as chokecherries or black cherries due to their smaller size, smaller clusters, and the fact that the trees usually do not bear them as heavily. Pin cherries are designed to be plucked and disseminated singly by birds rather than consumed in mouthfuls by mammals. The long stems often remain attached to the fruit. This forces one to remove them after picking or to pick more slowly to get stemless cherries. On a good tree I can usually collect about a gallon per hour. Unfortunately, pin cherry trees tend to hold much of their fruit out of reach – and they are usually too large and stiff to pull down with a berry hook, but too small and brittle to climb.

Preparation

Pin cherries are very tart, and the flavor is usually too strong to enjoy them straight from the tree. However, occasional pin cherry trees have fruit that is mild and delicious, and I eat these juicy jewels by the handful, spitting out the seeds along my way.

The main problem with using pin cherries for food is the many large, hard pits that one must separate from the pulp. You can employ a colander for this purpose, but it is still not easy, and there tends to be a lot of wasted pulp. Fortunately, a food strainer with the tension spring removed works very well on pin cherries. The resulting puree can be used to make one of the best jams ever tasted. While it is usually too sour to use alone as pie filling, it is also excellent mixed with other sweet fruits such as blueberries or serviceberries. I have dried

A typical clone of pin cherries in an open, sandy area.

a small amount of pin cherry pulp, but only that from the best trees is mild enough to make good fruit leather.

As always, the first step in making pin cherry jelly is to procure some juice. Cover the cherries with water and simmer for an hour or so, stirring occasionally and perhaps mashing them gently. (I say gently because pin cherry seeds, unlike those of chokecherry, hold a terrible flavor that will contaminate the juice if they are broken. This suggests that they are more toxic than chokecherry pits, which may help explain why pin cherry was used by Native Americans much less than its darker-fruited relative.) After simmering, pour the hot mess into a cheesecloth or jelly bag suspended over a container that the juice can drip into. Let it drip for a few hours until it cools down, and then squeeze out a little more juice if you want to.

Pin cherry juice is drinkable by itself, but it is so strong that it is best diluted and sweetened or mixed with another juice.

Pin cherry jam and jelly are well known to rural folk where the tree is common. Both have reputations as mighty fine confections. I couldn't agree more. In fact, the first time I made pin cherry jam I was forced to rearrange my favorite jam hierarchy. It seems ironic that something that I am so fond of today comes from a plant that, as a child, I was taught to fear as poison. When people mistrust and malign any unfamiliar wild plant, it robs them of a potentially rewarding experience.

Ground Bean, Hog Peanut

Amphicarpaea bracteata

Forest floor covered with ground bean vines in early October.

We have the tendency to imagine that excellent wild edibles must be elusive, hiding away where only the hardy and determined wanderer might happen upon them. It constantly amazes people to discover that the best wild food plants may be found in profusion just beyond their doorsteps. That elusive edible you have long sought may be a mundane sight: familiar but overlooked, abundant but unconsidered. Such was my experience with the ground bean.

There is a place where I often camped as a child, a land of vast hilly hardwood, hemlock, and pine forest interspersed with kettle lakes. I wandered for many miles in those woods and surely treaded over millions of ground bean plants before one day I knelt down and took a closer look at the tiny pea-like vines that sprawled across hundreds of acres of the forest floor. They looked like something that I had seen in one of my plant books, but I could not remember what, so I brought along some field guides the next time I ventured into those woods. When I discovered that this plant was the ground bean or hog peanut,

I was shocked. I had looked for the ground bean many times, and kept my eye out for it for a few years, but in those searches I had never considered that it might be *this plant*, because *this plant* was everywhere.

In our culture, we are taught that the old hunting and gathering way of life entailed an unrelenting search for scattered morsels of inferior food. The ground bean was one of my early indications that perhaps this was not the case.

Description

One will notice that I choose generally not to use the common name "hog peanut" for this plant. That name has lead to some confusion and is also rather unappetizing and cumbersome. Moreover, it is a derogatory term, meant to be demeaning to the Native Americans for whom this legume was common fare. Long ago in the American South, peanuts were considered food fit only for blacks; adding "hog" to the epithet suggested that this superb lentil, relished by Native Americans within its range, was even more lowly than the peanut and not fit for human consumption. This is typical of the way that Native Americans were made to feel ashamed of their heritage during the process of forced acculturation. The name has lost its derogatory connotation, but it still sounds terrible.

Ground bean vines in summer.

Ground bean is among the smallest herbaceous vines growing in North America. The stems are little thicker than sewing thread and are covered by fine hairs. Where there is moderate sunlight they will wind their way up the stalks of saplings, shrubs, brambles, and herbs, attaining heights of up to six feet; in heavy shade they sprawl over the ground in dense mats. The alternate compound leaves consist of three broadly ovate leaflets, each of which is from 0.75–3 inches (2–8 cm) long. The leaf is produced at the end of a proportionately long petiole 2–5 inches (5–13 cm) in length. The leaflets are very finely pubescent, paper-thin, and extremely delicate.

A cluster of aerial ground-bean flowers.

Ground bean is amazing in that it has two kinds of flowers and fruit. Its unique adaptations allow it to be one of the only annuals able to compete with long-lived perennials and persist year after year as a major part of the forest floor vegetation. If there is ample sunlight, ground bean will produce clusters of 2–12 white or purplish, two-lipped flowers that hang from leaf axils of climbing vines. These will mature into tiny pea-like pods, about one inch long, each of which contains three tiny, mottled, flattened beans or lentils. As these pods dry out the two halves will curl into a spiral and release the seeds.

If, as is often the case, the ground bean plant does not receive sufficient sunlight to produce these aerial beans, it has a superb backup plan: it starts acting like a perennial. It produces one or two inconspicuous flowers, without petals, at or near the ground. These flowers are self-fertile and guaranteed to set seed. Each produces a single bean that is much larger than an aerial seed. The parent vine then pushes these larger beans into the soil – in essence, planting itself. Functioning much like tubers, these beans store the energy from which a new plant will grow the following season.

There is considerable confusion in the literature about the fruiting habits of the ground bean. Because one of its common names is "hog peanut," and peanuts grow in pods, and perhaps also because hog peanut's aerial seeds and

Clusters of aerial beans, the vines climbing an *Elaeagnus umbellata* bush.

most other legume seeds are found in pods, many authors who write on hog-peanut have assumed that its underground seeds are borne in pods as well. Many edible wild plant books parrot this statement – making me doubt if the authors have actually collected or examined the seeds that they are talking about. The subterranean seeds of ground bean are covered with a thin, tight-fitting skin, and that's all. There is no technical, botanical, or commonplace definition by which this skin would be considered a pod. So don't expect to find your underground beans in pods; there are none.

The underground beans are generally shaped like a plump lima bean, but obstructions in the soil may coax them into odd forms. They range from .2 to .6 inch (5–15 mm) across. To the untrained eye these beans, especially the smaller ones, can be hard to tell from smooth pebbles – but you'll get the hang of it. When in doubt, see if you can slice the bean with your fingernail; if it's too hard for that, it's a stone. The beans are quite variable in coloration but are most commonly purple, cream, or some mottled mixture of the two.

Range and Habitat

The ground bean ranges from southern Manitoba south to northern Texas and east to Virginia and Maine. It is found through most of the hardwood forest region of eastern North America except for the Deep South, and it also abounds in the forested riparian corridors of the Great Plains. Ground bean likes medium levels of moisture and fertility; most well-drained soils in hardwood forests are suitable habitat. It does not grow well on heavy clays. It cannot survive extremely heavy shade, thus it is less common in rich mesic forests. It is sometimes found on the floodplains of large rivers but seems especially partial to the valleys of smaller rivers and streams.

In my region one finds the ground bean most strongly associated with basswood, red oak, white oak, white ash, and bitternut hickory. My best bean patch is in a stand dominated by aspen, red oak, paper birch, and white ash. Here there is a continuous tangle of vines encumbering twenty acres of the forest floor. Ground bean thrives in disturbed woods and often grows prolifically on the side of sand or gravel backroads through hardwood forests.

Harvest

The aerial seeds of the ground bean ripen in early autumn and can be harvested by stripping handfuls of them from the vines. When mature the beans become mottled; soon afterward the pods turn brown and begin to dry out. The earlier one collects them, the better, for as they dry out they split along their seams and release their seeds. These edible seeds can be collected even in the dead of winter, although fewer will remain at that time.

An aerial bean pod and palmful of the lentil-like seeds.

Since the seeds are small and need to be winnowed, it is not worth your time gathering them unless you find an area where they are produced copiously. Such is often the case after logging operations or windstorms open up the forest canopy. Only ground bean vines with a fairly generous dose of sunlight will produce any significant amount of aerial seeds; under such conditions they will produce few, if any, subterranean beans.

The underground bean, the "hog-peanut," is usually more worth your time to collect. These are scattered about in the soil as much as four inches deep underneath the tangled mat of creeping vines. For harvesting these, you want to look for the largest, most luxuriant plants that have few or no aerial seed-pods on them. Not only is collection easier where the soil is loose and coarse, but in these conditions the beans will also grow the largest. The subterranean beans can be collected from early autumn until the ground freezes at the end of fall, and again in the spring as soon as the ground thaws – if you can recognize the plant by the dead remains of its threadlike vines.

I have a small digging stick, about nine inches long, that I use primarily for collecting ground beans. It is held in my right hand and used to churn the soil while my left hand picks out the beans that are thereby exposed. In doing so I till a fair amount of dirt; I leave all of the smaller beans in the loose soil as seed for next year. Digging ground beans is somewhat addictive – and it's a great way to pass an afternoon in the woods spending quality time with a friend. However, be aware that in some places, especially where the soil is hard and heavy, it may not be worth your time to collect them—even if the plants are abundant.

Collecting ground beans is a slow process; I get about a cup of beans per hour. However, they can turn a soup of wild vegetables into something hearty by adding a great deal of protein, and they can be collected with minimal equipment. For these reasons, and because they are so abundant and widespread, they are one of the best wild foods for the survivalist to learn. Unfortunately, since it is difficult to amass large quantities of them, ground beans have not become a calorically important part of my diet.

Ground beans were once a very important food for many tribes of Native Americans. Ethnographic accounts of their use abound. The ethnobotanist Melvin Gilmore reported that these beans were eaten extensively by the tribes of the Missouri River Region, including the Omaha, Ponca, and Pawnee (Gilmore, 1919). Large quantities of ground beans were collected and stored by these tribes and others, to be used in the winter in stews with corn and other foods.

But how, one might ask, could the Natives afford to eat such a labor-intensive food source, and why would they choose to when other plant foods were available which could be gathered so much more quickly? Part of the answer lies in the nutritional quality of the beans; they complement corn, wild rice, or other grass seeds to form a complete protein, and there are few wild sources of protein which store well so that they are readily at hand if meat is scarce in the winter. Also, the collection rate of these beans may be slow, but unlike most beans, wild or domestic, these do not have to be shelled and thus have little processing time.

However, when it came to harvesting ground beans, the Indians had a trick that increased their efficiency many times over. Numerous accounts agree that ground beans were collected primarily by raiding the caches where rodents had stored large quantities of them. Philander Prescott (1849, as reported in Kindscher, 1987) reported that the Santee Dakota "sometimes find a peck at once, gathered by mice for their winter store." If this is true, it is an enormous time-saver, for a peck is roughly 30 times what I collect in an hour. I have never found a large store of these beans, however – just a few small caches that I believe were made by the pine mouse. Gilmore (1919) reports that the Dakota

Underground beans of ground bean, rubbed after rinsing, which caused some of the skins to come off.

women always repaid the mice from which they took the beans by leaving some corn or other food. Only when such stores could not be found did the women dig their own beans.

The old accounts do not agree as to which animal stores the beans. The industrious rodent has been reported variously as the bean mouse, field mouse, rat, meadow vole, mouse, and ground squirrel. Certainly more than one species collects and stores the beans. If I ever learn how to find these caches of ground beans, they will become a much more important article of food in my diet.

Preparation

The first thing you should do with your ground beans is rinse off the sand and dirt. Then pick out the basswood nuts and pebbles that you accidentally tossed into the pile. You will almost certainly miss some pebbles, so follow this simple procedure to assure yourself that you don't break any teeth: Put the beans into a large glass container with water and swish it around; if there are pebbles in it you will hear them clinking and scraping against the glass. If, as is almost certain, this is the case, take the beans out one handful at a time and swish them around in another glass container, listening for stones. Anytime you hear a pebble, carefully search that handful until you find it – and don't assume that there is only one stone in it – swish it around again until you don't hear any.

After all this swishing around the beans should be pretty clean. If you want to use them immediately, rub them forcefully between the palms of your hands to loosen the skins and then rinse them away. (It is not necessary that the skins be removed, but everybody prefers them that way.)

If you want to store them for later use, lay them out to dry once they are cleaned and checked for pebbles. Like other beans, they do not have to dry very quickly; as long as they are exposed to the air and are not piled up they should desiccate in a week or so. Once dried, the skins rub off these beans very easily and can be blown or winnowed away with little trouble. The dehydrated ground beans keep extremely well. Freshly picked beans can also be stored for months in a refrigerator or root cellar, as long as they are kept from drying out.

The small, lentil-like aerial seeds need to be removed and separated from their pods. To do this, dry them soon after they are collected and rub the dry pods between the palms of your hands to loosen the seeds. Sift out the coarse material with a colander that has holes large enough to let the lentils fall through. After that the smaller bits of trash can be winnowed out. These seeds are large enough to be separated by hand, but this is much more tedious.

Ground beans taste like cultivated beans, but they are better than most. You can use them in recipes instead of domestic beans with great success. I most often cook them in soup or simply boil them with wild rice. The fresh beans do not need to be boiled long before becoming tender, but dry ground beans should be soaked for several hours like other dry beans. The aerial seeds, despite their small size, should also be soaked and given a lengthy boiling, for they do not rehydrate or soften easily.

The peanut that is not a peanut, the bean without a pod, the annual that lives like a perennial, the sly producer of two kinds of flowers and two kinds of seeds, the legume that rodents collect for us – ground bean is full of surprises. Go out and surprise yourself with this fascinating wild food.

Hopniss, Groundnut

Apios americana

Hopniss leaves.

One day in early spring when I was thirteen years old, a friend and I were searching for water snakes along a small stream near my grandmother's house in southwestern Michigan. We came upon a place where the brush had been cleared and the ground bulldozed for the construction of a new home. Passing through the site, we were amazed to find hundreds upon hundreds of what looked like some odd variety of potatoes strewn over the ground. We figured that there had been a garden there, but it seemed like an odd locale.

A few minutes later, we found a string of eight small, round tubers dangling from the streambank where the sand had been washed away by spring floods. We immediately recognized them as groundnuts, having seen them in pictures, searched for them, and so often dreamed of this occasion. The next day, back at home some 320 miles away, we verified the identification and then proceeded to fry these precious groundnuts in bacon fat, as one of our books recommended. While enjoying my meager but tasty portion, I blurted out a most exciting hypothesis: "I think all those 'potatoes' were actually groundnuts!"

We instantly realized it was true, yet it seemed impossible. Some of those tubers were the size of large potatoes, and many were as big as my fist; we had never read of groundnuts growing this large. And there were literally bushels of them, just lying there for the picking! We felt like kicking ourselves for passing up *the mother lode* – and not even recognizing it.

234

Description

Hopniss *Apios americana* is a vigorously growing herbaceous vine that wraps around shrubs, small trees, tall herbs, and other vines. It also sprawls across low vegetation and open ground. Lush, elegant, and almost tropical in appearance, the vines grow from 10–20 feet (3–6 m) each season, dying back in the fall. The stems are thin and fragile-looking, rarely over .15 inch (4mm) in diameter, and thinly covered with very small hairs. Hopniss vines do not climb with tendrils; instead, they twine around and sprawl over their supports. The vines often grow profusely and form large, dense tangles.

The appearance of hopniss reveals its membership in the legume family; it looks much like an overgrown bean vine. The leaves are pinnately compound and often partly folded along the midrib. They consist of 5–9 ovate to lanceolate toothless leaflets, 1–2.5 inches (2.5–6 cm) long. Hopniss bears dense, small clusters of fragrant, dull purple flowers from July to September. In late summer and autumn, 2–5 inch (5–13 cm) pods appear, each containing a few edible beans. I have never tried or even seen these beans, but they were eaten by Native Americans and my friend Bill Blackmon tells me that they are fairly good. In the northern part of its range this plant rarely or never produces seed, but in the southern part of its range it does so regularly.

The principle edible part of hopniss is its tuber. These are produced in chains of anywhere from two to twenty, spaced from less than an inch to more than a foot apart. The tubers are connected by a rhizome of variable thickness that is fairly tough but not quite woody. These rhizomes often form an interconnected

Cluster of hopniss
flowers.

network under colonies of hopniss vines, but they usually break into many pieces when they are extracted from the soil.

Hopniss tubers range from the size of a grape to larger than a grapefruit. They range in shape from spherical to extremely elongated to amorphous and knobby. Most commonly they are about 1 inch (2.5 cm) thick, 1.5 inches (4 cm) long, and roughly egg-shaped. Hopniss tubers are protected by a rather thick skin, and a latex soon appears on damaged parts of the plant.

Hopniss is known by an unusually large number of common names, including Indian potato, ground potato, potato pea, pig potato, bog-potato, wild bean, wild sweet potato, white-apple, pomme de terre, and most commonly, groundnut. Although this latter name is the one more often used in

Hopniss beans. In many northern parts of its range hopniss never produces these. Photo by Bill Blackmon.

wild food literature, I disfavor it because it also refers to the peanut *Arachis hypogaea* (especially in England) and sometimes to the dwarf ginseng *Panax trifolia* of North America. All of the other names are problematic for one or more reasons. Hopniss is short, pleasant, one of the better-known names, and has never been applied to any other plant, so that is the name that I prefer.

Range and Habitat

Hopniss is widespread in eastern North America. It grows from southern Canada to the Gulf of Mexico and from the Great Plains to the East Coast.

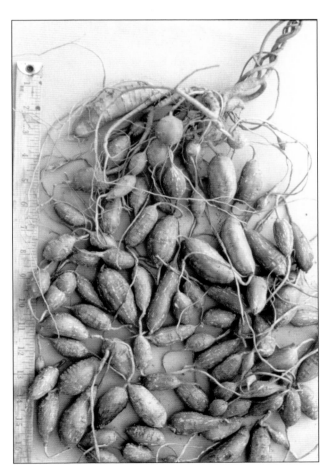

The favored habitat of this herb is sandy river bottoms, floodplains, lake edges, creek sides, and brushy wet areas. It thrives in full to partial sunlight. Common associates include swamp white oak, elderberry, jerusalem artichoke, poison ivy, and riverside grape. Hopniss is among the few plants adapted to both dry and water-logged conditions. The most vigorous stands that I have seen are in spring seepage areas with very loose, dark soil.

North America is home to one additional species of hopniss, *Apios priceana*. This vine produces one large tuber rather than a chain of several.

One year's production from a good selection of hopniss under cultivation. Photo by Bill Blackmon.

237

Confined mostly to Kentucky and southern Illinois, *A. priceana* is rare, protected, and should not be collected. Other species grow in Asia.

History

Hopniss was an important food for Native Americans throughout its range. There are possibly more historical and ethnographic accounts of the use of this tuber than of any other wild root vegetable in North America. Hopniss was sometimes planted near village sites to provide a readily accessible food source.

> "Hopniss or hapniss was the Indian name of a wild plant, which they ate . . . The roots resemble potatoes, and are boiled by the Indians, who eat them instead of bread. . . . the Indians who live farther in the country do not only eat these roots, which have as good taste as potatoes, but likewise take the peas which lie in the pods of this plant and eat them like common peas."
>
> — KALM, 1770

Hopniss is famous for having helped the Pilgrims through their first hard winters in North America, and probably more than once this plant kept European colonists from starving. Thoreau (2000) wrote of them extensively, saying, "In case of a famine, I should soon resort to these roots."

Attempts were made long ago to cultivate hopniss in Europe, but these were soon abandoned because the plant did not fit well with European-style agriculture. A breeding and research program was conducted at Louisiana State University during the 1980's with the aim of establishing hopniss as a food crop. Goals included improving yield and growth rate, and developing varieties with more closely spaced tubers. I believe that if we decide to implement a truly sustainable food economy, hopniss will again become an important source of food in Eastern North America, as it had been for thousands of years.

Harvest

Hopniss can be dug at any time of the year, provided that the ground is not frozen solid. This is one of the plant's greatest attributes: in early to mid summer, when starch is hard for a forager to come by, hopniss provides a ready source. I harvest the bulk of mine just before the ground freezes, when few other plants are in season.

Colonies of this plant are often large and prolific. I know of many places

Hopniss vines grown over brush, early winter. This is how one finds the plant at the best harvest time.

where hopniss vines form a tangled mess over several acres of brush. It only takes a small patch, however, to provide a good supply of tubers, for the tuber-bearing rhizomes run crisscross underground throughout the colony.

To dig hopniss seriously, I use a shovel, though a digging stick or even bare hands can be functional. Sometimes the tubers will be right on the surface of the ground, but most often they are one to six inches deep. Locate a vine and follow it to the point where it enters the soil. Insert your shovel near here and pry up a large scoop of dirt. Loosen the dirt from around any tubers or rhizomes, then follow them with your hands as far into the soil as you can before breaking them off.

Hopniss is heavily sought by certain wild animals, and half-gnawed tubers are a common find. (The latex is probably an adaptation to healing such wounds.) I suspect that cottontail rabbits, pocket gophers, and woodchucks are primary hopniss predators. To make themselves more difficult for these mammals to access, hopniss tubers have a definite affinity for wood; they grow around it, under it, between it, and sometimes even inside of it. If you see a clump of elderberry bushes draped with hopniss vines, the largest tubers almost invariably reside under and around the base of the bush. I do not suggest tearing out the shrubbery to get at the goodies underneath; dead bushes and stumps are just as likely to harbor a hopniss stash under their roots as are live ones, and you don't necessarily have to harm a bush to dig hopniss that is growing at its base.

Another thing to look for is places where spring floods have exposed hopniss chains. I have seen hundreds of pre-cleaned tubers flailing about in the current or hanging from sandy banks at times like this. Thoreau (2000) wrote of the rising waters of Walden Pond in rainy years creating similar conditions. Occasionally, construction projects will expose a windfall of hopniss.

In the most productive spring seepage areas, hopniss tubers grow so large that many of them protrude an inch or two above the surface. These can be just ripped out of the ground with no digging at all. An average tuber in such places is about the size of my fist, and the largest that I have found was 11 inches (28 cm) long and 6 inches (15 cm) wide. They are often so abundant that when I get down on my hands and knees, I can fill a twenty-pound sack in ten minutes, without crawling much more than my body length. You might think that I'm exaggerating, but I can take you there.

I don't want to inflate your expectations; it's generally not like that, and it

An average-sized new hopniss tuber compared to the "Hop-Ness Monster."

doesn't need to be. For many years I considered large tubers to be the size of a ping-pong ball, and I'm still delighted with hopniss of that stature. The best tubers are medium-sized, young, very firm, and as smooth as you can find them. In an average patch of hopniss, it takes two to three hours to gather a half-bushel (or five to ten minutes to get enough for a meal).

You can select a colony and return to it repeatedly. As long as you leave some tubers behind, they will take advantage of the ideal growing conditions that you leave them (loose soil and reduced competition) and produce a generous crop the next season. Once you find your first patch, you may begin to see them all over; in many regions hopniss is amazingly abundant. When you are familiar with the growing conditions that hopniss thrives in, you can transplant a few tubers to a promising locality nearer to home.

Hopniss is sensitive to frost and thus has a short growing season. In the northern states it shoots forth in early June, starts flowering in early August, and continues to do so until it dies back around the middle of September. When I gather the tubers in spring or fall, all that I usually have are dead stalks to guide me. It will take practice, but anyone can learn to identify them this way. Other herbaceous vines that might be confused with it are wild yam, bindweed, clematis, hops, and ground bean – all of which may share its habitat. Dry hopniss vines are fragile, quite pale and are almost uniform in thickness; they lack tendrils and have very inconspicuous leaf scars. If in doubt, excavate; there are no tubers that can be easily confused with hopniss.

After harvesting enough for a meal, you'll be ready for the next phase of the adventure.

Preparation

Hopniss should not be eaten raw, as it is not easily digested in this state. The raw plant contains potentially harmful protease inhibitors (chemicals that interfere with protein metabolism). These are destroyed by cooking (Reynolds et al, 1990). Plus, raw hopniss is hard, tastes terrible, and like many legumes causes horrendous gas.

The first step in hopniss preparation is to wash them. I like to do the initial rinsing in a lake or stream rather than in my sink. I simply use water and a vegetable brush, making sure there is no dirt or sand clinging to the tubers. You can clean them before or after cutting the individual tubers from their chains. Cut off the nodules and any rotten areas, and discard any soft tubers. Their insides should be white or slightly off-white.

You'll notice that some hopniss are relatively smooth, thin-skinned, light yellowish or reddish brown, and regularly shaped. These are ***new tubers***, less than a year old. They tend to be small to medium-sized and very hard. Their surface bears scattered lenticels (like the eyes of potatoes) oriented perpendicular to the rhizome.

The ***old tubers*** are a little softer with thicker, tougher skin, and their flesh appears somewhat marbled when cut due to fibers that form a latticework inside of them. Their lenticels develop into large lumps or knobs. Older tubers can range from small to very large. While both are considered edible, I find that the new tubers have a more appealing flavor and texture. (See the section on hopniss allergy for further considerations.)

After my hopniss are washed and cut from their chains, I separate them by size. I peel the larger tubers raw with a paring knife or carrot peeler. The smaller tubers I boil and then peel with my fingers. For certain applications such as frying, you may not feel that you need to peel the new hopniss at all, as their skins are relatively thin.

Once the tubers are washed and peeled, you have several options, depending on what you want to make from them. Nutritionally, hopniss is something like a cross between beans and potatoes. The tubers contain 11%–14% protein, higher than potatoes and other commonly eaten root vegetables, and

New tubers (top 2) compared to old tubers (bottom 3). Note the proportionately thicker rhizomes on the old tubers.

matching the protein content of wheat. The amino acid profile mirrors that of beans, which means that hopniss complements cereal grains to form a complete protein (Reynolds et al, 1990).

The flavor of hopniss has been likened to turnips. Being fond of both, I fail to find the comparison of any use. I would say that the flavor of this vegetable is somewhere between peanuts and potatoes, but unique and distinct.

To make hopniss flour, I first dice up the tubers and then roast them over low heat until they are dry. (These dry hopniss cubes will store perfectly for years.) I then grind them in my flourmill. You can also boil and mash the hopniss and then grind it. Fine hopniss flour can be used in pancakes, bread, and other baked goods; the coarse meal, when boiled, produces a hot cereal that is not bad with milk and brown sugar.

The fresh tubers can be baked or boiled whole, or they can be sliced or diced and used in many cooked dishes. They are a little bit harder than potatoes and have a different flavor, which sometimes goes well in potato recipes and sometimes does not. Few people find them particularly good all alone, but mashed and served with gravy, or fried and seasoned, they are liked by most. Hopniss is also excellent in casserole, stew, and stir-fry.

The most common way that I prepare this tuber is like refried beans as a filling for burritos and tacos. To give the hopniss this texture, I peel them, boil them, and run them through a meat grinder. (Other types of food processors, such as blenders, would probably suffice for this.) The key to making truly excellent "refried" hopniss is to add a proper dose of taco seasoning and something sour such as lime juice, or serve it with something acidic like salsa. Such burritos will please most lovers of Mexican food. I often mix the refried hopniss with ground venison, which is likewise delicious for tacos and burritos.

Since hopniss is a regular feature of my cooking, I have been forced to learn its keeping qualities. Fortunately, this vegetable excels here, too. The tubers keep very well in a root cellar as long as they don't dry out, and they can survive accidental freezing better than any cultivated vegetable. Dried hopniss products will store indefinitely. Sometimes I pressure-can burrito filling or soups that include hopniss.

I also make large batches of "refried" hopniss and then dehydrate it on baking trays over my woodstove. (It must dry quickly or it will spoil.) It is very important to flip this over as it dries so that it does not stick to the trays – it dries on like mortar. Refried hopniss dried in this fashion can be rehydrated by soaking and then boiling.

Warning: Potential Hopniss Allergy

I have eaten hundreds of pounds of hopniss over the last fifteen years and have fed the plant to hundreds of people. Five of those people have had allergic or intolerance reactions to it. The symptoms of all were nearly identical: two to three hours after eating the hopniss they felt severe nausea, which was followed by vomiting and diarrhea. The sickness lasted for a few hours.

Five out of a few hundred is a high rate of allergy, but this doesn't tell the whole story. Four of the allergic/intolerant individuals had eaten the plant on multiple occasions previously with no ill effect. After the initial adverse reaction, these individuals were extremely sensitive to hopniss – even in very small quantities. This suggests that many of those who have tried hopniss once or twice without reacting would or could develop an allergy after more exposures. It also suggests an alarmingly high rate of allergy. Since so few people eat this plant on a regular basis it is impossible to say how statistically prevalent such reactions may be, but it can be safely assumed that hopniss is far more likely than the average food to cause them.

To my knowledge this allergy is mentioned nowhere in the wild food literature. Bill Blackmon, who was head of the *Apios* breeding program at Louisiana State University for ten years, told me that he had encountered one case of suspected allergy/intolerance in that time, but he also noted that the researchers did not eat the plant regularly and that the people in their taste tests did not necessarily eat the plant on multiple occasions.

How could hopniss have been such an important food for Native Americans if so many people are allergic to it? Though I have long been searching for an explanation to this perplexing dilemma, I have but a few feeble hypotheses.

One answer could be genetics: Perhaps, after hundreds of generations of living with the plant as part of the economy, selection favored those Native Americans who could eat the plant. (This is not unlike the drastic reduction in the incidence of lactose intolerance that occurred in pastoral Eurasian populations after animal domestication.)

Another genetic possibility is that people of European descent, for unknown reasons, are anomalous in their high level of intolerance. This is comparable to the high incidence of severe intolerance to broad beans exhibited by certain tropical African and Asian populations.

Then again, perhaps the dilemma is dependent upon the growing conditions of the plant. As stated in the account, hopniss grows most commonly in sand but reaches its largest size in rich muck. Is it possible that these tubers, created underwater in anaerobic conditions, contain some chemical byproduct of their metabolism that some people are allergic to? I entertain this possibility because much of the hopniss that I have collected, eaten, and served over the years grew in such water-logged conditions.

What also seems possible is that the Native Americans who ate this plant simply knew something about it that we do not – some nuances of its harvest and preparation that were not recorded or not understood by European ethnographers.

I suspect that there is some substance found in all hopniss, but which is more concentrated in older tubers or those that grow in waterlogged soil. Perhaps the body initially reacts to this higher concentration of our mystery substance; once sensitized, however, it will not tolerate any amount of it. To play it safe, and to test this hypothesis, I now only harvest, eat, and serve new tubers from dry soil. Hopefully, feedback from readers can shed some light on this issue.

In any case, a person eating hopniss for the first few times should do so with caution, keeping in mind that this plant has a history of causing allergic or intolerance reactions.

How thoughtful of the Creator to have designed such a plant as hopniss. How lucky that such a food is not only easy to harvest, but delicious. How friendly and welcoming the woods feels to one who knows that a vine called hopniss is waiting there.

There was a time, not unfathomably distant, when everyone in this plant's range knew it well. Settlements were located with its bounty in mind, and hopniss daily found its ways into the hearty dinners of a healthy people. This vine put forth a beautiful proposition: in exchange for starch and protein, people would loosen its soil as they dug for its riches and plant occasional tubers where they knew they would thrive. Generations may have forgotten, but this offer still stands.

Black Locust

Robinia pseudoacacia

These black locust flowers are at the perfect stage for eating.

It is that time between spring and summer, when the lawn is growing so fast that you can't believe that it was cut only last week. Lamb's quarters is sprouting in the garden where there was nothing but dirt just days ago. The forest has gone from the sunlit joy of spring to the shadowy gloom of summer. The beaches are crowded with laughing children, the parks with cheeping ducklings. The days are again pleasant enough that you can rest your forearm on the sill of your open window as you drive leisurely down the backroads. And as you do . . . there is that smell.

It doesn't creep into your window like that of apple blossoms, or rise with heat waves under the relentless sun like that of pine and sweet fern; it hits you with a burst and fills your passages like an olfactory flood. How does one describe such airborne ambrosia? The human tongue has proven no match for our nose when it comes to articulating the nuances of Nature's perfumes. But if there were a superlative for scents, this one deserves it. When you're sure that you have caught a whiff of The Flower of All Flowers, the Queen of

Blossoming Sweetness, pull over. Chances are that you are on the trail of a flowering black locust.

You'll know when you've found her. Drooping clusters of white flowers will adorn her every twig, from the crown to the lowest limb, putting the most lavishly overdone Christmas tree to shame. At any other time of year you might consider the black locust nothing but a misshapen weed tree – but when she shows the world her colors for a week and a half each year in early summer, few can fail to appreciate her efforts. Some have learned to deepen that appreciation even further by partaking of the black locust's ephemeral gift with not only our eyes and noses, but also our watering mouths.

Description

A medium-sized tree, *Robinia pseudoacacia* rarely exceeds 20 inches (50 cm) in diameter or 80 feet (25 m) in height. The trees are typically found in dense clones and the trunks tend to be crooked. At a glance, the naked trunks in winter resemble sassafras, and both species are most common in open, dry sites with poor sandy or gravelly soil. Black locust, however, has thinner twigs and branches. Upon close inspection, small thorns (far more prevalent on saplings) can be seen near the ends of the twigs. Black locust bark is thick, furrowed, corky, and brown. This tree's wood is among the hardest, heaviest, and most rot resistant of any found in North America. The leaves are alternate and pinnately compound, 8–14 inches (20–35 cm) long, with numerous smooth-margined, delicate, oval leaflets about 1.5 inches (4 cm) long.

Black locust flowers are borne in loose, hanging clusters of more than a dozen individual blossoms. Clusters may be up to 8 inches (20 cm) long. The

Typical deeply-furrowed bark of black locust.

Typical form of a mature black locust.

flowers are pea-like and creamy with a yellow spot on the upper petal. The seedpods that it produces are 3–4 inches (8–10 cm) long and flattened, much like pea pods. They turn dark brown, almost black, after they dry and often cling to the tree through the winter. Each pod contains several small, dark-brown, bean-like seeds.

Range and Habitat

The black locust actually has a rather limited native range, mostly in the Ozarks and the central and southern Appalachians. However, it has been planted widely outside of this area and has reproduced successfully. It is now one of the most widespread trees in the world. It is common on roadsides, in old fields, and in urban areas and disturbed forests over most of the eastern half of North America, and at scattered sites in the West. In the Midwest it is so abundant that most people who are familiar with the tree assume that it is native.

Johnny Blacklocustseed has yet to receive the hero's recognition of his apple-toting counterpart, but perhaps he kept himself a little busier, for the black locust has spread around the world in only a fraction of the time that it took the apple to do so. John Robin, along with his father Vespasian, brought the tree to Europe in the 1500s and cultivated it, and the scientific name of the tree's genus was given in his honor. This tree now grows feral not only throughout North America, but also across the temperate regions of Eurasia.

The genus *Robinia* contains several other tree species in North America. Among these, the New Mexican locust *Robinia neomexicana* is reported to have edible flowers like those of black locust (Brill, 1994). This tree grows along mountain streams in parts of Arizona, New Mexico, Utah, Colorado, southern Nevada, western Texas, and Mexico. I could find no specific references to the edibility of clammy locust *R. viscosa*, found in the Appalachians, or Kelsey locust *R. kelseyi*, confined to the Smoky Mountain Region, but Brill states that "there are no similar trees in North America with poisonous flowers." Blanche Derby (1997) tells of eating the rosy-colored blossoms of bristly locust *R. hispida*, and it is probable that the flowers the other members of this genus are safe.

Harvest and Preparation

Black locust flowers are available for little more than a week in the early part of summer. Pick them as soon as you see them, for if you wait at all you'll probably have to wait until next year. You want to catch them either before they've fully opened, or within a couple of days after they've done so. After that they will lose both their fragrance and their flavor.

The blossoms that you should seek are succulent and healthy in appearance; slight wrinkles or dried and shriveled edges indicate flowers that have passed their prime. The yellow spot on the upper petal is important, for it indicates whether or not the flowers are good for eating. If this spot is bright yellow, the flowers are good to eat; if it is dull or faded, they are too old. Some people have tasted over-ripe black locust flowers and given up on this delicacy before giving it a fair shot. If the petals have reddish freckles or dried edges, they will be bitter and unpleasant. If they litter the ground under the tree like snow, you are too late.

So, what do you do with an edible flower? That's a good question, since there really are no flowers of wide culinary use in our traditional cuisine. Black locust blossoms taste something like sweet peas with a hint of vanilla, and their wonderful aroma and subtle flavor lend themselves magnificently in a variety of dishes. I once made fettuccine alfredo with a heap of locust flowers cooked into the cream sauce, and it was out-of-this-world; I also used the blossoms as a primary vegetable in a fantastic chicken soup. They are swell in salads: green salad, fruit salad, and potato salad. These golden blossoms go well on a grilled chicken sandwich or hamburger, in a stir-fry, stirred into hot cereal, or sprinkled over cold cereal. My favorite way to eat them, however, is straight from the tree. I just grab a cluster, shake it to make sure it is free of ants and bees, and then stuff it in my mouth.

For those traditionalists among us, there are of course the good ol' fritters, which you can make out of just about anything. After making, eating, and enjoying five batches of black locust flower fritters one summer, I thought to myself, "Didn't I quit eating doughnuts because I didn't think they were good for me?" So I quit eating locust flower fritters, too. But if you are looking for an excuse to indulge in homemade junk food, black locust fritters are a good one. On the other hand, Steve Brill has a recipe for locust flower ice cream, which deviates about as far from junk food as ice cream can get. Find this recipe in Steve's *The Wild Vegetarian Cookbook.*

I once gathered a large bag of black locust flowers in southern Michigan, then headed into the Upper Peninsula where the advance of spring was a month behind, giving me the opportunity to mix summer flowers with spring vegetables for the next three days. Wapato, walnuts, locust blossoms, and maple syrup for breakfast; wild rice and cooked locust blossoms with fiddleheads and other greens for lunch; black locust flowers in a salad of basswood, spring beauty, and violet greens. To each of these meals the locust flowers added a pleasant and delicate touch that few could fail to love. While camping in the Ottawa National Forest, I had a meal that would have cost me a day's wages if I could ever find it in a restaurant: pan-fried lake trout fillets with morels, wild rice, wild onions, and black locust blossoms all sautéed in the fish's oil.

Seeds

Another edible product of the black locust is the seeds. Some authors claim that these seeds are poisonous, but I have been able to find no verification of their toxicity. Euell Gibbons claimed that the shelled green beans of black

Black locust pods and beans in July, full-sized but still green.

locust, gathered when full-sized yet still soft, are excellent eating when boiled until tender; he stated that he and his family ate them freely (Gibbons and Tucker, 1979). Without citing any source for the origin of this information, Francois Couplan (1998) states that the boiled seeds were eaten by "Indians," but that the raw seeds contain toxins similar to those found in raw beans and lentils.

I have eaten black locust seeds collected late in the fall when they were dry and brown. After a lengthy soaking and boiling, they tasted like beans but were still too tough to really enjoy. When the pods are green or green and purple, as one finds them in July and early August, the seeds are much softer and cook into a nicely flavored, tender legume that few could find culinary objection to. These beans are remarkably easy to collect, but their drawback is the pitiful tediousness of shelling the seeds, which seem unduly small in proportion to the size of the pod. With my limited experience, I haven't even been unable to shell one cup per hour. Perhaps somebody will devise a faster method of shelling and render the black locust bean a more practical food source.

With all of its uses, utilitarian and culinary, I find it amazing that black locust is not a more popular tree. It is truly a gift to the world.

251

Sumac

Rhus spp.

Ripe staghorn sumac fruit cluster.

A friend's father taught me the name of the sumac tree when I was seven years old. On a hillside near this friend's house, where we often played, grew a large cluster of them. The exotic, almost tropical appearance of the sumacs had enchanted me long before I knew their name. I used to climb the trees, small and brittle as they were, and attempt to get to the next one in the clump without touching the ground. Large colonies of sumac grew in an abandoned field at the edge of the town where I lived. I spent many hours in the calming shade of these sumac thickets, following rabbit runs in the short grass below or just listening to the birds, daydreaming and staring skyward. Those memories have implanted an everlasting fondness for the staghorn sumac into my mind.

Description

The most common sumac in my region is the staghorn sumac *Rhus typhina*, which grows throughout the northeastern United States and southeastern Canada. Staghorn sumac is a small tree or large shrub, usually 8–20 feet (2.5–6 m) tall – although I've seen a few as tall as 35 feet (11 m). The twigs are sparse

Smooth sumac flower
cluster.

and very thick, and those of the current year's growth are covered with velvety hairs (like a stag's horns in velvet). The leaves are large – sometimes more than 2 feet (60 cm) long – and pinnately compound, with each leaflet lanceolate and serrate. The foliage closely resembles that of ailanthus and black walnut. Sumac bark is smooth and dark gray; the inner bark is light green. When damaged, these trees exude latex. This and other species of true sumac usually grow in clones.

Sumac colonies in the open have the classic appearance of clones: tallest in the center, getting gradually shorter towards the outside, creating the illusion of a gentle hill where there is none. In such a sumac clone the trees often have the habit of bearing leaves only at the canopy, so that when one ventures underneath he is struck with the impression of being under a gentle dome painstakingly coaxed into existence by some master gardener.

Poison sumac. Note the glossy leaves and drooping, grape-like clusters of round fruits, which will become whitish upon ripening.

Most true sumacs are very similar in appearance to the staghorn sumac, but a few species are small shrubs with smaller compound leaves and ovate, deeply-toothed or lobed leaflets. All of the edible sumacs have reddish or purple fruit borne in erect clusters, although on some species these clusters are quite small.

Poison sumac *Toxicodendron vernix* is usually classified in a different genus (along with poison ivy and poison oak). This shrub, which causes reactions even more readily and severely than its better-known brethren, is confined to the East. It can be differentiated from true sumacs in many ways. The most important distinction is in the berries, which are whitish, waxy, hairless, and hang in loose, grape-like clusters – quite unlike the berries of the edible sumacs. The leaves of poison sumac differ in being hairless and shiny with smooth margins. Poison sumac also differs in that it rarely grows in dense, pure stands, and it inhabits swamps.

Roadside thicket of staghorn sumac bearing fruit.

Range and Habitat

Staghorn sumac is common on roadsides, along railroad tracks and fencerows, and in old fields and other open habitats throughout the northeastern United States and adjacent Canada. It appears sporadically in hardwood forests after fires or logging and sometimes persists on dry banks of streams, lakes, and rivers. Sumacs require well-drained soil and thrive on dry sites. They are extremely intolerant of shade in general and are rarely found in any type of mature forest.

There are numerous other species of sumac in North America, and at least one is found in almost every inhabited part of the continent. Prairie sumac *Rhus lanceolata* occurs in Texas and parts of Oklahoma and New Mexico; Mearn's sumac *R. choriophylla* grows in southern Arizona and New Mexico; lemonade berry *R. integrifolia* grows in southern California; shining sumac *R. copallina* is found over the southern half of eastern North America, smooth sumac *R. glabra* is found throughout the eastern United States and scattered in the Rocky Mountains and Great Plains; fragrant sumac *R. aromatica* and the very similar basket bush *R. trilobata* are found in mountainous, dry, or rocky situations from coast to coast, south into Mexico and North into Canada. This is only a partial list, so wherever you are, you are probably near some useful species of sumac. Consult a field guide for your region. (Laurel sumac *Malosma laurina*, found in the West, is not a true sumac and is reported to be inedible.)

Collection and Preparation

Since sumac is related to cashews and mangoes, anyone allergic to those foods should avoid it or proceed with caution.

The various species of red-berried sumacs have been widely used to brew a tart, refreshing drink. This beverage has been called sumac-ade, rhus-ade, sumac lemonade, Indian lemonade, sumac tea, and probably a whole bunch of other terms. Whatever people call it, they usually pronounce it delicious. When made properly it is as universally liked as lemonade. I have personally brewed this beverage from staghorn, smooth, and shining sumacs on many occasions. Keep in mind that my experiences refer to these particular species in the Midwest, and other species might need to be treated a little differently.

Preparation of the beverage is simple. If done improperly, the drink can range from terrible to great; if made correctly, it is usually marvelous.

The first step is to harvest the berries. Sumac "berries" are really just seeds covered with a thin coating of an acidic substance and sometimes hairs. They are very easy to collect since the clusters are rather large. You can snap off the twig that bears the cluster by bending it quickly, although it is easier to use pruning shears or a knife.

You want to get the berries when they are dark red and fully mature, so that they have fully developed their tart flavor, but before the rain has had the opportunity to wash the flavor out. In some years this can be most difficult. In most of North America, the first clusters are ready to be plucked sometime in July, with the prime time being in early August. Taste each cluster as you harvest to assure yourself that you are collecting something with flavor, as often they are bland.

A dark purple coloration usually indicates that the flavor of the fruit has developed fully; yet some of the best clusters I've tasted were light pink, disdaining my rule of thumb. Sometimes a white, sticky substance coats the berry heads. This is nothing bad; it is pure essence of sumac flavor – just a dab packs enough sour punch to make you shudder. Sometimes, unfortunately, the heads are so full of grubs that you don't want them.

The flavor of sumac berries exhibits a strange and drastic variation from year to year. In some seasons they just don't have much flavor (and what they do have is poor), while in other years the taste is potent and wonderful. I know of no certain explanation for this, but it seems that the plants have better and stronger flavor in years of heavy rainfall. The variation in taste is strong enough that in some years I simply do not make any sumac-ade; while in other years I drink it regularly.

A common mistake with sumac is to harvest the berry heads long after their flavor has been washed out by rain. Although I have found good-tasting heads into April after the best flavor seasons, this is the exception. Around here, the vast majority of them are spent by the end of August. If you taste around, you might find good ones until early October and sometimes even later. To enjoy sumac-ade out of season, it pays to harvest the heads in their prime and dry them, so you don't have to worry about using mediocre material.

I pluck about six to eight average-sized clusters for a pitcher of sumac-ade. I cram these into a pitcher, pour *cold* water over them, crush them up with my hands a little, and then let the pitcher sit in a cool place for a while. Here is the second place where many a promising batch of rhus-ade has been downgraded: Some people pour hot, or even boiling water over their berries. This leaches tannin from the stems, causing the drink to become bitter. It will not necessarily be unpalatable, but people generally show a strong preference for sumac-ade steeped with cold water.

When you pour your sumac-ade, it is a good idea to strain it through a cheesecloth to keep from drinking the fine hairs that cover the fruit (and any grubs that may have been present in the center of the cluster). The drink is pleasantly tart with a light pink color. Some people add sugar, but I much prefer it without.

Despite having heard many assertions that staghorn is the best sumac to use, I have always preferred the flavor of both shining and smooth sumacs.

There are other things that can be done with sumac-ade. My sister used it to make one of the best wines that I have ever tasted. Following Steve Brill's suggestion, I made an incredibly potent sumac concentrate by soaking four sets of berry heads in the same water for half an hour each. This concentrate can be frozen and reconstituted at any time for a refreshing drink. I made a wonderful and very tart jelly from it, too. The flavor is transformed and

Staghorn sumac shoots and branch tips in early summer, some stripped of their leaves and peeled in preparation for eating.

weakened somewhat by the boiling, so be sure to use a very strong sumac brew for the jelly. Euell Gibbons (1962) recommended using sumac-ade instead of plain water for boiling elderberry and other fruits which need a touch of tartness to liven them up for making jam or jelly.

Shoots

Sumacs have one other important edible product: the peeled shoot. When I was a child my family lived beside a railway, and every year the railroad company would mow the brush along the tracks. Each spring the bushes would grow back vigorously from their stumps, and the sumacs along the tracks regularly produced massive shoots. In late spring and very early summer, I would gather these shoots on a daily basis and peel off the leaves and bitter outer bark, then eat the shoots raw. These are slightly sweet and delicious, tasting more like a fruit than a vegetable.

Since those good old days the railroad company has taken up spraying herbicide instead of mowing, so I don't eat the sumac shoots there anymore. (And I'm glad I made that choice, for in the first few years after the spraying began, all of the woodchucks that lived in the brushy railroad right-of-way died off.) I have never found another place with such large sumac shoots, but I still eat them whenever I get the chance.

Sumac shoots are largest and best in their first year growing as suckers or stump sprouts, but you can also collect the tips of the branches from older plants. The portion of the new growth that bends and snaps easily will make a good vegetable. (Examine the thick end of the shoot to see if it has developed a noticeable, light-colored pith. If it has, that part is too old; break off a few inches until the shoot is solid and opaque green all the way through.) The bark strips away easily by hand. The largest peeled shoots will be about an inch thick and 12 inches long, but half of that size is commonplace.

Sumac shoots are a refreshing fruity snack to enjoy on the long, pleasant days of early summer, before any fruit is ripe. Not only do I like them, I crave them. I have never cooked them, nor sliced them into salads, nor candied them. Although I have eaten many hundreds of these shoots, they were always simply peeled and eaten on the spot. They probably have excellent culinary uses that my voraciousness has never permitted them to achieve.

The sumac is a wonderful tree for food and drink, deserving of much more attention than it gets from those who love the outdoors. It wouldn't be fair to shun it simply because it shares its name with a dangerous relative.

Wild Grape

Vitis riparia and other *Vitis* species

Leaves of riverside grape *V. riparia*.

In high school I dated a girl whose father liked to make wine. One beautiful September weekend he took us on a drive around the countryside in search of wild fruit to fuel his hobby. Stopping the car along a little country road at a place where grape vines formed a dense tangle over a barbed-wire fence, he jumped out to check the fruit, then hurriedly returned to the car and grabbed a grocery bag. When I took a bag of my own and climbed up to the fence line I was struck speechless by the quantity of grapes that hung there. Meanwhile, he had begun filling his bag with the kind of excitement almost never observed in grown men. I took his cue and started frenetically pulling off juicy clusters and dropping them in my own sack.

In twenty minutes I had amassed five gallons of fruit from the laden vines, and I had only taken a few steps since I began picking. By the time we left, there were bags and boxes of grapes filling the entire back seat. The next day I sorted, mashed, pressed, strained, and squeezed wild grapes for many hours. After all was done we had seven gallons of the most potent grape juice on

Earth. We made five gallons of wine, some mead, some juice, and some jelly. Ever since that weekend I have had a special fondness for wild grapes.

Description

Wild grapes are produced on perennial, woody vines with dark gray-brown bark that is sloughed off in long, narrow strips. Grape vines grow thicker and higher than most other native vines, often climbing 60–80 feet (20–25 m) into the canopy of a hardwood forest. They cling by means of forking tendrils which coil themselves around tree limbs and other such supports; these tendrils are borne on the stalk opposite from a leaf.

Wild grape leaves are large, alternate, simple, and deciduous. They are three-lobed or heart-shaped with very coarsely or irregularly toothed margins and long petioles. The tiny, five-parted, greenish-white, fragrant flowers are borne in large clusters which, like the tendrils, grow from the main stalk opposite from a leaf. They bloom in early summer, after which clusters of hard, green grapes form. In late summer the grapes will soften and darken; when ripe they are dark purple and only about .3 inch (8mm) in diameter. They look like miniature clusters of store-bought grapes.

There are a few plants which can be confused with wild grapes. One of the more common is the Virginia creeper, also known as five-leaved ivy or woodbine (genus *Parthenocissus*). The leaves of *Parthenocissus* species are palmately compound, usually consisting of five elliptic or ovate leaflets, as opposed to the simple leaves of wild grape. The mildly toxic "grapes" of five-leaved ivy

The mildly poisonous fruit of Virginia creeper; note the palmately compound leaves and pink, spreading stems.

Canada moonseed *Menispermum canadense* leaves.

Canada moonseed fruit. Poisonous.

are produced in widely-spaced, umbel-like clusters in which the stems fork in equal divisions (as opposed to the large central-stem branching pattern of grapes). The stems of *Parthenocissus* fruit clusters are usually bright pink, while grape stems are generally green or straw-colored.

Canada moonseed *Menispermum canadense* has leaves that look rather like those of grapes in their general outline except that they are not toothed on the margins. Also, moonseed's petiole attaches to the underside of the leaf, setting it apart from grapes and most other vines. A grape usually contains 2–4 seeds, while the similar-looking toxic fruit of Canada moonseed contains a single crescent-shaped seed and tastes extremely bitter. Moonseed vines never attain the massive size that grape vines do. They climb by twining around their supports and have no tendrils.

Distribution and Habitat

Riverside grape *V. riparia* is probably the most common wild grape in North America; it is found across southern Canada from Manitoba to New Brunswick and throughout the eastern half of the United States, except the Southeast. Its primary natural habitat is river bottom forests, but it has become abundant in empty lots, young or disturbed woods, along roads, railroads, fencerows, and forest borders. It is a sun-loving vine that cannot survive in heavy shade.

There are more than a dozen other species of wild grape found growing in North America, from the East Coast to the West, south into Mexico and north into the southern parts of Canada. In the Southwest the canyon grape *Vitis arizonica* is found in ravines and near watercourses at middle elevations; it was

Although the size and form of grape leaves vary greatly, there is a thread of similarity that allows all of them to be recognized. The leaves in the top row are *V. riparia*; in the second row, *V. aestivalis*. The leaves in the foreground are overturned to show their differing undersides: *V. aestivalis* (right) and *V. riparia* (left).

263

Riverside grape flowers.

once cultivated by Pueblo Indians (Elmore, 1976). California grape *Vitis californica* is found in canyons and foothills of the northern two thirds of California and southern Oregon, while *V. girdiana*, the desert grape, is found in desert edge areas further south. Wild grapes are absent from the Pacific Northwest and higher elevations in the Rockies. In the East one finds the summer grape *Vitis aestivalis*, the frost grape *V. vulpina*, and several other species.

All of the wild grapes listed are small and extremely sour. The majority of my experience has been with riverside and summer grapes, but the information in this account can be applied to other small-fruited species with little difficulty. Problems arise, however, when all of North America's wild grapes are lumped together for discussion, because two well known species, the fox grape *V. labrusca* and the muscadine *V. rotundifolia* are standouts. These two species have totally different culinary qualities than the smaller grapes. The instructions in this chapter do not apply to fox grapes or muscadines. Likewise, recipes designed for these larger grapes (such as Euell Gibbons' grape pie) will prove disastrous if one attempts to substitute one of the smaller grape species.

Harvest and Preparation

Wild grapes begin to ripen in late summer and usually remain available through the fall. I once picked many gallons of riverside grapes on November 3, while standing in two inches of snow. Nevertheless, I prefer to harvest mine in late September or the early part of October.

Collecting wild grapes requires little explanation. I simply grab the stem of the cluster and break it off by jerking quickly downward. I pick whole clusters, not individual grapes. I drop the clusters loosely into a bag or bucket, where the springiness of the stems keeps the grapes from being crushed. In good locations you can get several gallons of wild grapes in an hour – and that hour will pass in a flurry of excitement.

Riverside grapes
in late August, just
getting ripe.

Crushed wild grapes will quickly begin to ferment, but if you are going to use them within a day or two you need not worry about it. If the grapes are not smashed they will store well in a refrigerator or on a cold porch for a week or more.

Wild grapes provide an extremely potent juice, which is the base for jelly, wine, and other products. To make this juice, I put some grape clusters into a bucket or tub (I remove the grapes from their stems only if there is a high stem-to-grape ratio, as sometimes occurs when the grapes grow in the shade or there is poor fruit-set at flowering time) and crush them *gently* (so as not to break the seeds and release their bitterness) with a mug or my stomper. Then I stuff some mashed grapes into a jelly bag and wring out the juice. (A cider or grape press also works wonderfully.) The resulting juice is thick, dark purple, and as sour as lemon juice. Strain it through a cheesecloth to remove bits of seed, skin, and stem.

If you drink more than a few sips of this freshly pressed juice it will give you a sore mouth and throat. This sensation is caused by tartrate, a substance

265

Grape vine with a moonseed vine wrapped around it.

found in grape juice that precipitates from it and forms irritating gritty crystals. In fact, when crushing the grapes, if the juice soaks into your skin it will make you burn about an hour later, and the pain can reach considerable levels. Limited contact with the juice will not cause this; it results from the kind of inundation that might accompany handling a lot of grapes and not rinsing the juice off for a while. Once the pain begins, washing your hands will help you none; the burning, tingling sensation will persist for as much as four hours. When I make grape juice I keep a pail of water close by to rinse my hands occasionally when I am forced to touch the mash or fruit juice.

Tartrate is present in all grapes but is highly concentrated in riverside grape and some of the other small-fruited species. Fortunately, it is easy to get rid of. Just let the juice sit in a container in the refrigerator or some other cool place for a day or two. The tartrate will settle to the bottom; you will recognize it because it forms an ugly grayish sludge. Pour off the good juice and then discard the tartrate sludge, which is usually about one-third of the volume of the grape juice. *Never make anything from fresh-pressed small wild grapes without subjecting the juice to this purification process.*

Wild grape juice prepared with care as I have described will be very strong but with a clean, refreshing grape flavor. I occasionally drink it by itself or mixed with other juices such as apple. For most palates it needs to be diluted or mixed with milder beverages.

If you like Concord grape jelly, the same thing made with wild grapes will probably seem heavenly, for it is far more potent. Many sources claim that unripe wild grapes contain much pectin and are an aid in getting your jelly to jell. This may be so, but unripe wild grapes are too hard to get crushed when I make juice, and they don't get boiled as would be necessary to release their pectin, so it's a moot point. For wild grape jelly, use 6 ½ cups of sugar, 5 cups of undiluted juice, and one package of Sure-Jell powdered pectin.

If you make jelly from wild grapes without removing the tartrate from the juice beforehand, the jelly will usually become saturated with annoying pieces of grit that, besides wrecking the texture, impart an unpleasant flavor to the confection. But you'd deserve it, because I warned you.

I make wild grape wine not for the alcohol, but for the taste. I generally do not drink alcoholic beverages, but I make a few rare exceptions; wild grape wine is *that good.* If you are the kind of person who likes a sweet, fruity wine, you'll probably love this one.

Making wild grape wine is also incredibly easy. First, prepare juice as I have described. (Do not leave seeds or skins in the wine as it ferments, as is often done with domestic grapes, or you will harm the flavor.) Bring the juice almost to a boil and stir in about a quart (1 liter) of sugar for each gallon (4 l) of juice. (This is a lot of sugar, but keep in mind that this juice is extremely sour to begin with, so it needs sweetness to balance the flavor.) Let it cool to lukewarm and then add your yeast and stir. Pour the juice into whatever container you are going to ferment it in. After a couple of weeks, when fermentation has slowed significantly, taste the wine and add sugar if you feel that it needs some. I let mine ferment for five to eight weeks before siphoning it into bottles.

When I do make wine, I give almost all of it away, and it goes fast. I have never kept any more than about a year, but none of it has ever gone bad. Making other wines can be a tricky and exacting art, but riverside grape juice seems

Young riverside grape leaves.

to want to become wine; it has never given me the slightest trouble, regardless of how careless I have been with it. If you've never made wine, or you've had trouble doing so successfully, this is the place to start.

I once took some purified and undiluted wild grape juice, added a little sugar, stirred until it dissolved, and then poured the grape juice onto a piece of waxed paper that was laid in a cookie sheet. I let the juice sit for a couple of days until it was mostly dried. Then I took a wooden block and carefully pushed the dried grape juice into globs. I rolled these globs around with my fingers until they formed round balls and then put them in the refrigerator on another piece of waxed paper. This made a very sour grape candy, which children who avidly seek sour flavors would love.

Another wild grape product that millions of children mysteriously learn to relish is the sour young tendrils and tender vine tips that the plant produces in early summer. These have a pleasant rhubarb-like tartness, and I often snack on them in season.

Stuffed grape leaves are a well-known dish, and some authors recommend using young wild grape leaves as greens. I do not like the flavor of riverside grape leaves, which have an astringent aftertaste, but summer grape leaves have a much better flavor. Whatever species you use, make sure to get the leaves when they are still young and tender, and look for the larger leaves growing in the shade.

Another possible food use of wild grapes is in making grapeseed oil. Indeed, edible vegetable oils from wild foods are hard to come by, and grapeseed oil is, in my opinion, the best cooking oil commercially available. I have not extracted it from wild grape seeds, but there is every reason to believe that it could be successfully done. Commercially, grapeseed oil is typically extracted using alcohol after grinding the seeds; the oil content is only around 10%, making it hard to extract oil by pressing.

All across North America, every year, there are thousands of pounds of wild grapes of diverse sizes and flavors free for the picking. They are among the most abundant and prolific wild fruits on the continent. Why not locate a vine near you and try out some of these wonderful wild grape products?

Basswood, Linden

Tilia spp.

Young basswod leaves, perfect for salad greens.

Most of the greens discussed in the wild food literature are weeds of overseas origin – as if the plants native to North America were inferior for such culinary uses. American writings strongly reflect our predominantly European heritage, exhibiting an enormous bias towards herbs imported from the Old Continent. Certainly no Native American tradition would choose to emphasize the same handful of Eurasian weeds that Caucasian foragers have seemed so reluctant to look beyond.

In fact, many of our native plants make superb greens – and I'd be willing to bet that some of those could-have-been foragers who were long ago turned away from wild foods by such propositions as dandelion salad or plantain pottage would jump right back on our little bandwagon if they got to experience some first class wild salad greens like young basswood leaves.

Description

The American basswood typically produces a straight trunk and narrow crown, sometimes exceeding 100 feet (30 m) in height and 3 feet (1 m) in diameter. In old age the trunks usually become hollow, making them important as dens for wildlife. Basswood has a peculiar habit of sending up sprouts around its base, often resulting in one large trunk ringed by several smaller ones.

On young trees the bark is thin, smooth, and light gray; on older trunks it becomes thicker and separated into long, narrow, almost parallel ridges. The inner bark is tough and fibrous, and this accounts for the tree's common name. (The "bass" in basswood is a corruption of *bast,* meaning cordage or textile fiber.) The inner bark of basswood saplings was widely used by natives throughout its range for making rope, twine, baskets, and bags.

A clump of basswod trunks.

The alternate leaves are 4–7 inches (10–18 cm) long and nearly as wide, glabrous, and grow on slender petioles about 1.5 inches (4 cm) long. Thin and usually asymmetrical, basswood leaves are roughly heart-shaped and coarsely toothed. The twigs are rather stout. The winter buds are smooth on the outside, sometimes green but usually reddish.

Basswood flowers appear in late June or early July, several weeks after the leaves are fully formed. They are yellowish-white, 5-petaled, and borne in drooping clusters of less than a dozen blossoms, each flower on a moderately long pedicel. The fruit of the basswood is a small round nut, about the size of a pea, which ripens in the fall.

Perhaps the most distinctive feature of the basswood tree is the oblong bract that is attached to each cluster of flowers or fruit. This strange, light-colored leaf looks like a tongue, and no other North American tree bears anything like it. These often cling to the twigs for the entire growing season after flowering,

Clusters of basswood flowers and flower buds, each cluster connected to its tongue-like bract.

and often they persist into the winter. Even if they are not present upon the tree, one can usually find them in the leaf litter beneath it.

There are three other species of basswood native to North America: Carolina basswood *Tilia caroliniana*, white basswood *T. heterophylla*, and Florida basswood *T. floridana* – plus several European and Asian species planted here as ornamentals. All share a similar leaf shape and the distinctive tongue-like bract, and all are reported to have similar edible properties.

Range and Habitat

The American basswood is found across eastern North America from Manitoba and the eastern Dakotas south to northern Arkansas, east to the Smoky Mountains and north to Maine. The ranges of the three other native species fill in the remainder of the southeastern United States.

Basswood is a common tree, preferring well-drained to slightly wet sites and rich soil. It is fairly shade tolerant and long-lived but grows fast, especially when sprouting from an established root. One of the most abundant and well-known trees in the East, basswood is an important component of mesic hardwood forests.

271

Harvest and Preparation

The basswood has several edible parts. The young leaves, just as they unfurl from their buds, make one of the best wild salad greens. Basswood leaves are best when less than half of their full size, light green, and shiny looking. The tips of young shoots remain good to eat a little past the shiny stage – as long

Basswood buds just opening up – my favorite time to eat them.

as the stem is tender and easy to pinch through or break. If you miss that cue, you'll be able to tell when they're too old because you won't like their texture in your mouth. The older leaves won't harm you, they'll just help you commiserate with cud-chewing livestock.

I eat more basswood leaves than any other wild salad green. Not only do they have a pleasant, mild taste and a soft, slightly mucilaginous texture, but they are also found in practically limitless quantity from mid-spring until early summer. I like to use basswood leaves as the base for a salad, mixed with other greens of the season. Basswood greens are good cooked, but I prefer them raw.

A very interesting source of food from the basswood is the cambium. This has a flavor that reminds me of cucumbers, only much sweeter. Cambium can be harvested during the fast growth period of early summer by peeling off the bark and scraping the soft, slushy cambium off the outside of the wood using a knife, spoon, chip of flint, or whatever utensil you may have. Or you can do it my way, by alternately chewing and slurping. It is best to take this from saplings that are cut for another purpose rather than kill the trees for it. In a real emergency you can chew on strips of inner bark (not cambium) and suck out the mucilage, which doesn't taste bad at all. I also like to pluck the large winter buds and eat them while hiking.

Better known is the tea made from basswood flowers steeped in hot water. I try this fairly often and think that it is overrated. Perhaps the reputation comes from the little-leaved linden *T. cordata*, a European species often planted ornamentally, which has sweeter and more fragrant blossoms.

Sometimes I take the unopened flower buds and cook them with wild rice or use them in stir-fry. They are rather firm, although not tough, and pleasant in flavor. The interesting texture is appreciated in some dishes. The main drawback of these unopened buds is the annoying necessity of removing the numerous stems, which makes it pretty impractical to use them.

The last, barely-known edible part of the basswood is the tiny nut. Individual trees often produce these by the thousands. They taste a lot like sunflower seeds, but the nutmeats are smaller than a pea and contained in a thick shell. I know of no method of efficient extraction and suspect that a person could die of starvation in a silo full of them. However, they are a food of major importance to chipmunks, flying squirrels, and deer mice.

All of these culinary and utilitarian uses make the linden a difficult tree not to love – if its natural beauty alone is insufficient to endear it to you. If you are going to plant a tree, I'd consider the basswood.

Mature American basswood leaves.

Evening Primrose

Oenothera biennis

Evening primrose rosette in the fall. This is a good one to dig for its root, but don't eat leaves such as those in this photo.

As a teenager I used to scour the abandoned gravel lots around our local train station for edible weeds, being careful to keep out of sight when possible. On one such excursion I found a jackpot of evening primrose rosettes growing near a factory parking lot. Nobody was around, so I took my shovel and began hastily unearthing evening primrose roots and stuffing them into my bag. Lost in the excitement, I was startled back to reality by the voice of a man yelling "Hey!" I would have run away, except that I had a shovel and a bag full of plants, so I decided to talk my way out of it. After all, I was only digging up weeds.

The man approached me and did something very startling. He asked enthusiastically, "Are you a botanist? What are you digging up?" He then queried me about several other weeds in the vicinity. I was so shocked to be taken seriously by an adult that I could hardly think to answer his questions, but I hope that whatever I said convinced him to bring a shovel to work and try some evening primrose roots on his own.

Description

Evening primrose is a biennial with a rosette of numerous densely-packed leaves. The largest leaves are lanceolate or linear and can reach 9 inches (23 cm) in length; they comprise the lowest layer of the rosette, usually lying flat on the ground. The rosette's topmost leaves are elliptic or ovate and only 1–2 inches (2.5–5 cm) long. Leaves of all sizes have prominent light green or reddish midribs which contrast sharply with the dark green leaf surface. Margins of the basal leaves usually have scattered teeth of irregular size.

Leaves on the stalk of evening primrose are alternate and usually lanceolate, about 3–6 inches (8–15 cm) long, and covered with fine hair. The leaves of the upper stalk are sessile, while those on the lower part are petioled. The

Evening primrose flower spike in midsummer, showing open blossoms and flower buds.

Mature evening primrose plants in a roadside meadow in August.

main stems are stiff, round in cross section, bumpy from leaf scars, and often tinged with purple; only very rarely do they branch. At maturity they are typically 3–6 feet (1–2 m) tall and .5–.75 inch (13–19 mm) in diameter at the base.

Evening primrose blooms from early summer until early fall. After attaining its full height, the upper one to two feet of the stalk is encircled by dozens of flowers and pods in various stages of development. The flowers are about an inch wide and yellow, with four broad petals that connect at the base to form a long, slender calyx tube. These blossoms open one evening and then close up late in the following morning; only a few will bloom at a time on a particular plant. After the flower dies, a narrow, woody, tubular seed capsule, about 1.5 inches (4 cm) in length, tapering towards its blunt tip and curving upward, forms in its place. This seedpod is full of tiny, hard, reddish-brown, elongated seeds.

It is worth noting here that the primrose *Primula veris* (also called cowslip in England) is an entirely different plant than the evening primrose, not closely related to it. None of this discussion of the evening primrose should be applied to the primrose.

Range and Habitat

The common evening primrose is found in most of the eastern half of North America and sporadically in the west. It has also been brought to Europe where it is cultivated for its edible taproot. A number of very similar related species of evening primrose are found in the West and East. Among these are *O. clelandii, O. oakesiana,* and *O. villosa.* All are considered edible, but they are not identical to the common evening primrose in quality.

You can find this beautiful herb in sunny localities in almost any soil, but it is especially fond of sand and gravel or loosened soil. Good places to search for them are construction sites, fallow farm fields or the edges of cultivated land, sand and gravel pits, lakeshores, meadows, river banks, or any other dry place where the ground is frequently disturbed.

Harvest and Preparation

Once you learn to recognize them, the old, dead stalks of evening primrose will tell you where to look for the rosettes. The abundance of the plants varies greatly from year to year in the same place, and so does the proportion of first and second-year plants; there may be many stalks and few rosettes, or vice-versa.

The rosettes of evening primrose

A spike of old, dried, opened seedpods. This is your clue for where to search for rosettes.

277

Spring-harvested roots.
Note the tiny rosettes
on top.

produce an edible taproot, averaging about .75 inch (2 cm) thick at the base
and about 8 inches (20 cm) in length, tapering strongly. They are whitish in
color, often with reddish parts, especially near the top. The largest roots I've
seen, on the beaches of the Great Lakes, were about 1.5 inches (4 cm) in diameter at the thick end and well over a foot (30 cm) long. Typically, however,
they are much smaller. Usually the largest rosettes have the largest roots, but
this is not consistent. Evening primrose roots can be harvested throughout the
root season. Once the flower stalks begin to grow in the second year, the roots
become tough and woody and should not be harvested.

Evening primrose roots are spicy when raw – to the extent that some people
find them unpleasant. As with most spicy foods, other people relish them.
The spiciness, toughness, and size of the roots varies across different growing

Spring growth of second-year evening primrose, with excellent greens and stalk. Note the prominent light midveins.

conditions, regions, and species, so don't count out evening primrose as a food source if you've tried it in one area and it was unpalatable. Eating evening primrose roots raw gives me an unpleasant, itchy feeling in the back of my throat, so I cook them, which reduces but does not totally eliminate this effect.

279

Some books recommend boiling the roots in multiple changes of water to rid them of their pungency. I have never found this to be necessary; boiling makes the flavor much milder and brings out the pleasant, slightly sweet, flavor. They remind me of beets, except they have a little bite.

The evening primrose has several edible parts besides the root. The young stalk leaves of the second-year plants are mildly spicy and can be eaten raw or cooked. Do not eat the basal leaves; they are tougher and less palatable than the stem leaves, plus they are almost always gritty. It is best to pick the stem leaves while the plant is growing vigorously in late spring or early summer, selecting the smaller, younger leaves. Some authors recommend boiling the leaves in multiple changes of water. I don't. (I suspect that this recommendation owes its existence to attempts to eat the strongly flavored rosette leaves.)

In late spring and early summer, when the stalks of second-year plants are growing very fast, they are still succulent and supple. You can cut these stalks and peel off the outer layer to get a light green vegetable that is very tender and slightly sweet and spicy.

Later in the summer the flower buds appear. These are a pleasant nibble and can be added to cooked vegetable dishes or soup. Don't get them confused with the seedpods, to which they look similar. The seedpods are hard and almost unchewable, while the flower buds are smaller and much softer. Although both will often be on the same plant at the same time, the flower buds will always be above the seedpods. The flowers are even better than the buds, with less spiciness than other parts of the plant. They can be surprisingly sweet, especially just after closing. Their texture, flavor, and appearance make them attractive for salads or as garnish.

Evening primrose seed oil contains the highest amount of gamma-linolenic acid of any known food substance (Balch and Balch, 1997). For this reason, it is highly regarded as a healthful dietary supplement. While millions of dollars are spent on evening primrose oil annually, it is very easy to collect the seeds on your own for free. After the pods have dried and split open along their sutures, break off the seedheads and shake the seeds into a bag or bucket. They have a pleasant flavor and can be eaten to receive their health benefits.

All of these uses make the evening primrose one of the best wild food plants to get to know. While it will never be a staple food source, it provides something edible at any time of the year.

I have been warned many times not to walk the primrose path. That's easy for me, since I prefer the evening primrose path anyway.

Parsnip

Pastinaca sativa

Typical wild parsnips from good soil.

Ever since it escaped from colonial gardens hundreds of years ago, the wild parsnip has been waiting patiently to be noticed by those who let it loose. Finally, in the last decade, that recognition has come, but in the ironic form of ignominy. Parsnip has come to be despised as an obnoxious, rash-causing weed and a non-native invader of the last prairie remnants. The very virtues for which it was originally cultivated and brought here have been utterly overlooked; many land managers and naturalists seem to have no idea that it is the same common vegetable available in nearly every grocery outlet in the country. As a wild food, the parsnip remains largely unknown. This is the story of how I discovered it.

A childhood friend and I used to take every opportunity to visit his grandmother in rural southwestern Wisconsin, where we would explore the creeks, meadows, bluffs, and steep wooded hills. On one visit in early July we took a three-mile hike to a special place called Trout Creek, where we spent the better part of the day fishing, watching birds, picking berries and watercress, catching frogs and snakes, and alternately swimming downstream in the icy current and sunning ourselves on the streambank.

Two days later both of us had a painful rash of large blisters that made a case of poison ivy seem enviable. The rash lasted for several tortuous weeks and left us both with scars that persisted for years. Fortunately, I did not know at that time that parsnips had caused the rash; if I had, I might never have dared to touch the plant on purpose.

That fall we returned to Trout Creek, armed with field guides. Along the edge of the steep bank I identified my first rosette of wild parsnip. Although I had no shovel, I easily unearthed its root from the loose bank with my bare hands. I was amazed by its size: easily as massive as ten average wild carrots.

I went down to the stream and washed the parsnip, calling to my friend about the discovery. In our excitement we ate it raw, despite the fact that it was underripe. We looked closely at the parsnip plants, and once we had their image ingrained in our minds, we noticed that they were the dominant herb of the valley in which we were standing. There were thousands upon thousands of them. The meadow along the creek had been transformed into a great garden. Before leaving I used a stick to pry a few more roots out of the soil and brought them home for my first taste of cooked parsnip. The plant has been one of my favorites ever since.

It was not until a few years later that I read about the ability of parsnip to cause a severe form of dermatitis. The light went on in my head, and the mystery rash from that summer trip was solved. However, that experience has never dampened my enthusiasm for collecting and eating wild parsnips.

Description

Wild parsnip *Pastinaca sativa* is exactly the same plant as the garden parsnip; it just happens to be growing wild. I demonstrated this in one class when I showed what our group had collected from the wild, side-by-side with the produce of a nearby organic farm. Nobody could tell the difference. Wild parsnips growing in fierce competition and poor soil are stunted and coarse, but so would be a domestic parsnip placed under the same conditions. Since the two are indistinguishable, anybody familiar with the garden parsnip also knows its wild kin.

Parsnip is a biennial. The basal rosette of the first-year plant, which produces

Close-up of parsnip leaflets.

the edible taproot, usually consists of 3–6 large, pinnately-compound leaves. At full size in autumn, the leaves may reach 2 feet (60 cm) in length. The midrib is fairly thin; it is green or sometimes purplish, especially near the base. The leaf usually has nine or eleven leaflets, but occasionally the number varies. The leaflets clasp the midrib and are usually notably ruffled. They are often described as "ladder-leaves" since the leaflets are not in plane with the midrib as is typical for compound leaves; instead they grow on a plane roughly perpendicular to it. This is one of the most distinctive features of the wild parsnip and is quite readily noticed. The leaflets are roughly ovate, 1–3 inches (2.5–8 cm) long, and very coarsely and irregularly toothed. Some of the larger leaflets will even be lobed.

The edible taproot, when mature, ranges from about 8–12 inches (20–30 cm) in length. It is normally 1–1.75 inches (2.5–4.5 cm) thick at the top, although I have gathered wild parsnips over 3 inches (8 cm) thick weighing almost a pound each. Massive parsnips taper very sharply, while small ones have a gentle taper; they all tend to be about the same length. Unless the soil is very rocky, the taproots have little tendency to fork. The color is off-white or cream. Parsnips bend a little, in the same way that domestic carrots are not supposed to. Their aroma is delicious, distinctive, and very potent.

The second-year parsnip plant (which does not provide an edible root) grows from 3–6 feet (1–2 m) tall. The stalk is very deeply and distinctly

Umbel of parsnip flowers.

grooved (or ridged, depending on how you look at it) and usually branches only near the top. It may be over an inch thick at the base. The shape of old, dead parsnip stalks can easily be learned, so that even at highway speed they indicate to the trained eye where parsnip patches are located.

The wild parsnip blooms from late June to the middle of July. This is a good time to locate your harvesting meadows because the flowering stalks are usually conspicuously taller than the herbs and grasses around them. The individual flowers are five-petaled, dull yellow, and tiny. They are borne in large, flat-topped clusters (compound umbels) and from a distance these clusters appear yellowish-green.

The flower arrangement and overall form of parsnip somewhat resemble water hemlock and poison hemlock, two extremely toxic plants. However, there are many substantial, consistent, pronounced, and easily observed characteristics which distinguish the parsnip from these poisonous relatives. In this case I must reemphasize the forager's first rule of safety: Never consume any plant unless you are absolutely confident of its identification and certain that the part you intend to eat is edible.

Due to the fear of such a mistake, the parsnip has been ignored in many wild food texts. That is unfortunate, since this vegetable is delicious, abundant, and in many places as easy to gather as if it were in your own garden. To the trained eye, wild parsnips are instantly, easily, and positively recognized – and anyone's eyes can be trained. So, if you are interested in wild foods, take some time and familiarize yourself with the parsnip.

Range and Habitat

The parsnip is an introduced plant, directly descended from the garden vegetable known by the same name and relished in Europe for thousands of years. Like many other introduced plants, it has a sporadic occurrence, influenced by human activities as well as the natural environment. It can pop up almost

Mature parsnip
stalks.

anywhere in North America where proper conditions exist and is still spreading in some regions. However, it is absent from the Deep South and is most abundant in the Midwest and Northeast.

Parsnip thrives in the best agricultural soils: deep, rich, sandy loam. It is therefore abundant in many farming regions, especially rugged farm country where there are still some fencerows, unplowed pastures, and streamside meadows for it to inhabit. In many regions, such as the driftless area of Wisconsin, Illinois, Iowa, and Minnesota; northeastern Ohio; and most of Pennsylvania and New York, it is a ubiquitous weed found on almost every roadside or other sunny, untilled place.

Parsnip rosette in very early spring, when the root still contains most of its energy.

Wild parsnips are despised by ecologists in the former tallgrass prairie region because they thrive in the famously rich soils of these native grasslands and compete with rare native wildflowers. Many thousands of dollars and volunteer hours are expended annually to control this "noxious weed." The best strategy, of course, would be to address the habitat loss that made prairie wildflowers rare in the first place, but if these ecologists must blame the parsnip for humanity's faults, perhaps they should consider eating it out of existence.

Poison Parsnip?

There is a persistent and foundationless myth that the wild parsnip is toxic. I suppose that this myth originated with well-meaning parents who worried that their children might mistake some poisonous relative for a wild specimen of this vegetable. In time, this tale (unlike "there's a monster in the attic") became generally accepted as fact.

The fallacy that wild parsnip is toxic has even been perpetuated by some respected botanists – and in one terrific case, by a cookbook author, Bert Greene. In *Greene on Greens* (1984) he provides the most ludicrous account of any wild plant that I have ever found.

Greene tells us that while parsnips were eaten in ancient Rome, wild parsnips came originally from northern Europe and were "exceedingly lethal." Brought to Rome as spearhead poison by Visigoth warriors, some parsnips were apparently left behind and managed to take root. When cultivated in their new land, the parsnips were not only innocuous but also edible and delicious. Greene then asserts that cultivated parsnips which have escaped and gone wild again have reverted to their former state of deadly toxicity.

Where Mr. Greene found this fabulous tale I cannot guess, but any human with even a moderate level of intelligence should be able to recognize it as not only false, but impossible. Would Germanic warriors really lug root vegetables across the continent? Could these vegetables be in viable condition after such a journey? (Perhaps they were kept in a root cellar hauled by chariot.) Would a parsnip simply dropped actually grow, or did one of these inept warriors accidentally bury it while relieving himself? How could the geographical difference effect the change from deadly to delicacy? Why would the Romans begin cultivating the Visigoths' spear poison plant as a food (since they, too, would probably be quite surprised by the transformation)? How do parsnips know if they are being cultivated? Do they sometimes get confused and mistakenly kill gardeners when poorly tended?

This is a fine example of the irrational fear with which many people view wild foods. Perhaps a day will come when otherwise intelligent people will stop suspending all logic when wild foods are discussed.

The parsnip *Pastinaca sativa* is not poisonous – not in your garden, not in the grocery store, and not in a meadow or pasture.

Harvest and Preparation

Parsnips can be collected throughout the root season, and a good, full-sized shovel is the best means of harvest. The roots reach their full size by the end of September, but their flavor improves the longer they are left in the ground. I collect most of mine in late October or early November, waiting until shortly before the ground freezes. Immediately after the soil thaws in spring you can dig more parsnips – this is when many people prefer to harvest them, since they are sweeter at this time. The spiciness of the roots also seems to diminish over time.

Parsnip is among the most labor-efficient wild foods to harvest. In many places it is entirely possible to dig thirty to fifty pounds in an hour, and it just takes a minute to get a root or two for a meal. If you collect parsnips wantonly with total disregard for the stand's future, annihilating entire populations, some local conservation group will probably give you a medal of honor for distinguished volunteer service. But if you *like* parsnips you may want to avoid doing that.

Parsnips consist of two distinct layers: the rind and the core. The difference between these two layers is slightly more noticeable in wild parsnips than it is with their domestic counterparts. The rind is slightly spongy and rather spicy, while the core is denser, sweeter, and not very spicy at all. The two layers separate easily. For most purposes, I use the whole parsnip, but occasionally I will use only the core if it is early in the season and the rind has a very strong flavor. The cores are my favorite part to eat raw.

Parsnip rosettes in October. This photo actually shows two growing side-by-side.

A century ago, parsnips were regular fare in most households in Canada and the northern half of the United States, but food choices change over time. Today this vegetable occupies only a small spot on the produce shelf, and few North Americans use them, although they remain more popular in Europe. There are hundreds of parsnip recipes scattered throughout the cooking literature: parsnip cake, stewed parsnips, parsnips and apples baked with brown sugar, and many more.

Parsnip is a wonderful soup ingredient, and this is probably its principal culinary use today. Its unique flavor and sweetness combine well with a great variety of other vegetables. Another way that I like to use parsnips is to grate them fine and cook them in casseroles. I enjoy very ripe parsnips raw, although not everybody shares this predilection.

Parsnips are easy to store. Traditionally, when harvested in the fall, they are kept in a root cellar packed in moist sand or sawdust and easily last until spring. For shorter-term storage (up to two months), place them in the refrigerator wrapped in a plastic bag to prevent drying.

The Parsnip Rash

I occasionally hear somebody describe a terrible case of "poison ivy" that includes enormous, burning blisters filled with clear liquid, and feel duty-bound to inform them that this was probably a parsnip rash. Until the last few years, when parsnip was adopted as a poster villain in the fight against evil invasive plants, the parsnip rash was virtually unknown. (Ironically, the rash is most often suffered by people pulling it out because it causes a rash – much like rattlesnakes, which bite people mostly when they try to kill them because they bite people.) The rash has been used effectively to stir up fear and anger against this intruder. I don't want to jump on the bandwagon, but anyone who plans to collect parsnips should know about it.

Parsnips will afflict you only under certain conditions. You must break the plant and get the juice on your skin while sweating and exposed to sunlight. Under these conditions, you *will* get the rash; it is not dependent on an allergic reaction like poison ivy. People rarely get the rash from parsnip rosettes; it is generally caused by the older plants in early summer. Garden parsnips can cause the same rash, but it is so unlikely to strike those harvesting the plants that this quality is virtually unknown to gardeners. In all my years of harvesting parsnips it has never been a problem. So don't let a little photodermatitis scare you away from this wonderful wild root.

Common Milkweed

Asclepias syriaca

A colony of common milkweed, one of the best-known wild plants in North America.

Most people know milkweed simply as food for the monarch caterpillar or as a tenacious, pesky weed of hayfields. If those butterflies weren't so beautiful, and if their annual migration to Mexico wasn't so amazing, few people would care what happened to this herb. But milkweed isn't your average weed.

In World War II, schoolchildren across the Midwest collected thousands of pounds of milkweed fluff to stuff life preservers for the armed forces in the Pacific, because kapok, the normal material used for this purpose, came from Japanese-occupied Indonesia and was unavailable. Today, you can buy pillows, jackets, and comforters stuffed with milkweed down – which is wonderfully soft and has a higher insulative value than goose down (Knudsen and Sayler, 1992). Native Americans used the fiber of milkweed stalks to make rope and twine.

I am amazed that, as much attention as milkweed has received as a fiber crop and a butterfly planting, so little has been said about its use as food. Ethnographic records show that common milkweed was eaten as a vegetable by tribes throughout its range, and often it was of great importance. It provides

edible shoots (like asparagus), flower bud clusters (like broccoli), and immature pods (like okra). The soft silk inside the immature pods is a unique food,
and the flowers are also edible. Milkweed conveniently provides one or more
edible parts from late spring until late summer, making it one of the most
useful wild edibles to learn.

Description

There are numerous kinds of milkweed in North America, but in this account
I am talking specifically about the abundant and well-known common milkweed *Asclepias syriaca*. What I say about this plant does not necessarily apply
to other milkweeds.

Common milkweed is a tall perennial herb that rarely branches. Typical
height is 3–6 feet (1–2 m). The leaves grow in opposite pairs all along the
stalk, borne on very short petioles. They are generally 4–9 inches (10–23 cm)
long and 2–4 inches (5–10 cm) wide, oblong or ovate in shape with smooth
margins, and thick but not succulent. All parts of the plant are covered with
a very fine pubescence, giving it a soft, velvety feel. The sap is a latex, which
often flows copiously and quickly when the plant is broken.

Milkweed flowers are borne on the upper third of the plant in tight umbels
that hang from the leaf axils. The clusters of flower buds look something like
miniature heads of broccoli, but the individual buds are larger. The distinctive
blossoms are some combination of white, pink, and purple; the five petals bend
sharply backward, and in front of each one there is a thick lobe or append-
age pointing forward, the
five appendages forming
a perfectly symmetrical
"crown" that is unique to
the milkweed family. The
pods that follow occur
singly or in small clusters.
They are teardrop-shaped
and range from 2.5–5
inches (6–13 cm) long
when mature. They are
typically bumpy on the
outside, but are some-
times smooth.

Common milkweed flowers.

The Great Milkweed Myth

The first time that I ate milkweed shoots, it was done with extreme care. I mean, **extreme**. I knew that the shoots were mildly poisonous when raw and that they would be terribly bitter and still a little toxic if not cooked properly. I knew that I had to boil them in three or more waters, making sure that the shoots were covered with boiling instead of cold water – for the use of cold water would "set" the bitter principle in the vegetable. I also knew that this bitterness was caused by a toxic, milky latex. I knew all of this because I had read it in half a dozen books.

Not surprisingly, such elaborate and exacting preparation requirements, with such severe consequences if wrongly performed, caused me to put off trying milkweed for several years. When so many excellent wild vegetables exist, why waste my time with one that requires such attention and is described as only "marginally edible?"

Nevertheless, one day in early May, responding to some insuppressible forager's curiosity, I brought home a handful of the thick, succulent shoots for a trial. I prepared them meticulously according to the instructions of my several books, then sampled hopefully. They were wonderful! I wanted to thank the genius who had discovered that such a distasteful and even toxic plant could be made delectable through this special process. Over the few weeks that followed, I ate milkweed shoots on several occasions, and grew to esteem them highly.

After a couple years I felt more comfortable with the plant and began to wonder if perhaps the three water changes that I had been using to cook milkweed parts were overkill, so I tried it with only two, still making sure to use boiling rather than cold water to refill the pot with each change. There was no perceivable difference in flavor. The next year I got even braver. All the warnings about terrible bitterness and mild toxicity notwithstanding, I changed the water only once when cooking my milkweed – again using boiling water as instructed. Still, there was no change in the flavor. That got me wondering, "Maybe milkweed isn't bitter at all? Maybe I don't need to change the water?"

Eventually I tried milkweed shoots boiled *without* changing the water; furthermore, I made sure to begin the process with *very cold* water so I could "set" this elusive bitter principle just to see what it tasted like. (I had expended so much time, water, and cooking fuel to fight this chemical culprit that I was becoming anxious to meet him.) The result was perfectly palatable without even a hint of bitterness. I drank the cooking water, too, and it tasted mild

Harvested common milkweed shoots, a few of them peeled.

and pleasant, reminding me of green beans. After that I went out and tasted some milkweed shoots raw, and they were pleasant, slightly sweet, and mild. So then I tasted the milky sap all by itself – only to find that it was without any noticeable unpleasant flavor. It turned out that our bitter enemy was too much of a coward to even show up.

This discovery begs the question: What the heck is going on here? At that point in my life I already owned a small heap of wild food books, and *every single one of them* stated that milkweed was unpalatably bitter unless prepared according to precisely these same elaborate instructions.

Since then I have tried common milkweed over many parts of its range and conducted some taste tests to see how others perceived the flavor. I have personally eaten milkweed at many localities in Wisconsin, Michigan, and Minnesota, as well as in Ontario, Nebraska, Ohio, Illinois, Pennsylvania, and New Jersey. Rather than varying in flavor from place to place as some plants do, it was not bitter in any of these regions. My ramblings on this topic have prompted correspondence from others, representing nearly every state in which the plant is found, who affirmed, often emphatically and angrily, that their local milkweed populations are not bitter either, and that the elaborate preparation instructions so often reported are absurd and unnecessary.

I gathered milkweed shoots in northern Wisconsin one May and boiled them without changing the water, then fed them to 19 people who agreed to give me feedback on their flavor. All of them said they liked them (an amazing consensus for any food), and none used the word "bitter" when asked to describe the flavor. In early August of the same year, I gathered immature pods in east-central Minnesota and again cooked them without changing the water. I had somebody else serve them to about twenty complete strangers. She reported to me that "everybody liked them." Later, I served two dishes containing milkweed, boiled without changing the water, at the 2000 Nature Wonder Wildfoods Weekend at North Bend State Park in West Virginia. These dishes were each tried by about 75 people. Not only were they liked almost unanimously, but nobody described the milkweed therein as bitter, to any degree – and one of these dishes won the cooking contest for the event. (Even two outspoken critics of my assertion that milkweed is not bitter both said, without equivocation or reservation, that the milkweed in these dishes was not bitter.)

In classes that I have taught over the last five years, I have had the opportunity to feed milkweed to hundreds of participants in three states, and on no occasion did I put it through the prescribed multiple-boiling process. Not only has it been among the more popular greens, but not one person has said that it was bitter. You may claim that these students are just trying not to hurt my feelings, but most of them dislike one or two greens that I teach them about, and nearly 100% of them pronounce winter cress, chicory, dandelion, and marsh marigold to be bitter.

One spring I had a class of seven people, all unfamiliar with this issue, read eight different accounts claiming that common milkweed was mildly toxic and too bitter to eat without leaching. Two members frankly stated that it would be stupid to eat such a dangerous plant that required tedious processing. I was afraid that one of them would walk out when I insisted in a naïve voice that we proceed to give it a try. We went to a field where I had recently seen (but not tried) some milkweed. I found a plant and told them that, while we shouldn't eat it raw, it would be safe to taste a bit to experience the bitterness firsthand.

They eyed me skeptically as I handed them small sections of stem, but seemed comforted by the fact that I didn't hesitate to pop one into my mouth. I watched their confused faces for a few seconds as they sampled the plant. Finally, one man asked, "Do you think maybe this milkweed doesn't have as much sap as it's supposed to?"

"Why do you think that?" I asked, pretending to be astonished.

"Because the sap is the bitter part, isn't it? This ain't bitter at all."

The entire group immediately rang out in an emphatic cacophony that can be summed up as, "This isn't bitter; it's sweet. What were all those books talking about?" They discussed the plant as I listened but did not participate, coming to the surprising consensus that raw milkweed tastes like plums.

I have been criticized hotly by a few for challenging the truism that milk-weed is bitter, but I am truly unable to locate a single person who eats common milkweed and finds it to be bitter. Native Americans did not consider common milkweed bitter; there are no ethnographic accounts that mention the plant being bitter or requiring any special process to render it edible, and the few Natives that I've met who eat milkweed today simply boil it before consumption. A few pre-1960 books on edible wild plants mention bitterness in milkweed, but none with the sense of danger or impending culinary doom expressed by more recent authors.

So where does the carefully delineated process of leaching out milkweed's terrible bitterness, parroted in nearly every wild food book written in the last forty years, come from? The answer to this one is fortunately quite obvious. An examination of the accounts in question clearly points to their being derived, directly or indirectly, from a single source: Euell Gibbons' 1962 classic *Stalking the Wild Asparagus*.

In his chapter on milkweed, Gibbons writes, "The milkweed has an extremely bitter principle that seems to permeate every part of the plant. Fortunately, this excessively bitter taste is easily removed with boiling water. . . The shoots, leaves, buds, or pods are put into a pot, covered with *boiling* water and placed over a high flame. When they have boiled one minute, drain and cover with fresh boiling water and return to the heat. This process is repeated at least three times . . . covering with cold water and then slowly bringing it to a boil . . . seems to cause the bitter principle to become fixed in the cooked product."

Euell Gibbons was by far the most influential wild food author of the 20th Century, and because of this influence, the extreme bitterness of milkweed, as well as the elaborate process necessary to remove this taste, became gospel truths in the wild edible plant field. The accounts of milkweed preparation given by most authors in the last 40 years are regurgitations of what Gibbons wrote.

At one point, Euell Gibbons probably made the same blunder that many foragers have made over the years: mistaking the horribly bitter shoots of common dogbane *Apocynum cannabinum,* or some toxic species of milkweed, for those of common milkweed *Asclepias syriaca.* He most likely took up the leaching process because of such an experience and just never quit doing it, despite the fact that it was not doing any good as long as he had the right plant. It seems highly improbable that the bitterness he described was actually found in a common milkweed plant – but if it was, it was certainly an exceptional specimen.

It is interesting to note that while Euell Gibbons was still alive he was challenged about this. One reader wrote to him, "Why did you say milkweed had to be boiled three times? I like it just cooked and eaten." His response that "not everyone prefers their food as bland as I do" certainly does not make it sound like he perceived leaching to be the only acceptable way to prepare milkweed (Akiyama, 1972).

Over the last few years, several reports have trickled back to me of people collecting common dogbane shoots, believing they were milkweed, and then attempting to eat them, only to be repulsed by their terrible bitterness. In four of these instances the mistaken foragers were quite experienced, just unfamiliar with the difference between these two plants. One person, unable to admit his mistake, forced himself to eat the "milkweed" and got sick.

There are many bitter and toxic species of milkweed out there, but most do not look much like *Asclepias syriaca.* An exception is *A. amplexicaulis,* the blunt-leaf milkweed, found in the northeastern United States and southern Ontario. This milkweed has a form very much like that of common milkweed, but the leaves are thinner and shiny, and all parts of the plant are smooth and hairless; the stems are coated with a white bloom. Blunt-leaf milkweed is extremely bitter and should not be eaten.

If Euell Gibbons made a simple mistake, that is excusable; we all do. What is not excusable is the blind, unquestioning acceptance of that mistake by later wild food authors, their failure to test his assertions, and their plagiaristic repetition of Gibbons' account under the guise of their own experience. Anybody who regularly eats milkweed will eventually discover that it is not bitter. In fact, thousands of foragers have made this realization; few regular milkweed-eaters practice the recommended leaching. This makes it especially disturbing that the authors of so many popular wild food books never figured it out. It was their irresponsibility that entrenched the misinformation that now prevails in the wild food literature.

So here I will set the record straight: Common milkweed is not bitter. It does not need to be boiled in multiple changes of water – simply boiling it is sufficient. Occasionally one may find an exceptional specimen that is slightly bitter, but not even within shouting distance of such greens as winter cress or dandelion. In fact, common milkweed has one of the most mild, neutral, and agreeable flavors of any vegetable you'll ever find, wild or cultivated. That is exactly why I like it, and exactly why it had such a broad and universal appeal to Native Americans.

Some foragers have been scared away from common milkweed by the claim that it is "mildly toxic." The harmful cardiac glycosides found in the inedible milkweeds and dogbanes are bitter to the taste (John Kallas, personal communication). If this is the case, then they are either absent in *A. syriaca* or found in an imperceptible trace. I have been unable to find any research demonstrating that common milkweed contains cardiac glycosides in levels that pose a threat to humans, or any evidence that the plant has ever poisoned anybody. None of the books warning us about milkweed's toxicity cite such sources for this "fact." The fact that millions of people have eaten this plant as a regular part of their diet strongly suggests that it is not harmful in normal use.

In conclusion, the stern warnings that follow the common milkweed like a felony conviction through the foraging literature are unnecessary and should be taken, not with a grain of salt, but with a big slab of it.

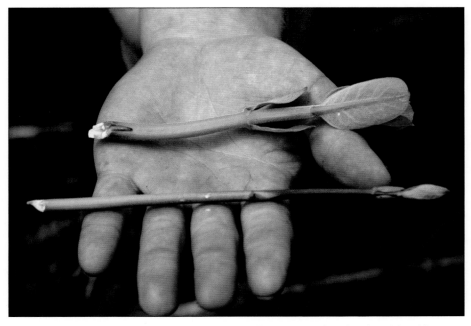

Shoots of spreading dogbane (bottom) and common milkweed (top). Photo by Glenn Schmukler.

Discriminating Common Milkweed From Common Dogbane

Because there is such a history of confusion between the shoots of these plants, a detailed discussion of their differences is in order. Steve Brill states that, "Tiny hairs on milkweed's hairy stem, visible only under magnification, provide the sole distinction," between common milkweed and dogbane. That is alarmist nonsense. The shoots can be readily distinguished by a multitude of easily observed characteristics. Novice foragers that I have taken afield, when shown these characteristics, found it a cinch to differentiate the plants. Note that there is another common species of dogbane, the spreading dogbane *Apocynum androsaemifolium*. This species has tiny hairs on the underside of the leaves but otherwise looks much less like milkweed than its larger relative.

Common milkweed shoot near last year's dead stalks, at a good size for harvest.

Shoot of common dogbane, a toxic plant often mistaken for milkweed, beside last year's dead stalks.

Common Milkweed *Asclepias syriaca*	**Common Dogbane** *Apocynum cannabinum*
Leaf bottom and stem pubescent	Leaf and stem smooth, hairless.
Veins on underside slightly lighter than those on top.	Veins on underside stand out as much lighter than those on top.
Top veins light green, more prominent.	Top veins cream colored, less prominent.
Few or no leaf axils contain buds.	Many leaf axils contain buds.
Leaves do not squeak.	Leaves squeak if rubbed together.
Leaf size decreases going up the stalk; when pressed against stem, leaves significantly overlap the set above them; leaves proportionately larger, ovate. (Not visible on youngest shoots.)	Leaf size increases slightly going up the stalk, leaves pressed flat overlap little to none, except at the top of the plant; proportionately much smaller, oblong. (Not visible on youngest shoots.)
Stem lacks bloom, usually light green color, slightly squared in cross section.	Stem has faint bloom, usually red spots or streaks, and is round in cross section.
Shoot form much shorter.	Shoot form much taller.
Stalk hollow, green inside.	Stalk solid, white or cream inside.
Exudes copious latex.	Exudes some latex.
Taste is sweet, pleasant.	Taste is extremely bitter.

**If your milkweed is bitter, it is not common milkweed.
Do not eat bitter milkweed!**

Range and Habitat

Common milkweed is found in eastern North America east of the dry Plains and south of the boreal forests of Canada, except for the Deep South. It also occurs sporadically farther west. Its native habitat is river bottoms, forest edges, clearings, and lakeshore or seashore dunes, but it has done extremely well in the wake of man's disturbance of the landscape. It is now a ubiquitous plant of roadsides, fencerows, waste places, agricultural fields, pastures, open woods, and abandoned farmland. It is one of the most well known wild plants in its range.

Although this chapter focuses on common milkweed *A. syriaca*, some other milkweed species are edible as well. Notable among these is showy milkweed *A. speciosa*, which occurs on the high western plains and in the lower elevations of the Rockies. In my limited experience, this plant is nearly as palatable as the common milkweed. I have not tried all the edible parts, however. Poke milkweed *A. exaltata,* common in wooded areas of much of eastern North America, is named for the resemblance of its greens to those of poke, a popular wild potherb. Its shoots are as good or better than those of the common milkweed, while its young leaves are more tender and make superb cooked greens. The flower buds of poke milkweed are also excellent. Readers should refer to reliable botanical manuals to identify these other species. Any milkweed species not specifically mentioned as edible should be considered poisonous.

Harvest and Preparation:

Shoots: Come late May, when oak and maple trees have just begun to adorn themselves with summer splendor, look for the thick shoots of common milkweed pushing up among the dead stalks of last year's plants. They appear asparagus-like, except they have a few pairs of small leaves – clasping their sides at first, but opening up later. The best size for picking is 6–14 inches (15–35 cm), as long as the leaves are not yet fully formed and the stems are still tender and break easily when pinched and bent. The skin of the shoot toughens before the interior does, so sometimes it is beneficial to peel off the stringy outside before cooking the milkweed shoots.

Boil the shoots until they are tender, which takes twenty minutes or so. Common milkweed shoots are almost universally liked, being most often compared to green beans. While their flavors are not identical, I think the comparison is a fair one. As the plants grow taller, you can still eat the tender top few inches, but these tops are never quite as good as the younger shoots.

Common milkweed with young clusters of flower buds.

I most often eat milkweed shoots by themselves, seasoned with a little salt and pepper. Some people like them creamed or with cheese melted over them. They are very good in soup as well, giving the water they are boiled in a delicious, hearty flavor and a nice green color.

Milkweed shoots are often easy to collect in quantity, since the plants grow in clones that are sometimes extensive. Every spring I can a few batches of them to vary my winter fare, and they retain their flavor fairly well. They can also be stored by blanching and freezing.

Some books suggest eating the smaller leaves at the top of the plant after boiling. I have done this a few times, but in my opinion these leaves are not flavorful enough to warrant much attention.

Flower Buds and Flowers: The clusters of unopened flower buds look like miniature heads of broccoli but are much less rigid. You can gather these at any size, but they are not quite as tender in the days immediately preceding the opening of the flowers. I prefer those that are about two-thirds of their full size. The collecting season for these buds spans most of July and August.

Dice up a handful of these flower buds and toss them into a soup, casserole,

Common milkweed bearing immature pods. All pods visible are good for eating.

pasta dish, stuffing, or stir-fry to excellent effect. To eat the flower buds alone, boil or steam them, drain the water, and season. Many people consider this the best part of the milkweed plant. It is often said that they taste like broccoli, but in my opinion, they taste almost identical to the shoots and the pods – they just *look* like broccoli. Before cooking the flower buds, check them for tiny, newborn monarch caterpillars, which often hide between the stems and buds.

The first milkweed flowers usually appear in early July, and the blossoming season is nearly two months long. The multicolored flowers have a sweet, musky odor and are a favorite of insects. They are often listed as edible; I have eaten them in small quantities, but they do not appeal to me.

Pods and Silk: After the flowers wither away, seedpods will form in their place along the upper parts of the stem. A cluster of flowers rarely produces more than four or five seedpods, and the average milkweed stalk produces only four to eight pods per season. These pods first appear about the size and shape of a teardrop, and when fully grown they will be 3–5 inches (8–13 cm) long.

Until about two-thirds grown, they make a superb vegetable. This is perhaps the best known and most highly esteemed milkweed product. The smallest pods, under an inch (2.5 cm) long and still firm, are the most desirable for eating whole, while the slightly larger but still immature pods are best for extracting the soft and sweet pre-silk. When the pods are fully formed, they become tough and unpalatable and should not be eaten.

Milkweed pods are excellent in stew, stir-fry, or eaten as a cooked vegetable. They are delicious with cheese and bread crumbs. Using your culinary creativity, you should be able to find many uses for this mild, unique, and delicious green vegetable.

Immature common milkweed pods with pre-silk showing.

The best time to gather milkweed pods is late summer (from early August to early September around here). The size of the pods varies greatly from one plant to the next. An immature pod on one specimen may be larger than a full-grown pod on another, so determining which pods are immature can be tricky. The pods that are too old tend to be rougher on the outside than the young pods. Their tips also tend to be more pointed and curved. These are tendencies, not rules, however. There are a few more reliable ways to determine the age of pods.

There is a line running the length of each pod, along which it will split open to release its seeds when mature. If you pull apart on both sides of this line and it splits open easily, the pod is probably too old to use. For the beginner, it is best to open up several pods and examine the insides to get an idea of which ones are in the proper stage for harvesting. In an immature milkweed pod (one that can be eaten) all of the seeds will be *completely* white, without even a hint of browning. The silk should be soft and juicy, not fibrous. It should be easy to pinch through the bundle of silk or to pull it in half. Immature pods are also plumper and harder than mature ones. Don't let this seem more complicated than it really is – with time you will know, at a glance, which pods to collect.

Occasionally I gather a large quantity of milkweed pods. I work my way through my favorite patch and fill a cloth bag, which doesn't take very long since milkweed often grows in large, prodigious colonies. I let the tiny pods grow and ignore those that are questionably old. When I get home I sort through the pods, keeping those less than about 1.25 inches (3 cm) long to be eaten whole. If I do not use these immediately, I can them or freeze them after parboiling. Milkweed pods begin to toughen in a few hours after they are picked and may become unpalatable in a day or two, so try to use them or prepare them for storage without undue delay.

The immature pods that are more than 1.5 inches (4 cm) long are used to make a unique food product that is called *milkweed white* at our house. Milkweed white is simply the pre-silk and soft white seeds from immature pods. I open up each pod, remove the white from the inside, and discard the rind. (The rind is actually edible, but I don't find myself having the desire to eat all of it.) When raw, milkweed white is sweet and juicy. (I only eat small amounts of it raw, however.) When boiled, it has a mild, pleasant flavor and a chewy texture. Mixed with other foods, the boiled white looks, tastes, and behaves surprisingly like melted cheese. In fact, most people assume that it *is* cheese until I tell them otherwise. I often add this boiled silk to rice, pasta, casseroles, and soup, and it has never disappointed me.

To Cook, or Not To Cook

The fact that milkweed does not require repeated boilings to rid it of bitterness does not mean that it should be eaten raw. I have eaten small quantities of all parts of the plant raw with no ill effects, and I know some people who eat it raw without reservation and have had no problem. I even witnessed one friend eat about quart of milkweed greens, flower buds, and pods over the course of an afternoon while we were camping, and he felt fine afterward.

On the other hand, I have talked to two individuals who had upset stomachs after eating raw milkweed parts. I also know that when working with the plants for a few hours and having the juice continually on my hands, such as happens when I am preparing a batch for canning, my skin sometimes itches and the area underneath my fingernails gets tender and sore. It is reported that milkweed contains chemicals that tenderize meat, and this may be related to my observation that eating raw milkweed gives me heartburn. Also, I have not found any ethnographic accounts indicating that the plant was eaten raw by Native Americans. In light of this evidence, I recommend cooking milkweed before eating it, even though I cannot conclusively state that the plant is harmful when raw.

The lowly common milkweed provides two different useful kinds of fiber (stalk fiber and down), plus six different vegetables (shoots, leafy tops, flower buds, flowers, immature pods, and white). It is abundant, easy to recognize, familiar to many of us, and it appears in the same place year after year. Its blossoms feed numerous kinds of butterflies as well as hummingbirds and honeybees.

Because of the myths surrounding the plant, many people have kept their distance from the common milkweed. This is sad because it is one of our best tasting, easiest to harvest, and most abundant edible wild plants. This wonderful weed should be a lesson to us all. What other treasures have we been ignoring, though they abound beside us?

Virginia Waterleaf

Hydrophyllum virginianum

Newly emerged, watermarked leaves of Virginia waterleaf, at their best stage for eating.

This herb is so common and plain looking that it is likely to be overlooked. A few consider it a weed – yet it is so small and unobtrusive, hiding in the shadows of brush and taller herbs, that it hardly seems to earn that title. Slowly, patiently, it creeps out of the woods and fencerows to conquer shady backyards, flowerbeds, and that little area between the lilacs and the silver maple where nobody ever walks. And if we do notice it, there's a pretty good chance that we'll just smile, fondle a delicate leaf, and let it grow. Because waterleaf doesn't get in anybody's way.

Description

Virginia waterleaf is a small perennial herb, rarely growing more than 2 feet (60 cm) tall. It has a few large basal leaves that reach as much as 9 inches (23 cm) in length, plus a few smaller alternate leaves upon the stalk. The leaves are deeply lobed or pinnately divided and very coarsely toothed. The petioles of the basal leaves are quite long and somewhat channeled. When young, the leaves usually have distinct whitish-gray "watermarks" on them, accounting for the name. As they age, however, the leaves become darker and usually lose these watermarks.

The basal leaves of non-flowering specimens of *Rudbeckia laciniata*, an herb with almost as many common names as chromosomes, can be confused with those of Virginia waterleaf. They are larger, darker, rougher, tougher, and never watermarked, but the two often grow side-by-side. *Rudbeckia laciniata* leaves are unpleasant to eat but not dangerous.

This photo shows the striking similarity of *Rudbeckia laciniata* (which I call *cut-leaf coneflower*) and *Hydrophyllum virginianum* (Virginia waterleaf), two plants commonly found growing together. On the top of the photo are two leaves of Virginia waterleaf (one partially covered by fallen leaves and one with watermarks). Across the bottom, from left to right, one sees the following leaves: coneflower, very small coneflower, waterleaf without watermarks, damaged coneflower, and an oddly-shaped coneflower. Note the larger teeth and more pointed lobes of waterleaf, and the darker coneflower leaves with more prominent light venation. Cut-leaf coneflower is not toxic, but the leaves are generally too tough and coarse to eat. However, the tenderest new leaves, such as the one near the waterleaf at bottom center, are edible (I ate this one) with a flavor very different from waterleaf.

The flowers, appearing in late spring and early summer, are borne in a tight, rounded cluster at the end of a long stalk that usually protrudes well above the leaves. About .3–.5 inch (8–13 mm) wide, these bell-like flowers have five united petals. Their five stamens are borne on long filaments that protrude like whiskers far beyond the petals, giving the flowers a distinctive look. The blossoms range from white to purple, usually starting out light and darkening as they age.

Virginia waterleaf is what I call an "optional ephemeral." It is very abundant in the spring, but many or most of the plants disappear by midsummer. However, a few persist through the growing season. A very small proportion persist through the winter, lying frozen and limp but still green on the cold ground.

Range and Habitat

Virginia waterleaf grows in rich hardwood forests or thickets near them, especially along rivers or streams. It sometimes colonizes open, weedy sites near its wooded strongholds, and in these sunny locations it grows much larger than it does in the shade. This herb survives human activity better than most woodland wildflowers; it is often extremely abundant in disturbed hardwood stands, carpeting areas of the forest floor. In more pristine forests it shares the available space with spring ephemerals and other herbs.

Virginia waterleaf *Hydrophyllum virginianum* is one of at least eight species of waterleaf found in North America. I chose it as the focus of this chapter because it is the one that grows all over my woods, and it is the one that I nibble on from April to November. I have no experience eating the other species, but they are all considered edible.

The West is blessed with such species as Cali-

Cluster of Virginia waterleaf flowers.

Edible flower stalk of Virginia waterleaf in late spring, bearing clusters of edible flower buds. Note the absence of watermarks on the new leaves.

fornia waterleaf *H. occidentale*, Pacific waterleaf *H. tenuipes*, dwarf or ball-head waterleaf *H. capitatum*, and Fendler's waterleaf *H. fendleri*. The East has large waterleaf *H. macrophyllum*, broad waterleaf *H. canadense*, appendaged waterleaf *H. appendiculatum*, and Virginia waterleaf *H. virginianum*.

Harvest and Preparation

In early spring the splotched foliage of Virginia waterleaf appears in small rosettes of two to four leaves. Pluck one leaf from each cluster so as not to unduly harm the plant. The smaller the leaves, the better their flavor and texture. Waterleaf can be eaten raw as a snack or in salad, or it can be served as a potherb. In my opinion, it is much better raw, but occasionally I toss some into a soup or other cooked dish.

As with most greens, preparation is straightforward and simple. Don't wash them; pick only clean ones. If they are dirty, their surface texture will not allow you to get them clean. As with most greens, there is a limit to how much of this plant one would happily consume; it is a side dish or a snack but not a main course. Some people object to the slightly dry and fuzzy feeling of the leaves in their mouths. The young leaves of spring are best, both in flavor and texture, but this waterleaf is passably good throughout the growing season. It becomes immensely appreciated in October and November, when it is among the only woodland greens available.

I happily eat Virginia waterleaf several times a week when it is in season, most often as a trailside nibble. It is very abundant and fairly good. The plant has a mild astringency and bitterness (much milder than dandelion or chicory) and a slight crunch to it. I like it, but I wouldn't travel across the county to get some. I have never tried to store this green for out-of-season use.

The flower stalks, when they are about 12–16 inches (30–40 cm) high and not yet very stiff, *before the flowers have opened*, are sweet, juicy, and crunchy. I snack on these flower stalks anytime that I walk the woods while they are in season, but I have not tried cooking them. The clusters of unopened flower buds, found atop the stalk, are edible raw but better when cooked. Both of these parts are available in late spring and early summer. Although I like the flavor of the flower stalks and buds, both of them can leave a lingering, unpleasant astringent feeling in one's mouth after eating them.

There are reports of Native Americans eating the enlarged taproots or rhizomes of some of the waterleafs, in both the East and the West, but all reports that I have seen contained minimal detail. I have never tried waterleaf roots, since those of Virginia waterleaf are not edible.

Virginia waterleaf is certainly not going to become a staple food, but with three edible parts, a long season of availability, and the plant's great abundance, it is a wild food well worth learning.

Nannyberry, Wild Raisin, Black Haw

Viburnum lentago

Cluster of ripe nannyberries. Note the claw-like bud at the top.

It is hard to explain a nannyberry to the uninitiated. They don't fit any of the stereotypes that we associate with wild berries, and they're downright ugly to those who have not learned to love them. Although nannyberries are abundant and quite delicious, they are virtually unknown – even among those who spend an occasional weekend picking wild fruit. Perhaps this is because they ripen in late September and October, when most people are done looking for wild berries. Perhaps it is because they are black and wrinkly, like little else that we eat – or because they are the wrong texture for jam or jelly. Maybe it is because they grow in swampy areas and thick brush, where few have wandered to find them, or because they contain seeds, which civilized people resent in their food. It seems that nature and human nature have conspired to keep the nannyberry a secret. But I'm inspired to get the secret out.

Description

Nannyberry is a large shrub or small tree, typically 8–15 feet (2.5–5 m) tall and 1–2 inches (2.5–5 cm) in diameter, usually found in dense clumps or clones. The bark is thin and dark, almost black; on older stems (more than two inches thick) it becomes broken into many small plates or chips.

Nannyberry leaves are opposite and ovate, with rounded bottoms and pointed tips. They are 2–4 inches (5–10 cm) long, finely toothed, smooth, and somewhat shiny. In autumn, when the fruit is harvested, the foliage turns to a brownish purple.

One of the best ways to recognize the nannyberry, especially in winter, is by the long, pointed, beak-like buds. A bulge at the base of one of these buds indicates that it will produce flowers the following year. Flowers appear in late May or early June, and nannyberry is one of the showiest of our native shrubs. The large flat-topped clusters (cymes) of creamy white blossoms are easily spotted against the typical backdrop of glossy green. When ripe, the fruit is blue-black with a bloom that often wears off. It is oblong and slightly flattened, with a single large, flattened, rather soft seed – like a small watermelon seed with sharper edges. Nannyberries are borne in large, pink-stemmed clusters.

Nannyberry flower cluster.

Mature nannyberry leaves.

Range and Habitat

Nannyberry is found in the northeastern United States and the southern parts of Ontario and Quebec. It is typical of river bottoms, streamsides, shrub swamps, the edges of marshes and ponds, or other moist, sunny areas. Like most river-bottom species, however, nannyberries do just fine on upland sites and are common in young woods, brushy areas, and field edges. Nannyberries will inhabit almost any soil type. The bushes are short-lived and only tolerate light shade. Although the fruit is relished by many birds and mammals, which spread the seeds to new localities, spreading by underground runners or stolons remains the nannyberry's principle form of reproduction.

Besides *V. lentago*, which is the focus of this chapter, there are several other dark-fruited viburnums with edible berries, and their names can be quite confusing. The black haw *V. prunifolium* (also called wild raisin, sheep berry, and nannyberry) is found over much of the eastern U.S., and it looks very similar

313

to the nannyberry but tends to be more branchy and usually grows in drier situations. I like this fruit, but not quite as much as I like the nannyberry. Some other edible dark-fruited viburnums that I have not tried are *V. nudum* and *V. rufidulum* (which share all of the common names of the last two species), *V. cassinoides* (witherod, wild raisin), and *V. alnifolium* (hobblebush, moosewood). The information in this account refers specifically to nannyberry *V. lentago* because that is the species with which I have extensive experience. However, much of the information may apply to the other species, especially those that share its common names.

Harvest

Nannyberries are among the most consistently productive of our wild fruits. This is probably at least partly because of their late flowering season, when frost is very unlikely. Nannyberries also have fewer pest problems than most wild fruits; I think this is because the fruit almost never falls to the ground beneath the tree. Instead, they are held until birds pluck them and carry them elsewhere.

Fruit-laden nannyberry bush in early October.

Through most of the summer the berries will be light green and hard. By the end of August some of them will turn rosy, though remaining hard. From rosy, the fruit will turn to dark blue and soft, beginning in mid September. Clusters often have one or two precocious fruits that ripen weeks before the rest of them; these are poor representatives of their kind, often being very dry and bitter.

Thoreau, who was an avid admirer of nannyberries, states that the unripe fruit, if plucked, will ripen in a day or two in the house – even if picked when green and hard (Thoreau, 2000). I have found this to be the case as well, but would add that these fruits do not achieve the fullness of flavor attained by those that ripen on the bush. Also, the berries which remain attached to a plucked stem ripen sooner than those which do not; the latter may take a week to turn black. For all practical purposes, I recommend that you wait to harvest your nannyberries until they ripen on the bush.

The vast majority of nannyberries ripen in the last week of September and the first week of October. A cluster that is ready to be harvested will at first have berries that are smooth and black, but over time the berries dry out and get ripples or wrinkles as they shrink (hence the name "wild raisin"). I prefer to harvest mine in early to mid October while they are still moist – and before the birds have had the opportunity to clean them off. As the season progresses, both the quantity and quality of the berries diminishes.

Bark of nannyberry, on a trunk about 2 inches (5 cm) thick.

In most years they are gone by the end of November, but after some bumper crops they hang from the twigs until the snow melts in spring.

The flavor of nannyberries, I tell people, is like a cross between bananas and prunes. Most people who try the fruit like that description and commend it as accurate, but I'm afraid that if I mixed equal parts of bananas and prunes in a blender it would produce a sorry imitation of nannyberry puree.

Occasionally a clump of nannyberry bushes will produce fruit that is somewhat bitter. Don't be discouraged; find another patch. When you find good fruit, you can generally pick it very fast. The berries of each cluster can be quickly worked off into your hand and then thrown into a bag or tub. Any stems or leaves incidentally harvested can be picked out later. It is quite possible to pick two or three gallons of fruit in an hour this way.

I love to eat nannyberries fresh off the bush while I am picking. I chew gently on a mouthful of berries, and the pulp just kind of melts away from the seeds. Then, of course, I spit the seeds out. Nannyberries contain more calories and are more filling than most wild berries. They are doubly appreciated in late fall when there are few other fruits available.

The thin black skins of nannyberries often stick to the enamel of your teeth, giving the appearance of a horrendous cavity. We call this cosmetic dental affliction "nannyberry tooth." Symptoms include the sudden, uncontrolled laughter of a companion or the wide-eyed stare of a stranger – but the afflicted can't even feel it. Nannyberry tooth can be readily cured by drinking a glass of water.

Preparation

Nannyberries do not mold or spoil quickly like so many small fruits. Refrigerated, they can sit for a few weeks without harm, and they last for several days at room temperature. They store well in the freezer. This allows one to save the fruit from multiple excursions and combine them into a large batch.

Before making anything from this fruit you need to separate the seeds from the pulp to make a puree. I put my berries in a large pot with a small amount of water (not quite enough to cover the berries) and let it simmer on low heat for about an hour, stirring occasionally. When the fruit is well cooked I run it through my food strainer to separate the seeds from the pulp. (It will not go through my strainer unless it is hot.) The resulting puree is thick, almost like prune butter. Unlike most cooked berries, this puree is thick enough to use for spreads without adding pectin and sugar to make it jell. For those who want a spreadable fruit confection without all the sugar required to make jam or jelly, nannyberry is perfect.

To make the most of the nannyberry, it is best to start thinking of it as a mealy or starchy fruit, such as a banana, rather than a juicy berry. When looked at this way, the nannyberry's unique characteristics become advantages rather than hindrances. Some authors tell us to use nannyberries for jam or jelly. I think that would be a waste. You don't hear of anyone making banana jam or fig jelly, so why try to turn nannyberry into something that it obviously wasn't intended for?

Nannyberry puree can also be dried into fruit leather, or mixed with oatmeal and sugar to form a kind of pudding. Used to replace the banana in a banana bread recipe, nannyberries give the final product a delicious flavor and a nice chocolate-brown color.

I have successfully used three principal methods to store nannyberries for the long term. I preserve the puree (or different nannyberry-based spreads) by water-bath canning, I freeze the puree or whole fruit, and I dry the puree into fruit leather. That way I can enjoy this delicious and unique fruit at any time of the year.

Nannyberry puree is dark like prune butter and thick enough to hold up a spoon.

Highbush Cranberry

Viburnum trilobum, V. edule

A cluster of highbush cranberries in September. (They don't grow on the trunk like that – I put them there.) Note the pale gray bark.

It's late in the afternoon and the temperature has just broken the freezing mark for the first time today. I've been awake since long before dawn, meandering six miles with nothing to eat. My footsteps are slow and careful, my senses keen and my attention rapt. I'm so focused on sensing the deer before it senses me that I do not notice that I am tired, or hungry, or thirsty. On a slope heading towards a stream, I crouch and carefully weave my body between hazel and alder bushes. As I come to the rushing waters a bit of red catches my eye a few yards away, standing out like a Christmas decoration among the drab winter twigs and their backdrop of fresh snow. My mouth waters, and suddenly I am famished, thirsty, and fatigued. I grab the cluster of highbush cranberries and sit down upon a fallen tree to enjoy them one-by-one as their frozen juice melts into my mouth. And at that moment there's nothing in the world that I like better.

Description

For decades there has been an uninformed debate over highbush cranberries; some people insist that the fruit is bitter and unpalatable, even when cooked into jelly or sauce, while others say that the fruit is very tart but tasty, like the true cranberry. This divergence of opinion is due to the fact that there are actually three widespread and closely related species which go by the name "highbush cranberry," and their eating qualities differ greatly. (The highbush cranberry, by the way, is not closely related to the true cranberry *Vaccinium macrocarpon*.) The two native highbush cranberry species, *Viburnum edule* and *V. trilobum*, are generally highly esteemed for their flavor, while the introduced European *V. opulus* has terrible fruit. The general description given here refers to *V. trilobum,* the American highbush cranberry, because that is the species with which I am most familiar. The differences of the other species will be mentioned thereafter.

The American highbush cranberry is a multi-stemmed shrub that is generally 8–12 feet (2.5–4 m) tall. The twigs are fairly stout and smooth, hairless, and very pale gray in color. On the trunks the bark becomes rougher and a little darker. All parts of the plant contain a bitter chemical known as viburnin that has been used since antiquity for relieving menstrual cramps. This accounts for another common name, cramp-bark, which is most often applied to the European species. The winter buds are large, plump, glabrous, and bright green or red.

The maple-like, three-lobed leaves, 2–4 inches (5–10 cm) long and about as wide, are borne in opposite pairs on grooved petioles about 1 inch (2.5 cm) long. The margins may be slightly and irregularly toothed, or they may be smooth.

Highbush cranberry blooms in early summer, and at this time the bushes are very showy and easy to spot. The white flowers appear in flat-topped clusters called cymes. The perimeter of the cluster is composed of large, five-"petaled" infertile flowers, built for nothing but show, while the center of the cyme

Highbush cranberry flower cluster, with false flowers on the outside and true flowers inside.

consists of tiny, drab, fertile blossoms. The fruit is a rounded drupe that turns bright red at the end of the summer. It contains a single flattened, soft seed.

When growing in shade, the highbush cranberry spreads by layering. The stems on the outside of the clump lean further and further outward until eventually their tips touch the ground. As soon as this happens the branches send roots into the soil and produce new shoots, which grow vigorously since they are connected to and partially fed by the parent tree. After a few years the stem connecting the new shoot to the original plant will die, leaving the daughter shrub to fend for itself.

The other native species, *V. edule*, also called mooseberry or squashberry, is a smaller shrub, rarely exceeding 6 feet (2 m) in height. Its leaves have more dentate margins and less deeply cut lobes than *V. trilobum*. Perhaps the best distinguishing characteristic of this shrub is that the fruit is produced in smaller clusters than its larger cousin, in the leaf axils along the branches rather than at the tips. The fruit of this species is reputed to be the best of the highbush cranberries, but I have not had the pleasure of confirming this, since it does not grow where I live.

The European highbush cranberry *V. opulus*, also called guelder rose, is very similar in appearance to the native *V. trilobum*. Some botanists even consider them the same species, which adds to the confusion and seems to have created a loophole by which many tree nurseries sell the distasteful European type labeled

Leaves of *V. trilobum*.

as the preferable American one. You can differentiate the two by vegetative characteristics (the European has smaller, wider, more dentate leaves and thinner, darker twigs), but it is easier just to taste the fruit: the European species is extremely bitter, accentuated by other bad flavors, while the native type tastes much like cranberries. In fact, European highbush cranberries are so terrible that I don't even consider them edible, despite the claims of some bitter-plant apologists – and frost emphatically *does not* improve their flavor. Birds typically refuse to eat them until the desperate times of late winter, and they often hang on the bushes untouched until spring. The fruit of the North American species, on the other hand, is normally picked clean by the end of November.

Range and Habitat

The two desirable species of highbush cranberry range across the northern United States and all of the forested regions of Canada. Of these two, *V. trilobum* is the more southerly in its distribution, growing down to northern Illinois and Ohio. *V. edule* is found across the far north; it is the famous highbush cranberry of Alaska and the Yukon. The European highbush cranberry is most common in the northeastern and midwestern United States, the Pacific Northwest, and southeastern Canada, where it persists as an escaped ornamental shrub in towns and around farms.

Leaves of *V. opulus* (the species you don't want). Compared to leaves of *V. trilobum*, note their smaller size, less pointed lobes, and more prominent teeth.

Native highbush cranberries grow along streams, ponds, rivers, and lakes, and in damp woods or shrub swamps. They sometimes occur on upland sites, especially the squashberry. Highbush cranberries thrive in full sun or light shade.

Harvest and Preparation

The small fruits of *V. trilobum*, about a half-inch long, begin to ripen in late August. As soon as they turn red they are ready to eat, though they will still be hard and crunchy. At this stage they taste almost exactly like true cranberries, although they differ in that they contain a large seed, which is somewhat bitter if chewed. You will often read that the flavor of highbush cranberries improves after frost, but this is contrary to the truth. This myth came about as people who were unaware that there are in fact distinctly good and distinctly bad highbush cranberries tried to explain why some tasted so much better than others. It is a hypothesis that remains untested by those who proclaim it as truth. Highbush cranberries taste the best when they first become fully ripe; the flavor goes downhill from there, frost or no frost. American highbush cranberries vary significantly from one bush to another; the best tasting ones tend to have large, brightly-colored fruit. I try to pick all of my highbush cranberries before the middle of October when the leaves fall, for soon after this they begin to shrink with evaporation and lose some of the freshness of their flavor.

One endearing quality of highbush cranberry is that it is generally easy to pick in large quantities. The fruit is conveniently arranged in clusters at the ends of the thornless and limber branches – which virtually beg you to remove their cumbersome scarlet burden. I have often gathered more than a gallon from a single bush in only 20 minutes. Highbush cranberry is the most consistently productive fruit in my area and has one of the longest seasons of availability – so I've never had to endure an autumn without any. These qualities make it an ideal fruit to store up for the winter, and every year I gather pails of them to make juice for winter and spring.

To make juice from the still-hard, just-ripened highbush cranberries you must freeze them and then thaw them, which makes them soft and juicy. This is an extra step, and if you pick them a little later, when they have softened on their own, you can avoid it. (Note that they do not require frost to soften when ripening naturally.) Either way, the next step is to crush them. I do this by placing about two gallons of berries in a five-gallon bucket or other container and thoroughly mashing them (but gently, so as not to break the seeds) with

Viburnum trilobum, fruiting bush.

my wooden pestle. If I want juice, I stir in about a quart of water per gallon of cranberries; if I want to make cranberry sauce or jam I leave the extra water out. Then I press the mashed fruit in a jelly bag (for juice) or a colander (for pulp). I do not boil the whole fruit, for this seems to release some of the bitterness of the seeds into the product.

I like to use highbush cranberry pulp to make jam, cranberry sauce, or cranberry-applesauce. The juice makes a wonderful jelly. It can also be diluted and sweetened for drinking, or added to juice mixes. It can even be taken at full-strength, in tiny sips – which is how I prefer it.

You can give your juice a finer color and flavor by letting it sit in a pitcher in the refrigerator for a day or two so the solids can settle to the bottom of the container. Then carefully pour the cleaner-looking, more brightly colored juice into another container, leaving the sludge on the bottom. I have stored my highbush cranberry juice by canning it in a water bath, but it tastes much better when frozen. Fortunately, the fresh juice lasts a long time in the refrigerator due to its natural antibiotic properties.

Because they are mostly seed, skin, and juice, highbush cranberries are poor candidates for drying.

If you like cranberries, you will probably like our native highbush cranberry. If you taste some that you find disgusting, understand that they are probably its evil twin; don't judge all highbush cranberries accordingly. It would be your loss.

Burdock

Arctium minus, A. lappa

Mature common burdock plant, about to flower.

When I was a child some of my friends and I made a regular sport of catching opossums by hand. The method was to walk along slowly in likely areas, listening for their telltale rustle in the dried leaves. When an opossum was found we'd charge, outrunning him and forcing him to take defensive posture (sitting on his haunches with jaws agape). Then, if there were two of us, one would get his attention while the other simply grabbed him by the tail. If, however, as was more often the case, I was alone, it became a real challenge. I'd jump over the opossum repeatedly, and each time he'd turn to face me. Eventually the animal would become dizzy and lose track of where I was. Finally, at the opportune moment when the opossum was hissing intently at a place where I had just been standing, I would grab his tail and carry him around for a while, showing him off to sometimes less-than-impressed passers-by before letting him go.

On just such an excursion, I encountered one of these hapless marsupials in a formidable tangle of burdock along some railroad tracks. Being familiar with the area, I knew that the direction he was headed would soon bring him to a woodchuck burrow, down which he would surely disappear when attacked – unless I did so immediately. I weighed the consequences: glory or burs?

The infamous burs of the burdock.

It didn't take long to decide. I made my move while he was still in the dreaded burdocks, oblivious of the fact that I was wearing brand new sweatpants and a sweatshirt. He thrashed and scrambled about while I jumped over him frantically and blocked his route to safety. Soon enough the ordeal was over and I was standing on the railroad tracks with my living trophy, but we were both so matted with burs as to defy easy identification. To onlookers, we may well have been the Sasquatch and her baby. I went home quite uncomfortably, pulling off huge masses of burs all the way, and ended up throwing away my unrecoverable clothes and getting my hair cut. The unfortunate opossum didn't have those options, but I think he was happy just to have survived the incident.

It is for these stick-tight burs, the worst of all kinds, that the burdock is generally known – and it is thoroughly detested by most people. It comes to many as quite a surprise that the burdock is actually an escaped domestic vegetable, still grown widely in Japan where it was first cultivated thousands of years ago. It is sometimes sold in Asian markets or health food stores in North America under the name of "gobo."

Description

Burdock is a massive biennial or perennial herb. The rosettes consist of 2–5 very large ovate or wedge-shaped leaves with heart-like lobes at the base; they are dark green above but whitish and densely covered with fine wool beneath. Borne on a long, grooved petiole that is often tinted purple, these ruffled leaves grow as much as 28 inches (70 cm) long and more than 14 inches (36 cm) wide. They have a prominent, light-colored midrib and main veins, which are depressed on the upper surface and form raised ridges on the lower surface. The margins of the leaves are rough and irregularly wavy but not toothed. Burdock rosettes remind people of rhubarb. Their overall form is indeed similar, but rhubarb leaves are glossy, have no wool underneath, and have smoother petioles.

Common burdock's flowering stalk is very stout, strongly tapered, grooved, slightly zigzagged, and green – usually with purple highlights, especially near the base. It grows to about 6.5 feet (2 m) tall. The stalk leaves are alternate and much smaller than the basal ones. Their margins tend to be less wavy and their bases are usually less prominently lobed. Mature stalks and rosettes are usually found growing together.

Common burdock in flower. Note the tightly clustered burs, some of them sessile. Photo by Glenn Schmukler.

Flowers are borne at the top of the plant in clusters of several composite heads, each consisting of numerous tubular purple florets. Common burdock flower heads are about .8 inch (2 cm) in diameter and have the same "shaving-brush" shape as those of its close relative, the thistle. After the seeds develop, the flower head retains its many hook-like bracts, becoming the vexing bur for which the plant is named.

Although at first glance they

Great burdock *A. lappa* flowering. Note the long pedicels, spreading clusters, and larger, rounder heads.

may appear dissimilar, burdocks are very closely related to thistles, and it is helpful to think of them as wild food "twins." The structure of the flowers, the life cycle, the general form, and the edible parts of these plants are almost identical. The main difference is that, while the thistles have chosen to protect themselves with thorns, the burdocks accomplish this by covering their outer surface with an incredibly bitter substance that repels herbivores.

There are two species of burdock, both edible. The common burdock *Arctium minus* is far more common, and this is the species most of us are familiar with. The great burdock *A. lappa* is locally common but is absent in most of North America. The literature often propagates the misconception that great burdock is notably larger than the common species, but this is untrue; typical size for the two plants is about the same. Compared to *A. minus*, *A. lappa* has much larger inflorescences, and these are spread out widely on individual stems rather than clumped together. Where the two grow near each other, *A. lappa* usually flowers about two weeks earlier than *A. minus*. The leaves of great burdock are more rounded, slightly thinner, and are less ruffled, especially on the margins; their undersides are also more silvery than those of common burdock. Great burdock stalks are proportionately thinner and less tapered, giving the flowering plant a more graceful look. Finally, the petiole of common burdock is grooved and hollow, while that of great burdock is grooved but not hollow. The two species are not hard to differentiate.

Range and Habitat

The two species of burdock are introduced to North America. They range from coast to coast across the northern two thirds of the United States and southern Canada. These plants are common weeds of disturbed ground, often abundant in old fields, barnyards, roadsides, along footpaths and railroad tracks, in vacant urban lots, gardens, yards, fencerows, and other such places. They occasionally show up in wild areas along river banks. Where I live, burdock is often found under wild apple and plum trees; perhaps this is due to the trampling caused by animals that come to eat the fruit.

Harvest and Preparation

Roots: Burdock taproots are very thick and run deep into the soil. Except in unusual circumstances, one must employ a shovel and a little labor to harvest them. The largest burdock roots are as much as 3 inches (8 cm) thick, but the best size for eating is .75–1.5 inches (2–4 cm) thick. Especially on larger roots, the top three to eight inches is often dark and rough on the outside. This rough part usually corresponds to a tough, poorly flavored, and partly hollow interior; such sections of the root should be discarded. The good portion for eating will be relatively smooth, creamy or light brown in color, and solid all the way through. The bottom 40% or so of the burdock root is the best part for eating – but this is unfortunately the hardest part to extract from the dirt. Indeed, were it not for this dilemma I would collect these roots more often and recommend them more highly.

Only collect burdock roots from plants without stalks. (I told this to a class once, and a participant, in defiant disbelief, went and dug up a flowering, second-year burdock. He held it up and said, "What do you mean? This one's got roots, too!" My point wasn't that older plants don't *have* roots – for that would be strange indeed – it was that the roots of older plants are tough and woody.)

Euell Gibbons (1962) claims that the best time to harvest the roots (of *A. lappa)* is in early summer, and that afterward they become tough. This is not necessarily true. Some of the roots may be best in summer, but others are ideal in the typical root season of fall and spring. This variation occurs because individual burdock plants do not necessarily follow the typical biennial pattern that they are pigeon-holed into. At the end of the first growing season, some burdock rosettes have stored enough energy that they are ready to send up a shoot in the spring of their second year (the classic biennial pattern). A few persist as a rosette into the second growing season, only producing a stalk later in summer after having stored enough energy to do so in extravagant burdock fashion. (That's why you never see tiny burdock stalks.) Quite often, the burdock plant spends its entire second year in the rosette form, storing more energy in the root and postponing flowering until the third year. This means that under wild conditions you can find burdock roots in many stages of growth at any one time.

I collect roots from burdock rosettes anytime from the middle of summer until late in the fall, and then again in the early spring before the plants begin to grow. (Even plants with small stalks in early summer will have a small portion of good root at the tip.) At any of these times, in my opinion, their flavor is good, but the texture is a little tougher than I like, whether they are eaten raw or boiled. Oftentimes the rind is tender while the core is unpleasantly tough.

Bigger is not always better. With burdock, don't look for large plants with

These fine folks show off some large roots of common burdock, about 32 inches (80 cm) long.

massive roots; these are so difficult to work out of the soil that the best parts almost always break off and are left in the dirt. Instead, select medium-sized rosettes, which should have medium-sized roots. The best way to get these out of the dirt is to dig a deep hole in the middle of an area where several burdocks are growing close together, then pull the plants neighboring the excavation sideways into it, being careful not to break their roots. If only a few inches of the root go deeper than your hole, you can probably extract it by pulling upward steadily (rather than jerking) until it is released. Burdock roots of ideal quality are generally 14–26 inches (36–66 cm) long, so your hole needs to be well more than the depth of a shovel blade. If you break off all of your roots a few inches below the surface, as often happens with sloppy use of a shovel, all you'll get from each plant is the section that should be tossed out anyway.

The burdock root consists of a distinct rind and core, which separate with ease. Many books say that the rind should be peeled and discarded, while others say to discard the core and keep the rind. I do neither and see no reason to.

Common burdock rosette in early spring.

The rind is two thirds of the root; it tastes as good as the core and is no tougher. The core is one third of the root; it tastes as good as the rind. I just scrub and rinse the root, cutting off any dirty ends, hollow sections, and coarse parts. Then I usually scrape off the outside with a knife or vegetable peeler.

I like to put finely chopped burdock roots into stew or fried vegetable dishes, or cook them with wild rice. The sweetest burdock roots I'll snack on raw or sometimes eat as a boiled vegetable.

Burdock root is available today in many health food stores, and it is becoming increasingly popular. The root is considered invigorating, detoxifying, and an all-around vegetable of good health. The species cultivated for the market is the great burdock, *A. lappa*, which has better-tasting, more tender roots than the common burdock.

Leaves and Petioles: Some authors report that the young leaves of burdock are edible, adding that they should be parboiled in a few changes of water before consumption. Perhaps there is some semantic loophole by which such horrific greens can be admitted to the "edible" classification, but burdock leaves have achieved quite a level of infamy among wild food enthusiasts. They are so bitter, in fact, that handling them will leave a bitter residue on your fingers that will pollute any food you touch thereafter. The few times I have tasted raw burdock leaves my tongue actually became insensitive to bitter flavors for a while, allowing me the temporary freedom to enjoy greens that are normally too potent for my palate. But that was not exciting enough to make me want to eat them again.

The long, thick petioles of burdock are another matter. They are bitter on the outside, but if the skin is carefully scraped off, the inside of the petiole can be boiled to make a fairly good vegetable. There are long fibers that run the length of these leaf stalks, much like those found in celery, and on older leaves these become pretty tough, so you want to get them in early summer before the leaves are fully grown. Chopping them into short sections also makes the fibers less noticeable.

Burdock stalks at exactly the right stage to harvest.

Stalks: The best food product that the burdock supplies, in my opinion, is the core of the young stalk. These are harvested in late spring and early summer when the shoots are one to three feet tall and not yet stiff – weeks before the flowers appear. Cut the stalks at the base, pull off any leaves or small side branches, and then carefully peel off the bitter and stringy rind. I do this by biting onto the fibers at the base of the stalk and then pulling the whole stalk away from my teeth; the finishing touches are done with a fillet knife or carrot peeler. It is important to remove *all* of the outer layer, which is green, for it contains a potent, disagreeable bitter flavor. The core you end up with should be entirely of an opaque whitish color. It will be 6–20 inches (15–50 cm) in length, up to 1.5 inches (4 cm) thick, and should show no fibers.

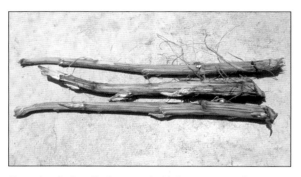

Young burdock stalks, harvested with leaves removed.

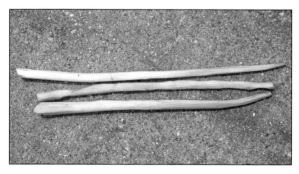

The same burdock stalks, peeled to show the edible core.

Peeled burdock stalks are edible raw, but cooked they are superb. When steamed or boiled for a long time they become very soft like new potatoes; they are starchy and not at all fibrous like the roots or petioles. I like them served alone as a vegetable dish, and their mild, slightly sweet flavor can't go wrong in soup or stir fry. When burdock stalks are in season, they are a truly fine vegetable.

That's a pretty good list of edible parts for what is probably one of the most accursed plants on the continent. Next time you run into this widespread weed, try to see it in a different light. Call it gobo. Tell people it is a delicacy in Japan, first cultivated there thousands of years ago. Then, if you must get rid of it, do so by eating it.

Thistle

Cirsium spp. and *Carduus nutans*

Pasture thistle flower. Photo by Glenn Schmukler.

The bull thistle looms large in the recollection of my early years of eating wild foods. Like most lawns, mine had its share of thistles. And perhaps more often than the feet of most children, mine were bare. The inevitable came to pass early on – and it happened again and again. Like most children, after a number of barefoot encounters with thistles I began to dislike them.

Bull thistle rosette in spring, when the leaf midribs are best. Photo by Glenn Schmukler.

Then one day, after stepping on a thistle, I wondered to myself in frustration, "Why do they have those thorns? The other plants don't have any!" Then it dawned on me – they must need that armor to keep from being eaten. Every time I saw a thistle plant after that, I pondered that question, and again would think to myself, "It needs thorns so that it doesn't get eaten." Somehow, on some level, I just *knew* that the bull thistle must be edible, so when I finally found a book that verified this, I excitedly went to try some. I carefully picked a thistle leaf from a rosette on the lawn and wondered how I was going to eat it. In the process of removing the thorns I ended up stripping off nearly all of the surface of the leaf, leaving just the light green midrib. I bit into this carefully and chewed. Compared to dandelion, dock, and the few other wild greens that I knew at that time, it seemed like a mighty fine vegetable. And so I ate my first thistle leaf. A few years later, when I gave an edible wild plant presentation to my seventh-grade science class, peeling and eating a bull thistle leaf was the first thing that I demonstrated – much to the horror of my classmates.

In the edible plant programs I teach today, I tell students to think of the burdock and thistle as wild food twins. The main difference between these closely related plants is that, while the thistle protects its edible interior with thorns, the burdock repels herbivores by covering its surface with an incredibly bitter and distasteful chemical. Once you get past the plants' defenses, their food uses are nearly identical.

Description

This account refers to the "true" thistles of the genus *Cirsium* as well as the nodding thistle *Carduus nutans*; it does not refer to *Sonchus* (sow thistle) or *Silybum* (milk thistle). The United States and Canada have dozens of species of true thistles, both native and introduced, found in nearly every region and habitat. Most can be used in similar ways as food, and several were eaten by Native Americans. None of the true thistles are known to be toxic, but of course, they vary in their palatability. The only part of the Canada thistle *C. arvense* that I use for food is the stalk; its other parts are inferior in quality.

Thistles spend one or more years as a basal rosette accumulating energy before finally sending up a flower stalk and dying. The basal leaves that comprise the rosette can be as much as 2 feet (60 cm) long. They are deeply and irregularly lobed or divided, especially near the base. The tips of the lobes are armed with extremely sharp, light-colored thorns, the size and density of which varies from one species to the next. The midrib of each leaf is large, distinct, and very thick. It is very light in color, contrasting sharply with the dark green of the leaf's main surface. Most species have basal leaves that are woolly, especially on the underside. Thistle leaves tend to have a wavy, ruffled appearance, particularly when

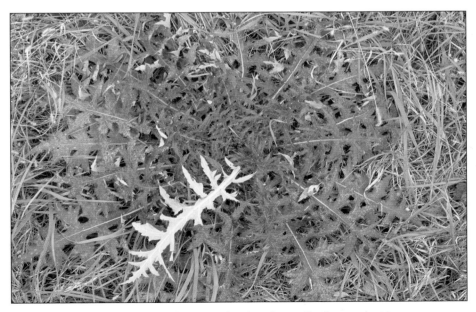

Pasture thistle rosette in fall, with leaf overturned to show the woolly, silvery underside.

growing vigorously in full sunlight. Stem leaves are similar to the basal leaves but tend to be smaller, less deeply lobed, and less woolly.

Flowering thistle plants produce a single, erect, robust stalk that is generally straight and tends not to branch except near the apex. These flower stalks often reach more than 1.5 inches (4 cm) in thickness and 6 feet (2 m) in height. Leaves are borne alternately along the length of the stem, and there is a thorn-bearing wing on the stalk under the stem leaves of some species.

Atop the mature thistle plant will be several 1–2 inch (2.5–5 cm) wide composite clusters of pinkish or purple florets, protected by thorn-bearing bracts. Many have likened the form of these flowers clusters to an old-fashioned shaving brush. Thistles bloom from early to late summer, producing heads of small, dark, elongated seeds equipped with a down parachute for the purpose of dissemination by wind.

Range and Habitat

The introduced bull thistle *Cirsium vulgare* is found from East Coast to West, at most latitudes, as long as there is ample moisture. It inhabits fields, pastures, lawns, roadsides, and clearings in the woods. Pasture thistle *C. discolor*, found

Tall thistle rosette in fall, showing leaf underside.

in the East, is abundant in many open woodlands, fields, and pastures where the soil is well drained. Tall thistle *C. altissimum* inhabits woodlands and forest edges in Eastern North America, sometimes growing out into fields where the soil is rich. The nodding or musk thistle *Carduus nutans*, an introduced plant that now grows widespread, is found in fields and disturbed ground.

There are many additional edible species of thistle distributed through most of North America. This includes: the swamp thistle *C. muticum*, an eastern wetland species; the introduced European swamp thistle *C. palustre*; edible thistle *C. edule*, growing in meadows and forest openings at middle to high elevations in the Northwest; Indian thistle *C. brevistylum*, a plant of lower elevations in the Northwest; wavy-leaved or woolly thistle *C. undulatum*, found in dry, open areas of the Great Plains, Rocky Mountains, and semi-arid West; Texas thistle *C. texanum*, common in parts of Texas, Oklahoma, and New Mexico; and the prairie thistle *C. flodmanii*.

Collection and Preparation

Leaves and Petioles: The part of the thistle that I eat most often is the midrib of the leaf, after the rest has been carefully stripped off. Steve Brill says that anyone who ever tried to cut all the spines from a thistle leaf "died of old age first." I must have lived through eons by now, because I've done it thousands of times. Plucking the leaf from the plant without getting pricked is the hardest part; once your hands get used to the task, stripping the leaf is no problem. I don't try to remove individual thorns; I peel off the entire leafy portion and all the spines come off with it. After practice the whole process takes no more than fifteen or twenty seconds.

Thistle midribs are large and crisp like celery, with a few large fibers and a pleasantly sweet flavor. I find them an almost addictive trailside nibble. During junior high, I would usually peel and eat several a day on my walk to and from school. While deer hunting one recent October, I found massive bull thistle rosettes more than four feet wide growing on tip-up mounds produced by a recent windstorm; the midribs of these leaves were as thick as my little finger. It took a long time to crunch my way down one 18-inch piece of this "thistle celery," but it was delicious and absolutely refreshing. All that noise must have been what scared away the deer.

Some people object to the wooliness of the leaves, but most of this can be rubbed off easily by pulling the midrib between two fingers. Thistle leaf midribs taste the best and seem the least stringy in spring and fall. I prefer the basal leaves, probably for no reason other than size. In my experience, the bull thistle has the best midribs for eating.

Euell Gibbons (1971) reported eating the entire thistle leaf as a cooked green after the spines were carefully cut off, and he rated them highly: "almost good enough to make all that trimming worthwhile." He did not specify the species of thistle, however.

Stalks: In late spring and early summer one can collect the still-soft, vigorously-growing stalks of thistles, remove the leaves, and peel off the outer layer of the stem to procure a vegetable that is fairly good raw and excellent cooked. You should gather this stalk when it can still be bent easily – long before the flowers appear. Normally such stalks are less than 3 feet (1 m) tall.

This is one of the few outdoors tasks for which it is clearly preferable to have

Young bull thistle stalk in early summer at the stage when you want to harvest it.

Harvested stalks of young bull thistle with leaves removed.

The same bull thistle stalks after peeling, ready to be eaten or cooked.

a very long knife. I cut off the thistle's stem leaves while the plant is still standing, working my way from the top toward the base so that I can take advantage of the continually increasing work space as I try to avoid getting pricked. After this I cut the stalk at the base and sever the top. On large specimens the unpeeled shoot might be 1.5 inches (4 cm) thick at the base and as much as 16 inches (40 cm) long. Typical dimensions are about half of that, however. The final step is to peel off the outer dark green, fibrous layer – leaving a soft, moist, hollow, opaque core.

The flavor of the peeled shoot is slightly sweet, mild, and very pleasant. The texture is soft but not mushy, with no fiber. Most who try this vegetable will like it. I enjoy it chopped up and cooked in a variety of dishes. I have eaten the peeled stalks of marsh, bull, Canada, tall, pasture, and nodding thistles, and all were very good. There are ethnographic records of other species being eaten in this fashion as well.

Roots: Our wild thistles provide yet a third edible product: the taproot. Thistle roots are light in color, firm, and almost crisp (but usually not as tough or woody as common burdock roots). Their inner and outer layers do not separate as easily as do those of burdock or parsnip, and the texture of the skin is such that it does not hold much dirt and is therefore fairly easy to clean. Thistle roots are sometimes well over a foot long, often having no taper for the first half of their length. Collect them during the root season from plants that lack a stalk, and store them as one would store other root vegetables.

Thistle roots vary in quality from one species to another. The best kinds taste remarkably like those of burdock but are simply better. Those of bull thistle taper quickly and are often surprisingly small, but they are not bad. Nodding thistle has very large taproots, but they tend to be unpleasantly tough. Swamp and Canada thistle roots tend to be small and fibrous. Pasture thistle *C. discolor* has very large taproots. They are quite long and taper slowly, sometimes being wider in the middle than at the top. Pasture thistle roots are sweeter and less fibrous than bull thistle roots.

Large pasture thistle root. This one stopped abruptly when it hit a rock - normally they are much longer.

Tall thistle roots of typical size and shape.

The best thistle roots, in my experience, belong to the tall thistle *C. altissi-mum*. Taproots of this species are long, slender, and rather smooth, making them easy to clean. When raw they are crisp, crunchy, and sweet, but not tough – a delight to eat like a carrot. When cooked they become tender. These are among my favorite root vegetables.

Flower buds: The globe artichoke is the giant flower bud of a plant very closely related to our wild thistles. It is possible (although not necessarily pleasant) to peel the bristly bracts from the outside of a thistle flower bud (well before flowering time) and expose a tiny, tender, delicious, artichoke-like heart. Un-fortunately, this vegetable is less than a half inch in diameter – so small that it is hardly worth mentioning except as a curiosity.

As you can see, the much-maligned thistle has many culinary uses. It should not be passed off as unworthy of attention due to its prickly nature, as many wild food enthusiasts have done. If the ground is cursed to produce thorns and thistles for us, perhaps that's not such a bad thing after all.

341

References and Recommended Reading

My dissatisfaction with the majority of existing wild food references only makes the few good ones seem more precious. The list that follows contains only those books that I am familiar with, that are readily available, and that I feel adhere reasonably well to responsible writing and research practices. These are the references that I think a beginning forager will be at an advantage to equip herself with: *Stalking the Wild Asparagus, Stalking the Blue-Eyed Scallop,* and *Stalking the Healthful Herbs,* by Euell Gibbons; *Food Plants of British Columbia Indians, Vol. 1, Vol.2,* by Nancy Turner; *Edible Wild Plants of the Prairie,* by Kelly Kindscher; *Abundantly Wild,* by Teresa Marrone, *Guide to Wild Foods and Useful Plants,* by Christopher Nyerges; *Edible Wild Plants,* by Weatherbee and Bruce; and *The Wild Food Adventurer,* a periodical edited and published by John Kallas.

A few other books contain numerous statements of questionable accuracy but have still compiled information in a fashion that is highly useful to readers. Among the more popular of these are: *Identifying and Harvesting Edible and Medicinal Plants,* by Steve Brill (the best); *Field Guide to North American Edible Wild Plants,* by Elias and Dykeman (good); *Edible and Medicinal Plants of the West,* by Gregory Tilford (good); and *A Field Guide to Edible Wild Plants,* by Lee Peterson (hard for me to include, but does often prove useful). These titles make the beginnings of an excellent foraging library.

For identifying plants, it is best to have several reliable regional references. The most reliable identification guides cover plants in general, not just the edible species. Look for books with high-quality graphics, whether these are drawings or photographs. Look for books that have detailed technical descriptions that will help you verify the characteristics of your plant. If a book does not use scientific names, do not rely on it for plant identification. The absence of a glossary should also be viewed with suspicion.

In the following bibliography I list the references cited throughout this book, as well as additional uncited references that I use regularly when researching wild food.

Bibliography

Akiyama, Takao. *"The Plowboy Interview: Euell Gibbons."* In *Mother Earth News*, Issue #15, May/June 1972.

Angier, Bradford. *Field Guide to Edible Wild Plants*. Harrisburg, PA: Stackpole Books, 1974.

Balch, James F. and Balch, Phyllis A. *Prescription for Nutritional Healing*, 3rd Ed. New York: Penguin Putnam, 2000.

Barnes, Burton V. and Wagner, Warren H. Jr. *Michigan Trees*. Ann Arbor: University of Michigan Press, 1981.

Brill, Steve. *Identifying and Harvesting Edible and Medicinal Plants in Wild (and Not So Wild) Places*. New York: William Morrow, 1994.

Brown, Tom Jr. *Tom Brown's Field Guide to Wild Edible and Medicinal Plants*. New York: Berkley, 1985.

Clarke, Charlotte Bringle. *Edible and Useful Plants of California*. Berkeley: University of California Press, 1977.

Cobb, Boughton. *A Field Guide to Ferns*. Boston: Houghton Mifflin, 1956.

Coon, Nelson. *Using Wayside Plants*. New York: Hearthside, 1957.

Couplan, Francois. *The Encyclopedia of Edible Plants of North America*. New Canaan, CT: Keats Publishing, 1998.

Derby, Blanche Cybele. *My Wild Friends: Free Food From Field and Forest*. Northampton, MA: White Star Press, 1997.

Elias, Thomas S. *Trees of North America*. New York: Times Mirror, 1980.

Elias, Thomas S. and Dykeman, Peter A. *Field Guide to North American Edible Wild Plants*. New York: Outdoor Life Books, 1982.

Elmore, Frances. *Shrubs and Trees of the Southwest Uplands*. Tucson: Southwest Parks and Monuments Association, 1976.

Elpel, Thomas J. *Botany in a Day*, 4th ed. Pony, Montana: HOPS Press, 2000.

Elpel, Thomas J. *Participating in Nature*, 5th ed. Pony, Montana: HOPS Press, 2002.

Fernald, Merritt Lyndon and Kinsey, Alfred Charles. *Edible Wild Plants of Eastern North America*. New York: Harper and Row, 1943.

Gibbons, Euell. *Stalking the Wild Asparagus*. New York: David McKay, 1962.

Gibbons, Euell. *Stalking the Blue-Eyed Scallop*. New York: David McKay, 1964.

Gibbons, Euell. *Stalking the Healthful Herbs*. New York: David McKay, 1966.

Gibbons, Euell. *Stalking the Good Life*. New York: David McKay, 1971.

Gibbons, Euell. *Stalking the Faraway Places*. New York: David McKay, 1973.

Gibbons, Euell and Tucker, Gordon. *Euell Gibbons' Handbook of Edible Wild Plants*. Virginia Beach: Donning, 1979.

Gilmore, Melvin R. *Uses of Plants by the Indians of the Missouri River Region*. University of Nebraska Press, 1977. (Reprint; first publication 1919)

Greene, Bert. *Greene on Greens*. New York: Workman, 1984.

Hall, Alan. *The Wild Food Trailguide*. New York: Holt, Rhinehart, and Winston, 1973.

Hamerstrom, Frances. *The Wild Food Cookbook, From the Fields and Forests of the Great Lakes States*. Amherst, WI: Amherst Press, 1989.

Harrington, H.D. *Edible Native Plants of the Rocky Mountains*. Albuquerque: University of New Mexico Press, 1967.

Harris, Ben Charles. *Eat the Weeds*. Barre, MA: Barre, 1961.

Henderson, Robert K. *The Neighborhood Forager: A Guide for the Wild Food Gourmet*. White River Junction, VT: Chelsea Green, 2000.

Kallas, John. *The Wild Food Adventurer*. Vol. 1, No. 4, "Wapato, Indian Potato." Portland, Oregon: Wild Food Adventures, 1996.

Kallas, John. *The Wild Food Adventurer*. Vol. 6 No. 3, "Oxalates Schmokulates." Portland, Oregon: Wild Food Adventures, 2001.

Kalm, Peter. *America of 1750: Peter Kalm's Travels in North America: The English Version of 1770*. Revised and edited by Adolph B. Benson. New York: Dover, 1966.

Kindscher, Kelly. *Edible Wild Plants of the Prairie*. Lawrence, KS: University Press of Kansas, 1987.

Knudsen, Herbert D. "Milkweed: The Worth of a Weed," in *New Crops, New Uses, New Markets: 1992 Yearbook of Agriculture*, 118–123. U.S. Department of Agriculture, 1992.

Marrone, Teresa. *Abundantly Wild: Collecting and Cooking Wild Edibles in the Upper Midwest*. Cambridge, MN: Adventure Publications, 2004.

Medsger, Oliver Perry. *Edible Wild Plants*. New York: Macmillan, 1939.

Meuninck, Jim. *Basic Essentials: Edible Wild Plants and Useful Herbs*. Guilford, CT: Globe Pequot, 1988.

MMWR (Morbidity and Mortality Weekly Report), Vol. 43 No. 37 pg. 677, Sept. 23, 1994.

Morgan, P., Morton, T., and Iverson F. "Ostrich Fern Poisoning," in *Canada Communicable Disease Report*, 1994; 20.

Newcomb, Lawrence. *Newcomb's Wildflower Guide*. Boston: Little, Brown and Company, 1977.

Nyerges, Christopher. *Guide to Wild Foods and Useful Plants*. Chicago: Chicago Review Press, 1999.

Peterson, Lee. *A Field Guide to Edible Wild Plants of Eastern and Central North America*. Boston: Houghton Mifflin, 1977.

Pojar, Jim and Mackinnon, Andy, Eds. *Plants of the Pacific Northwest Coast*. Vancouver, BC: Lone Pine, 1994.

Ray, Bibek. *Fundamental Food Microbiology*. Boca Raton, FL: CRC Press, 1996.

Reynolds, B.D. et al. "Domestication of *Apios americana*" in *Advances in New Crops*, Eds. Janick, Jules and Simon, James. Portland, Oregon: Timber Press, 1990.

Saunders, Charles Francis. *Edible and Useful Wild Plants of the United States and Canada*. New York: Dover, 1976. (Reprint; first publication 1920)

Smith, Bruce D. *Rivers of Change*. Washington: Smithsonian Institution Press, 1992.

Smith, Bruce D. *The Emergence of Agriculture*. W.H. Freeman, 1999.

Soper, James H. and Margaret Heimburger. *Shrubs of Ontario*. Toronto: The Royal Ontario Museum, 1982.

Tatum, Billy Jo. *Billy Jo Tatum's Wild Foods Field Guide and Cookbook*. New York: Workman Publishing Company, 1976.

Thoreau, Henry David. *Wild Fruits*. (Ed. Bradley Dean.) New York: W.W. Norton, 2000.

Tilford, Gregory L. *Edible and Medicinal Plants of the West*. Missoula, Montana: Mountain Press, 1997.

Tull, Delena. *Edible ands Useful Plants of Texas and the Southwest*. Austin: University of Texas Press, 1987.

Turner, Nancy J. *Food Plants of British Columbia Indians, Part 1/Coastal Peoples*. Victoria, BC: British Columbia Provincial Museum, 1975.

Turner, Nancy J. *Food Plants of British Columbia Indians, Part 2/Interior Peoples*. Victoria, BC: British Columbia Provincial Museum, 1978.

Turner, Nancy J. and Szczawinski, Adam F. *Common Poisonous Plants and Mushrooms of North America*. Portland, Oregon: Timber Press, 1991.

Vennum, Thomas Jr. *Wild Rice and the Ojibway People*. Saint Paul: Minnesota Historical Society Press, 1988.

Voss, Edward. *Michigan Flora*, 3 Vols. Ann Arbor: University of Michigan Press, 1972, 1985, 1996.

Wardlaw, Gordon M. *Perspectives in Nutrition*. Boston: McGraw-Hill, 1999.

Weatherbee, Ellen Elliot and Bruce, James Garnett. *Edible Wild Plants: A Guide to Collecting and Cooking*. Weatherbee and Bruce, 1979.

Young, Kay. *Wild Seasons: Gathering and Cooking Wild Plants of the Great Plains*. University of Nebraska Press, 1993.

Glossary

Acuminate: Tapering to a long, narrow, needle-like point.

Alternate: Growing from opposite sides of a stalk at different points along its length (rather than at the same point as in opposite leaves). Not paired.

Awn: An elongated bristle, often found on the lemma of a grass seed.

Axil: The upper angle where a leaf or petiole joins a stem.

Basal: Growing from the base of the plant, attached near ground level.

Berry hook: A pole or stick with a hook on the end, used to pull down and hold out-of-reach branches for fruit picking.

Biennial: A plant that normally has a two-year life cycle, spending the first year as a stalkless rosette storing energy, and using that energy to produce a flowering stalk the second year, after which the plant dies. Biennials may spend several years as a rosette before flowering, however, if the growing conditions are poor.

Blanch: To briefly boil a vegetable in order to destroy enzymes and kill individual cells; generally done before freezing. Also, to cover growing plants so as to keep light from them, making them grow lighter in color, more tender, and less strong in flavor.

Blickey: A berry-picking container that straps onto the waist, leaving both hands free.

Bloom: A thin waxy or powdery coating that can be rubbed off. Often found on fruit and smooth herb stems, bloom gives the surface a lighter hue.

Boreal forest: The plant community that dominates most of Canada's forested regions, characterized by fir, spruce, aspen, white birch, and other northern plants.

Bract: A small, modified leaf found directly beneath a flower or flower cluster.

Bulb: A modified bud, such as an onion, in which the leaves are enlarged and thickened to store energy.

Calyx: The sepals of a flower, collectively. These sometimes remain attached to fruit after the flower has been fertilized.

Cambium: The layer of dividing cells that lies between the wood (xylem) and bark (phloem), and which produces both. Cambium is often erroneously called "inner bark." It would be more proper to call it "outer wood" because it generally remains attached to the trunk when bark is peeled off. In truth, however, it is neither bark nor wood.

Chaff: The unwanted, inedible dried flower and fruit parts that are separated from a grain by rubbing and then removed by winnowing.

Chambered: Divided into compartments, often with hollow spaces, by transverse partitions; said of pith.

Channeled: Having a groove or depression running its length; usually said of petioles.

Climax community: A plant community that persists indefinitely in the absence of significant environmental disturbances; the last stage in plant succession on a particular site.

Clone: A colony of genetically identical plants or stems that have propagated themselves through some form of vegetative reproduction; a clone is essentially one large plant with many stems.

Cold storage: Storing produce in a cool but not frozen environment.

Colony: A group of many individuals or stems of the same species of plant found growing together.

Composite: A flower cluster that appears as one flower (such as dandelion) in which many tiny florets are clustered on a receptacle. Also, any plant of the Composite family, all of which share this characteristic.

Compound leaf: A leaf that consists of multiple leaflets connected by petioles, usually to a main axis or rachis. The stems within a compound leaf never become woody.

Contradictory confidence: Such absolute certainty in a plant's identity that you would be willing to contradict anybody who told you otherwise.

Corm: The base of an upright stem, enlarged to store energy.

Corrugated: Having a rough surface texture formed by valleys, ridges, wrinkles, or folds.

Cyme: A broad, flat-topped or convex cluster of flowers, which is not an umbel.

Deciduous: Dying and falling away from the plant at the end of the growing season.

Dermatitis: Rash or irritation of the skin.

Dichotomous key: A tool used for identifying a plant by repeatedly deciding which of two technical descriptions applies to it, narrowing down the number of possibilities with each set of descriptions until the species is determined.

Dicot: (Short for dicotyledon) One of the two major divisions within the Angiosperms (typical flowering plants). Dicots generally have net-patterned veins, a main central root, and two seed-leaves (cotyledons) when germinating. Examples include maple, strawberry, dandelion, and clover.

Drupe: A fruit with pulp surrounding a seed with a tough outer layer.

Parts of a Regular Flower

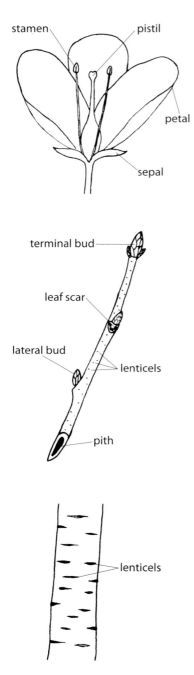

Edible plant: A plant, one or more parts of which can normally be consumed at a certain stage of growth, prepared in a particular fashion, and eaten in a certain manner, with no significant ill effects. Edible plants can also be poisonous!

Entire: A leaf or leaflet with no divisions, lobes, or teeth.

Fiddlehead: The shoot of a fern, upon which the end parts are coiled or drooping rather than pointed.

Floret: One of the many tiny flowers in a composite cluster; also, a grass flower.

Flower bud: A flower that is not ready to open; the bud that will later become a flower.

Flower stalk: A stalk that bears a flower or flowers; sometimes used in distinction to the leaf-stalk or petiole.

Frond: The leaf or above-ground stem of a fern.

Fruit leather: Thin sheets of dried fruit pulp.

Glabrous: Smooth; lacking hairs or bristles.

Globose: Spherical or roughly spherical.

Greens: The edible leaves or leafy portion of a plant.

Inflorescence: A flower or cluster of flowers and all that comes with it, such as stems and bracts; the whole flowering portion of the plant.

Inulin: A non-digestible starch that can be broken down by prolonged cooking, inulin is found in many underground vegetables, which convert it to simpler, digestible sugars before using it to fuel growth.

Kernel: An edible seed, or the edible portion of a seed.

Lanceolate: Shaped like a lance head: much longer than wide, broadest near the base, tapering to a pointed tip.

Latex: A white, milky sap that dries as a rubbery substance, used to heal wounds.

Layering: To spread or propagate by rooting from the branches where these come in contact with the soil.

Leaflet: One of the smaller leaves or blades within a compound leaf.

Leaf scar: The mark left on a stem or twig where a leaf or petiole was formerly attached.

Lenticel: A small corky spot on the bark of small trees and shrubs.

Lobe: An extension of a leaf blade; a division of a leaf that is broadly attached rather than constricted or stalked at the base, as on the leaves of white and red oak.

Margin: The outer edge of a leaf.

Mast: Collectively, the crop of nuts produced by a group of trees; originally referring primarily to beech but now used more generally.

Mesic forest: A forest with a medium level of soil moisture; rich hardwood forest dominated by long-lived species such as sugar maple, beech, basswood, yellow birch, hemlock, and white ash.

Midrib: The main vein of a leaf, especially one that is enlarged and provides support, as on most divided leaves; sometimes also used to refer to the rachis (main stalk) of a compound leaf.

Midvein: The main vein of a leaf. Same as midrib, except in connotation; the main vein is more commonly called a midvein if it is relatively small, as one finds on most simple leaves.

Flower/Fruit Clusters

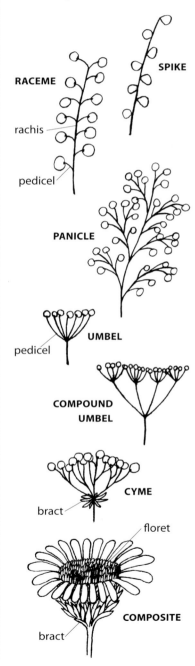

349

Simple Leaf Shapes

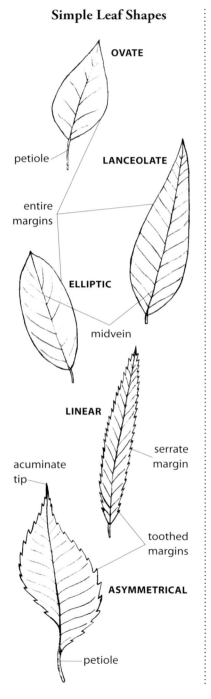

OVATE

petiole

LANCEOLATE

entire
margins

ELLIPTIC

midvein

LINEAR

serrate
margin

acuminate
tip

toothed
margins

ASYMMETRICAL

petiole

Monocot: (Short for monocotyledon) One of the two main divisions within the Angiosperms (typical flowering plants). Monocots generally have parallel veins, no main taproot, and a single seed-leaf (cotyledon) when germinating. Examples include grasses, sedges, arums, onions, Solomon's seals, and lilies.

Mucilage: A sticky or slimy substance, usually indicating the presence of dissolved starches. Mucilaginous refers to plants or plant parts containing mucilage, or which produce mucilage when chewed.

Node: The point on a stem where one or more leaves are borne.

Nutmeat: The edible portion of a nut.

Opposite: Growing from the same point along a stalk but on opposite sides of it; paired. (Alternate leaves grow on opposite sides at different points.)

Ovate: Roughly egg-shaped; somewhat longer than broad, with the widest part near the base.

Palmate: Hand-shaped, having several finger-like lobes.

Palmately compound: Having several leaflets radiate from the same point.

Panicle: A flower cluster with a compound branching pattern, the branches growing from an elongated central stalk. Grapes are a well-known example.

Parch: To heat and cook (a grain) to harden the kernel and make the chaff brittle.

Pedicel: The stem of an individual flower or fruit within a cluster.

Perennial: Any plant that typically lives for more than two years.

Petal: One of the innermost set of modified leaves of a flower, usually brightly colored.

Petiole: The stem or stalk of a leaf.

Phenology: The timing and sequence of seasonal biological events, and the study of this timing and sequence.

Pinna: A primary division of a pinnate fern frond.

Pinnate: Feather-like; with leaflets, branches, or veins arranged in two rows along opposite sides of a midvein or midrib; the most common form for ferns, also seen in most legume leaves and compound tree leaves such as walnut, hickory, and ash.

Pistil: The central female part of the flower, which receives the pollen. It is usually much larger than the stamens (if both present).

Pith: The soft, spongy material found in the center of many stems.

Poisonous plant: A plant, one or more parts of which can be harmful if consumed. The same plant may have both poisonous and edible parts.

Potherb: A green eaten after boiling or steaming.

Pubescent: Covered with hairs.

Puree: The pulp of fruit after the seeds, skins, and stems have been removed by straining.

Raceme: A flower cluster in which each flower is borne on a stem emanating from an elongated central stem.

Rachis: The primary stem of a compound leaf or flower cluster.

Rhizome: A horizontal stem of a perennial plant, found under or on the ground, usually thick and rooting at the nodes; its purpose is to spread the plant and store energy. (The term rhizome is, perhaps erroneously, also applied to completely different underground storage structures of many ferns.)

Leaf Shapes

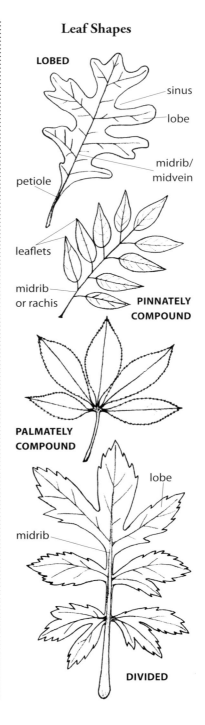

Leaf Patterns

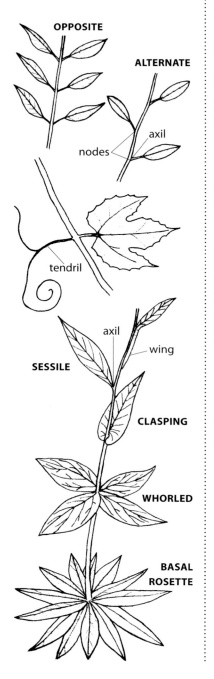

OPPOSITE

ALTERNATE

axil

nodes

tendril

axil

SESSILE

wing

CLASPING

WHORLED

BASAL
ROSETTE

Rib : A pronounced vein (nerve) in a leaf.

Root: The part of a plant which serves to anchor it and absorb water and dissolved nutrients. The root does not have leaves or buds.

Root crown: The transition area from root to stem.

Root season: The time of year when most underground vegetables should be harvested: from late summer to mid spring (being best from late fall to very early spring).

Rootstock: A rhizome that is enlarged to store energy. Also used to refer to fern "rhizomes."

Rosette: A circular cluster of leaves radiating from the same point, usually a root crown or the base of a stem.

Sagittate: Arrow or arrowhead-shaped, with two sharp lobes at the base of the leaf.

Samara: A winged fruit, such as maple, ash, and elm seeds.

Sepal: One of the outer ring of modified leaves in a flower. Sepals may be green or they may be colored like typical petals.

Serrated: With sharp teeth of somewhat uniform size.

Sessile: Attached directly, without a stalk or petiole.

Shoot: Rapidly growing stem or stalk of a plant, like asparagus. Leaves may be present, but are not fully formed and comprise a small portion of the shoot's volume.

Simple: Not compound; a single-leaf unit.

Sinus: The space between two lobes of a leaf.

Spike: An elongated, unbranched flower cluster in which the flowers are attached directly to a main stem without individual stems.

Spring ephemeral: A plant with a brief

growing season in spring, the visible growth usually dying back in late spring or early summer.

Stamen: The male, pollen-bearing part of a flower. Usually multiple.

Stone: A seed with a hard shell that is enclosed in a fruit; a pit.

Straining: The process of removing seeds, skins, stems, and other unwanted coarse material from fruit or berry pulp.

Succulent: Thick, fleshy, and juicy.

Taproot: A primary, central root that grows downward rather than laterally or horizontally.

Tendril: A modified leaf or branch that grasps or coils around other objects to support a vine.

Tip-up mound: The mound of dirt formed by the soil attached to a tree's roots when a tree falls.

Tuber: An enlargement of a stem in which energy is stored, primarily in the form of starch.

Umbel: A flower cluster in which all of the flower stalks radiate from the same point.

Vegetative reproduction: Any form of reproduction or propagation that does not involve seeds, such as spreading by tubers, suckers, or rhizomes.

Wing: A thin, flat, usually leafy extension from a stalk, petiole, fruit, or other plant part.

Winnow: To separate kernels or seeds from chaff using wind, air, or the different rates that different materials fall or travel through the air.

Wool: Long, matted hair, lying on the surface of a plant rather than erect.

Underground Parts

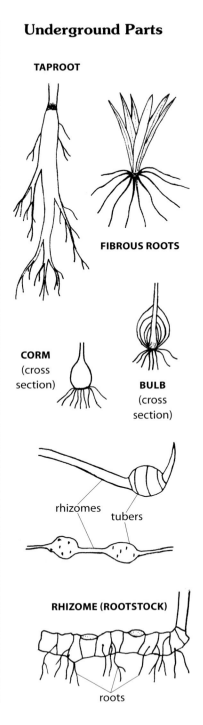

TAPROOT

FIBROUS ROOTS

CORM
(cross section)

BULB
(cross section)

rhizomes tubers

RHIZOME (ROOTSTOCK)

roots

Index